LEARNING

'Teaching machines' and 'programmed
learning' are phrases which are only now
beginning to penetrate the consciousness of
the man in the street. Even for students of
psychology there are few simple descriptions of the theories that lie behind these
modern applications soon to become part
of our daily lives.

The present work by an American psychologist provides an elementary but fairly
solid account of these theories. It deals with
the learning process, largely in the classroom, and the laboratory, and then proceeds to the various theorists from Watson
to the contemporaries such as Skinner,
Gagñe, Underwood and others.

UNIVERSITY PAPERBACKS

UP 97

Learning

A SURVEY OF PSYCHOLOGICAL
INTERPRETATIONS
BY

Winfred F. Hill

NORTHWESTERN UNIVERSITY
ILLINOIS

UNIVERSITY PAPERBACKS

METHUEN : LONDON

First published 1963 by Chandler Publishing Company
© 1963 by Chandler Publishing Company
First published in this series 1964
Printed in Great Britain by
Lowe & Brydone (Printers) Ltd, London

LB
1051
H524
1964

University Paperbacks are published by
METHUEN & CO LTD
11 New Fetter Lane EC4

To my father:
a devoted educator

Contents

Illustrations

Preface

SYSTEMATIC INTERPRETATIONS OF learning have an important place both in the science of psychology and in the application of psychology to education. This introductory survey of contemporary learning theories is designed to provide a fairly elementary but nonetheless solid account of this topic for students in the psychology of learning and in educational psychology.

In planning this book particularly for educators, I have tried to point up educational and related applications. However, I have been particularly concerned with what J. M. Stephens calls the "teacher as a theorist," so that much of the emphasis is on learning theory as an attempt to provide basic understanding of the learning process. The discussions in this book are therefore fully as appropriate for students in the liberal arts as for those in education.

In attempting to classify psychological interpretations of learning, I find the familiar division into connectionist and cognitive theories still the most useful. However, much of the interest in this classification is in the ways that these two kinds of theory have been moving closer together. The latter half of this book has as one of its main themes the attempts that have been made to combine the advantages of these two approaches.

Another basis of classification, especially significant for the beginning student, is the degree of formality of the theory, varying from the chattiest of verbal interpretations to the most abstract of mathematical models. The former kind are both easier for the student and in most cases more oriented toward practical applications, but a balanced picture of learning theory requires that both be considered. In general, the discussion in this book proceeds from the more simple and practical to the more complex and abstract. Chapter 1 provides an introduction to learning theory and its uses. Chapters 2 through 4 deal with relatively nontechnical interpretations of learning, oriented toward educational and other applications. Chapters 5 and 6 treat more technical interpretations, and may be omitted if only a simple and practically-oriented coverage is desired. The final two chapters explore various aspects of current learning theory, highlighting unsettled issues and attempting to predict future trends.

Special thanks are due to Ernest R. Hilgard, both for his thorough critical reading of the manuscript and for his many contributions to my thinking about learning theory. I also wish to thank David Ryans and Ruth Wylie for their many helpful comments, Elaine Johnson and Irene Nolte for their efforts in typing the manuscript, and my wife, Libby, for help in all stages of preparation.

WINFRED F. HILL

Evanston, Illinois
January, 1963

LEARNING:

A Survey of Psychological Interpretations

Chapter 1

Understanding and Explaining Learning

THEORETICAL SYSTEMS FOR the interpretation of learning have grown up along with the experimental study of learning, and to understand one it is necessary to understand the other. Although the experimental study of learning to a large extent grew out of everyday problems, particularly problems in education, it soon became involved with theoretical issues and with the experiments appropriate for dealing with them. This theoretical involvement proceeded to such an extent that the original problems became barely recognizable. It is therefore worthwhile to take a long look at the interrelations among theory, research, and applications in the field of learning before undertaking a detailed survey of different theoretical systems.

The reader should be warned at the outset that psychologists use the term "learning" more broadly than it is used in popular speech. While it is almost impossible to give an exact definition of learning that will be generally acceptable to psychologists, we can at least note certain phenomena to which the term is or is not applied. In psychological usage, what is learned need not be "correct" or adaptive (we learn bad habits as well as good), need not be conscious or deliberate (one of the advantages of coaching in a skill is that it makes us aware of mistakes we have unconsciously learned to make), and need not involve any overt act (attitudes and emotions can be learned as well as knowledge and skills). Reactions as diverse as driving a car, remembering a pleasant vacation, believing in democracy, and disliking one's boss all represent the results of learning.

1

How does learning take place? What factors determine what we will learn and how rapidly we will learn it? There are innumerable people in situations in which it would be useful to have answers to these questions. We think at once of students looking for better methods of study, of teachers wanting to improve their classroom techniques, and of people in industry seeking better ways of training new workers. We may also consider the mother looking for the best way of raising her children, the counselor trying to improve his client's emotional and social adjustment, the animal trainer preparing seeing-eye dogs for their work, and the advertiser trying to develop a preference on the part of consumers for his client's product. In all of these cases, knowledge about the learning process represents power.

The above practical needs are not the only reasons for wanting to know more about learning. Man has always been curious about himself, always wanted to know more about what "makes him tick." Since learning is such an important factor in what man is and does, a greater understanding of the learning process would go far toward increasing his self-knowledge. Consequently people are motivated to study learning, not only by the practical benefits to be gained but also by curiosity about themselves and how they came to be as they are.

LEARNING IN SCHOOL

Let us begin our discussion by looking at a setting in which learning is the primary focus: the school. A child in school faces a bewilderingly complex learning situation. It is complex from his point of view; it is even more so from the point of view of the psychologist who bravely attempts to analyze it. The child is influenced in countless ways by the varied aspects of the classroom situation. He learns much from the teacher, including many things not prescribed in the curriculum and some things of which neither teacher nor pupil is aware. He also learns from his books, from his fellow students, and from the physical arrangements of the school. Part of what he learns is measurable as specific knowledge and skills, while another part involves changes, some very subtle but a few quite dramatic, in attitudes, emotions, social behavior, and a variety of other reactions. The psychologist's job is to analyze such complex situations into their component parts and to try to understand the principles of learning and motivation involved.

Let us consider some incidents in the school day of a particular sixth-grader, Alex B. We meet Alex first as he is studying a vocabulary list in his reading book. His teacher (a trifle old-fashioned) has instructed the class to learn to spell these words. He is thus confronted with a list of twelve words for which he must learn to give the correct written form when presented with the spoken form. However, in studying from his book he faces a slightly different task, since only the written form is before him and he must provide the spoken version (subvocally) himself. He goes through the list, pronouncing and spelling the words to himself, but finds his attention wandering. He looks out the window and remembers how much he enjoyed the previous weekend. Snapping back to the spelling book, he continues dutifully to the end of the list. Then he tries covering all but the first letter of each word with his hand and trying to spell the word to himself. At "r" he proceeds cautiously, trying to remember the rule for "i" and "e." Finally he decides on "receive," moves his hand away, and relaxes a bit as he finds his guess confirmed. At "s" he spells to himself without hesitation, "seperate," then frowns as he sees his mistake. He stares for a moment at the "ar," trying to fix it in his memory, then continues through the list. Half way through, he finds himself unable to remember a word from the first letter.

Annoyed, he looks at the word and then concentrates heavily on trying to remember it. Two words later, the same thing happens again. He looks at the word, wonders why it should be hard to remember, and begins to feel discouraged. He stares at the picture on the wall of Washington crossing the Delaware, and imagines himself leading such an expedition. Catching the teacher's eye, he returns quickly to his book and finishes the list. He spells the last word confidently, "cematary," only to find "cemetery," staring back at him from the page. Puzzled, he looks back and forth from "separate" to "cemetery" and thinks, "I hate spelling."

We see Alex next at recess running excitedly out to join a softball game. He begins the game in the outfield. As the batter hits a ground ball in his direction, he starts running, his speed and direction adjusted to make his path intercept that of the ball. As he nears the ball he bends over, puts his hands in front of it, and closes them at just the right moment to catch the ball. He then looks up, notes the position of the runner, and throws the ball in the direction of first base, his arm motion just forceful enough to carry the ball to the first baseman. This whole sequence of coordinated, purposeful behavior occurs rapidly, almost automatically, with no evidence of thought or verbal self-instruction. Watching him, the teacher is impressed by how much Alex has improved at softball since she has known him.

During the game, Alex calls frequently, "Wait'll I get to bat!" and "When'm I up?" Finally his turn comes. He pounds the plate and shouts, "Put it over!" When the pitcher throws the ball, Alex takes a mighty swing at it, and misses. He looks chagrined, but shouts, "Let's have another!" Again he swings and misses. This time he frowns and says nothing. He stands more rigidly at the plate, his teeth clenched. His swing at the third pitch is more tense, less free, and again he misses. He throws the bat down and stalks away. At his next turn in the outfield, he does no shouting, and his fielding is less coordinated. When recess ends, he returns quietly to the classroom, ignoring the chatter around him. He seems relieved that recess is over.

Later we see Alex during his math lesson. The class has been learning how to find the areas of rectangles. Now the teacher raises the problem of how to find the area of a triangle. She draws a right triangle with a 4″ and a 3″ side on the blackboard and asks the students what the area is. Alex likes math and enjoys learning how to solve new problems, so he eagerly tries to figure this one out. He tries to apply the rule for rectangles, but can't see how to do it. Then the teacher draws two more lines, making a rectangle with the hypotenuse of the triangle as its diagonal. Alex stares at this for a moment, then grins and excitedly holds up his hand. "The area is six. The whole rectangle is 12, and there are two triangles, and each triangle is half of the rectangle!" The teacher smiles. "Very good. The area is half of 4 times 3. Math makes a lot of sense when you figure it out like that." Alex basks in his success, pleased both with the teacher's approval and with his triumph over the impersonal challenge of the problem.

We leave Alex now, happy that a rather frustrating day for him has ended with success. However, the challenge to a psychologist to analyze Alex's experiences lasts long after the incidents are over. In fact, the narrative of Alex's day might be used as a hidden-picture puzzle: "How many aspects of learning can you find illustrated in these incidents?" Consider, for example, the similarities and differences among the three situations in which we saw Alex. All involved learning, motivation, goal-directed behavior, and success or failure. All could be analyzed in terms of the responses that Alex made to various stimuli in his environment, and also in terms of the way he perceived the environment. All occurred in social situations and against a background of norms and values shared (though not completely) by Alex, his teacher, and his fellow students. However, the three situations differed in the principal kind of learning involved (verbal memorization of the spelling list, motor skill on the softball field, and logical insight in the math problem). The situations also differed in the emotional learning that occurred and in some of the subsidiary principles. In each situation we may ask what factors contributed to Alex's successes and failures. How much did his difficulty in spelling "cemetery," for example, depend on the word itself, on its position in the list, on the fact that "separate" came earlier in the same lesson, on distractions in the room at that moment, or on a variety of other facts about Alex, the lesson, and the general situation? There are endless possibilities for the psychologist to analyze in these three everyday situations.

However, such analysis assumes that we already know a great deal about the principles of learning. In cases where a number of factors might have influenced Alex's behavior, we cannot make worthwhile guesses about how important each was unless we have information about how important each has been in other similar situations. For example, we cannot judge whether the word "cemetery" itself or the situation in which Alex encountered it contributed more to his error unless we know something about the relative importance of words and their context in other cases of

B

memorization. It is to provide such information about the regularities in behavior that we do experimental studies. If we know from such studies that certain situations cause special difficulty in memorizing, we are in a much better position both to explain Alex's errors and to find ways of helping him.

LEARNING IN THE LABORATORY

Let us now look at some typical laboratory learning situations. As compared with Alex's experiences, some of these may appear artificial or trivial. This difference is the price we pay in order to have situations in which we can manipulate certain variables, hold others constant, and measure precisely the resultant changes in behavior. We will see many relations between the complex situations in which Alex learned and these simpler, better controlled, laboratory learning situations.

Two Complex Learning Situations

In the first laboratory situation, as in Alex's math lesson, the learner (commonly called the subject) is presented with a problem for which he must find a solution. A common problem for use with college students requires the subject to tie together two strings hanging from the ceiling. The strings are so far apart that when he holds one, he cannot reach the other, which is why this otherwise easy task constitutes a problem. The only equipment available to help him do the job is a pair of pliers. Can he find a way of tying the strings together? (There need not be an actual room with two strings; problem and solution can all be given with pencil and paper.)

What commonly happens in this situation is that the subject tries a variety of approaches, all unsuccessful. The pliers might be used as an extension of his arm to reach the second string, but they are too short. It might be possible to cut a piece off one of the strings and tie it to the other, but the two strings could still not be brought together. Finally the thought of swinging the strings occurs to most people. Given this lead, the solution usually comes quickly: tie the pliers to one of the strings, start the string swinging as a pendulum, then run over the other string, bring it as close as possible to the one that is swinging, and catch the swinging one at the closest point of its arc. Since the subject is now holding both strings, he can easily tie them together.

How does this laboratory problem differ from the geometric problem that Alex solved in the classroom? In principle, very little. Both have simple solutions drawing on the solver's past experience, but both are difficult because they require the use of this past experience in new ways. The solution in each case usually involves a period of futile search followed by a flash of insight. A hint, such as the two extra lines the teacher drew, or the word "pendulum" in the two-string problem, often results in quick solution of the problem. And although we have spoken of these as problem-solving situations, they are quite impressive as learning situations, since the ability to tie the strings or compute the area not only appears suddenly but is also very well retained as compared with most other learned material.

The important difference is not between the two problems but between the classroom and the laboratory. In the classroom case, we do not know how soon (if at all) Alex would have solved the problem without the teacher's hint, or why Alex rather than another student solved it first, or how many other students would have found the solution if he had not beaten them to it, or how the presence of other students helped or hindered him. In the laboratory, on the other hand, all of these questions can be systematically studied. The problem can be presented to subjects singly or in groups, with hints at predetermined points, and each person's time to solution (and his mistaken "solutions") recorded. This laboratory situation makes it possible to investigate both sets of factors—those in the situation and those in the individual—that contribute to this learning. (If the reader feels uncomfortable about calling such problem solving "learning," since it does not involve improvement with practice, he should note that a major theoretical approach to learning is built around just such "perceptual restructuring" as is involved in solving these problems.)

Another laboratory example of learning, closer to the popular image of a learning situation, involves rote memorization. The items to be memorized are usually either words or nonsense syllables (such as *deg* or *czr*), and the task may either be to learn a series of them in order (as would be the case in memorizing a chemical formula) or to learn a number of pairs of items with one member of a pair always given as the response to the other (comparable to learning a foreign-language vocabulary). The items are typically presented in a memory drum, a machine that displays them one by one at a controlled rate through a small window. As each item appears in the window, the subject tries to say what the next item will be. The whole series of items is repeated again and again until the learner is able to anticipate each item correctly before it appears.

The contrast between such a learning task and Alex's spelling lesson is again largely in the precision of control that the laboratory setup permits. Alex could approach the words to be learned in any order and divide his time among them in any way he chose. Moreover, he had to study from a book, even though the test of his mastery would consist of writing the words in response to oral dictation. This difference forced him to devise techniques of practice that would as nearly as possible match the test procedure. Finally, he was subjected to the distractions of the classroom situations. The laboratory subject, on the other hand, sees the items in a predetermined order and for constant amounts of time in a small room with a minimum of distractions. Since he is automatically tested on each item each time through the list, there is a continuous record of his mastery of each item at each stage in the learning. This record makes possible separate analyses of different stages of learning, different parts of the list, and different individual items.

Three Simpler Learning Situations

Both the problem-solving and the rote learning situations in the laboratory represent refinements of learning situations found in the classroom and elsewhere in everyday life outside the laboratory. However, many psychological experimenters analyze these and other examples of learning (e.g., Alex's learning of the motor skills involved in fielding a softball) into simpler components and then study these components separately. Rather than working with complex patterns of responses such as Alex learned, they study changes in the frequency or magnitude or speed of a single response. Their object is not to study everyday kinds of learning under better-controlled conditions, but to study the underlying components of everyday learning in order to get a better under-standing of what learning is. Such understanding, it is hoped, can then be used to predict learning in a great variety of more com-plex situations. This approach is comparable to that in other sci-ences, where complex chemical substances are analyzed into their component elements, or where the speed of a falling body is stud-ied as a function of the distance it has fallen, without regard to whether the body is a mail bag, a person, or a hydrogen bomb.

Since research of this sort attempts to reduce learning to its sim-plest essentials, animals have often been found more satisfactory subjects than humans. Animals lack the complexities of language and cultural traditions, their background of previous experience is both simpler and (at least if they are reared in the lab) less variable than that of humans, and their heredity as well as their rearing can to a considerable extent be controlled. All of these factors make it easier to study one aspect of the animal's learning processes at a time while holding others constant. For example, if we want to study the rate at which a dog learns to flex his leg to avoid an elec-tric shock, we probably do not have to worry about his interpre-tation of the purpose of the experiment or about his concern with behaving bravely, politely, or rationally, all of which would be factors if we were studying the same behavior in humans. This is not to say that humans cannot usefully be studied in such situa-tions, for they often are, but to point out why for certain purposes animals are often preferred.

One simple animal response which has been extensively stud-ied is the pecking response in pigeons. If a hungry pigeon is occa-sionally rewarded with food for pecking a lighted key on the side of its cage, it will peck the key at a high rate. This pecking rate is quite sensitive to changes in level of hunger, frequency of food re-ward, and other variables. It can thus be used to investigate many of the phenomena of simple learning.

The low rate at which the pigeon pecks before food is in-troduced is called the *operant rate*. When food first begins to be presented as soon as the pigeon pecks the key, the rate of pecking rises. In technical terms, this change indicates that the food *rein-forces* the pecking, or that it is a *reinforcer*. If some but not all pecks are followed by food, the particular pattern used (*e.g.,* food after every tenth peck, or after one peck each minute) is known as the *schedule of reinforcement*. If pecking is no longer followed by food, the rate drops. This decline in rate resulting from the removal of the reinforcer is known as *extinction*. If after extinction takes place there is an interval of time during which the pigeon does not have access to the key, and then the key is presented again, the pecking rate is likely to be higher than it was at the end of extinction. This increase in rate is called, naturally enough, *spontaneous recovery*. If a key that the pigeon has been reinforced for pecking is replaced by another key of a different color, the pigeon will peck at this key also, though not as much as at the original one. This tendency to respond to stimuli other than the one used in training is known as *generalization*. If, however, the two keys are presented alternately, with pecking at one reinforced and pecking at the other nonreinforced (extinguished), the pigeon will learn to peck the reinforced key at a high rate and the nonreinforced key very little. We then say that a *discrimination* between the keys has been formed.

Many aspects of the above learning phenomena have been studied experimentally. How does the rate of pecking vary with the amount of food given, the schedule of reinforcement, or the delay between peck and food? How does spontaneous recovery vary with the time interval between extinction and test, or generalization vary with the difference in color between the two keys? Will making a pigeon more hungry increase or decrease his ability to form a discrimination? Questions of this sort may be studied, not only with regard to the rate of key-pecking in pigeons, but with regard to many other forms of behavior in a variety of species.

These learning phenomena, established in experimental studies, can be applied (though often with some modification) to complex learning in everyday life. Though we did not see Alex over a long enough period of time to observe the effects of reinforcement and extinction in his behavior, we can note a number of cases where these processes were probably occurring for him. His statement about the area of the triangle was reinforced by the teacher's praise, his techniques of fielding the softball by the approval of his fellow players, and his correct spellings by seeing his spellings confirmed by the printed words. On the other hand, his incorrect spellings, his batting techniques, and his competent manner with regard to batting were not reinforced and hence presumably underwent some extinction. The disappearance of his confident shouting after he struck out might be taken as evidence of extinction. If the shouting reappeared at his next softball game, this renewal could be interpreted as spontaneous recovery. The problem of spelling "separate" with an "ar" and "cemetery" with an "er" clearly involved making a discrimination between two similar situations, and it might also be interpreted as extinguishing the tendency to spell phonetically.

Not only can we identify these learning processes operating in everyday life; we can also make predictions from learning experiments to everyday learning situations. For example, it is commonly found in experiments that a delay between the response and the reinforcer results in poorer performance of the learned response. From this finding we could make predictions about the efficacy of different teaching methods. If Alex had taken a spelling quiz on one day but had not found out which words he got right until the papers were handed back the next day, he probably would have learned less spelling than he did with his book, in consequence of the delay of reinforcement. On the other hand, it is possible that the opposite might be true, either because correctness on a graded test is more reinforcing than correctness on a private self-test, or because writing from dictation is a better way of studying spelling, or for a variety of other reasons. This example thus points up both the usefulness of laboratory study in making suggestions about everyday learning and the danger in taking such suggestions uncritically.

A fourth example of laboratory learning, and one even less like the ordinary picture of a learning situation, occurs in experiments on *classical conditioning*. The first of these, and still the most famous, were those in which the Russian physiologist Ivan Pavlov used the procedure to train dogs to salivate. Another version of this procedure (less famous than Pavlov's salivating dogs, but currently more popular in American labs) is the conditioning of the eyeblink reflex in humans. If a person who is watching a dim light sees the light grow somewhat brighter, he ordinarily does not blink his eyes in response to this stimulus. If, however, he is hit in the eye by a vigorous puff of air, he does blink. The conditioning procedure consists in pairing these two stimuli, with the brightening of the light coming a fraction of a second before the puff of air. Each time this sequence occurs, the subject blinks in response to the air puff. Presently, however, he begins to blink as soon as the light changes, before the puff comes. Since the changing light now produces a blinking response which it formerly did not produce, learning has taken place. In this setup the puff, which already produced blinking, is called the *unconditioned stimulus,* and blinking to the puff is the *unconditioned response.* The increase in brightness of the light is called the *conditioned stimulus,* and the learned response of blinking to it is the *conditioned response.* The whole learning sequence is known as *conditioning.* The same principles of reinforcement, extinction, spontaneous recovery, generalization, and discrimination that were illustrated by the pigeon pecking a key can also be demonstrated in classical conditioning situations.

The distinctive characteristic of this kind of learning is that a certain stimulus elicits a response after the learning experience that it did not elicit before. (Because some authorities use the term "conditioning" rather broadly, the adjective "classical" is often added to "conditioning" to make clear that this form of learning is meant.) Since classical conditioning does not involve learning new responses, solving problems, or carrying out goal-directed activity, it seems at first glance to be of little importance compared to the other forms of learning so far discussed. Some theorists have concurred in this judgment, regarding conditioning as nothing more than a laboratory curiosity. Others, as we shall see, have regarded it as of central importance. One modern viewpoint is that its importance is mainly for the learning of emotional reactions. When Alex experienced failures at spelling and at batting, he reacted with discouragement and anger. These can be considered unconditioned responses to the unconditioned stimulus of failure. When he said, "I hate spelling," this opinion may have indicated that conditioning was taking place, with the spelling lesson as the conditioned stimulus and discouragement and anger as the conditioned response. This interpretation makes classical conditioning of emotional responses crucial to our learning of attitudes toward all the people, objects, and situations we encounter in our lives.

A fifth and final laboratory example of learning is the *maze*. The principles involved in maze learning are similar to those in the key-pecking experiments already mentioned, but the maze has been used so widely in learning experiments that it deserves separate mention. The original mazes were modeled after the Hampton Court maze in England, where tall hedges formed an intricate pattern of winding pathways through which visitors tried to find their way. Miniature versions of this maze were used to study the ways in which both humans and animals learned to avoid the many blind alleys and find the correct path from the starting point to the goal. Over the years mazes have become simpler and simpler as psychologists tried to find the basic principles involved in learning them. The winding pathways of the Hampton Court maze have been replaced by alleys with simple series of left and right turns. Even these, however, have been considered too complicated, and have been largely replaced with "mazes" in which there is only a single choice to be made, between a right and a left turn. Because of their shape, these are known as T mazes. These are too easy to be useful with humans, but are widely used with animals. The learner (typically a well-domesticated white rat) runs along the stem of the T and then enters one of the arms. If he chooses the correct one, he finds food at the end of the arm. The rate at which he learns which side is correct can be studied in relation to the amount of food he gets, how hungry he is, and other more complex variables. Finally, even the one choice point may be eliminated, leaving only a straight runway. Here one can study only how fast the animal runs and whether he runs at all. Simple as it is, the runway has proved valuable for studying many aspects of reinforcement, extinction, and even discrimination.

Advantages of Laboratory Study

Hopefully, the preceding examples have helped to indicate the relation between the sorts of learning situations studied in the laboratory and the sorts of most interest to educators and to others directly concerned with the problems of learning in everyday life. However, it may be well to discuss certain aspects of the relationships more explicitly. Two main points need to be considered: (1) what psychologists gain by studying learning under the somewhat artificial conditions of the laboratory, and (2) what difficulties are involved in applying the results to other, nonlaboratory, situations.

There are two main respects in which the psychologist gains by taking questions about learning into the laboratory. One of these pertains to *measurement*. The laboratory situation permits the experimenter to measure the subject's behavior more adequately than is usually possible outside the laboratory. He can keep an accurate record of how long it takes a subject to memorize certain material or to solve a given problem, of how many and what kind of errors a subject makes, and of the successive stages by which mastery is reached. This improved measurement is valuable for three reasons. First, it gives a more complete picture of the learning process. Details are recorded that otherwise would be overlooked or quickly forgotten. Second, it protects the researcher against the mistake of noticing and remembering only what he expects. Thus a teacher who is convinced that a certain new method of teaching long division will work better than the old method may remember clearly her striking successes with the new method, while overlooking the failures as unimportant exceptions. It is possible, of course, that in this case the failures are unimportant exceptions, but whether they are should be decided by careful consideration, not by spur-of-the-moment intuition. If both successes and failures are recorded as they occur, and if extenuating considerations are noted for the successes as well as for the failures, the effect of teaching with the new method can be more objectively evaluated. Third, apart from such systematic biases as this teacher's, careful measurement also protects the researcher against all the unsystematic errors of observation and memory that are likely to occur when research is carried on as part of everyday work. Thus measurement in the laboratory is likely to be more thorough, more precise, and more objective than measurement in comparable situations elsewhere.

The other gain from studying learning in the lab is in *control*. Essentially, this gain is associated with our ability to study one thing at a time. When we control a variable, we hold it constant so that it will not interfere with our studying another variable. Suppose, for example, that we want to find out whether it is easier to learn spelling when words that are likely to cause confusion with one another (e.g., "separate" and "cemetery") are in the same lesson or in different lessons. We can study this problem by preparing two sets of lessons, one according to each principle, and using them with two sets of students. However, we must see to it that the two sets of students do not differ in intelligence, interest in spelling, previous experience with these words, or motivation to do well in their studies. We must also see that the groups are taught by teachers who do not differ in teaching ability or in enthusiasm. In other words, we must control intelligence, motivation, and all the other above variables except arrangement of the words in the spelling lessons. Only then can we be confident that any difference we find in mastery of the spelling lessons is due to arrangement of the words rather than to some other difference between the two sets of students. Because the practical demands of the classroom make it difficult to obtain such control, or even to know whether one has obtained it, it is valuable to have laboratories specially arranged for doing well-controlled experiments.

Though laboratory studies of learning provide great advantages in measurement and in control, we must not suppose that they provide easy answers to questions about the practical management of learning. Because they typically study single variables out of their usual context, laboratory experiments can seldom give direct answers to questions about how these variables work together in that context. For example, it has been established in a number of experiments that larger reinforcers lead to better performance in a learning situation. Does it follow that the more lavishly a teacher praises students for their successes, the better the students will do their work? Perhaps, but there are various reasons why this result might not follow. The students might become so used to this effusive praise that it would soon be no more reinforcing to them than mild praise would be to other students. Or, perhaps, those who failed to win the praise might be all the more frustrated because the praise they missed was so desirable, which might result in more disappointment and anger becoming conditioned as responses to the stimuli of the whole situation. Moreover, neither the reinforcers nor the learning tasks used in the laboratory are likely to be the same ones used in the classroom (in fact, many of the studies on reinforcement magnitude were done with animals); this kind of difference will probably make the outcomes different in degree, and possibly in kind. Finally, even if the subjects, tasks, and reinforcers are all similar in the laboratory and in the classroom, the difference between working alone in an unfamiliar situation (the laboratory) and working in a familiar group situation (the classroom) may produce considerable differences in behavior. For all of these reasons we would be rash to generalize from the laboratory studies to the classroom application.

VARIABLES, LAWS, AND THE PROCESS OF ABSTRACTION

Researchers in the field of learning, like those in any other branch of science, are concerned with discovering scientific *laws*. All the experimental procedures we have discussed are directed toward such discovery. A law is a statement about the conditions under which certain things occur. Some laws are highly precise and accurate, as in the physicist's statement that the period of a pendulum is proportional to the square root of its length. Other laws are much less precise and much more subject to error, as when the amateur weather prophet maintains, "Red at night, sailor's delight; red in the morning, sailor's warning." In both cases, however, we are being told that certain events occur under certain conditions. Given those conditions, we can predict that these events will occur. The prediction need not always be correct, so long as it is correct often enough to be useful. If bad weather occurs 75 per cent of the time when the morning sky is red and only 20 per cent of the time when the morning sky is gray, the amatuer weather prophet has a valid law, even though not a wholly accurate one, for predicting the weather.

Kinds of Variables and Laws

All laws state a relationship between a *dependent variable* and one or more *independent variables*. A dependent variable is one about which we make a prediction; an independent variable is one we use to make the prediction. In the above examples, the length of the pendulum and the color of the sky were independent variables while the period of the pendulum (the time it takes to make its complete swing) and the weather were dependent variables. In a study of learning, the dependent variable is some aspect of the learner's performance, while the independent variables may be any characteristics of the learner, the task, or the situation.

In some cases these variables and the laws relating them to one another involve merely the presence or absence of something. This is the case with the weather-prediction law. Red in the evening indicates good weather and red in the morning bad weather; that is all we are told. Does it matter whether the red is pale or deep? Will the bad weather be a drizzle or a hurricane? The law does not tell us. In other words, it deals with *qualitative* information only, information about the *kinds* of events that occur. In other cases, however, degrees of the independent variable are related to degrees of the dependent variable. The physicist's law tells us how much of a change in pendulum length will produce how much of a change in period. This, then, is a *quantitative* law, one that gives information about *amounts* of things, about the degree to which certain events occur. In learning, the statement that removal of a reinforcer produces extinction is a qualitative law, since it refers only to whether or not reinforcement is removed and whether or not extinction occurs. On the other hand, the statement that a larger reward results in a higher level of performance is quantitative, since it deals with different amounts of reward and different levels of performance. Both qualitative and quantitative laws are found in all branches of science, but in general the more highly developed sciences tend to have more quantitative laws.

Independent variables also differ in another respect. Some independent variables can be directly varied by an experimenter. He can arrange the independent variable to suit himself and then see what happens to the dependent variable. For example, a physicist can change the length of a pendulum in order to see how this difference affects the rate at which the pendulum swings. Likewise, a psychologist can stop reinforcing a pigeon for pecking a key and watch what happens to the rate of pecking. Such a study, in which the independent variable is manipulated by the researcher, is called an experiment. If the experiment is properly controlled, we can conclude definitely that the changes in the independent variable caused the changes in the dependent variable.

There are other independent variables, however, that cannot be manipulated by an experimenter. The weather prophet cannot make the sky red in order to see what will happen to the weather. He has to wait until the sky gets red by itself and then watch for changes in the weather. This is still a perfectly valid scientific study, but it is not an experiment, for the researcher does not manipulate the independent variable. A similar example in learning would be a study of memorization rate in people of varying IQs. Here IQ would be the independent variable and rate of learning the dependent variable. The researcher could not change a person's IQ; he could only choose subjects who already had different IQs and then compare their learning rates. A difficulty with this kind of nonexperimental study is that we can seldom be sure just what is causing what. We would not be likely to say that red in the evening sky caused good weather; presumably some atmospheric condition caused both. The red sky was merely an indicator of good weather, not its cause. We might say that high IQ caused faster memorizing (if we found such a relation, as we quite likely would not), but perhaps it would be just as reasonable to say that high memorizing ability was responsible, over a lifetime, for the development of a high IQ. These nonexperimental studies still give us laws that are valuable for prediction, but for telling us what causes what they are definitely inferior. For this and other reasons, experimental studies are preferable wherever it is possible to do them, and the great majority of psychological studies of learning are experiments.

As we have seen, scientific laws may differ in several ways. They may indicate simply that when something happens, something else will happen, or they may relate the amount of something to the amount of something else. They may be based on experiments or on nonexperimental observations. They may be very precise or they may allow for a large amount of error. In all cases, however, they state a relationship between an independent and a dependent variable in such a way as to make possible prediction from the independent to the dependent variable. These laws are the primary focus of science in general and hence of the psychology of learning in particular.

Abstraction

Scientific laws are statements about the way the world operates, and like all statements they involve abstractions. Whenever we apply words to things and events, we ignore a great deal of what is there in order to focus attention on what this particular thing or event has in common with others. For example, when we call something a car, we are ignoring its make, model, year, and color in order to emphasize the features it has in common with other cars. In other words, we are abstracting its "carness" from all the other characteristics of this particular battered, brown, eight-year-old, two-door Ford. The same is true when we use the term "discrimination" to describe the behavior both of a rat learning whether to turn right or left in a T maze and of a child learning whether to use "ar" or "er" in spelling a word. Again, we are dealing with an abstract concept, ignoring most aspects of the two situations in order to concentrate on one thing that they have in common.

Since some degree of abstraction is inescapable, any statement, however concretely "factual," is an abstract formulation that tells only a part of the truth. To say, "Columbus crossed the ocean blue in 1492," is to give only the barest outline of that momentous event. Even to say, "John Doe dropped a copy of *A Tale of Two Cities* from his school desk to the floor in the middle of an arithmetic lesson in Room 6 on the morning of March 17" is to give only a minute fraction of the detail that could have been observed. For all their tremendous value, words are only pale shadows of the things they represent.

This process of abstraction goes on in all description and in all thought. Every intellectual activity involves the organization and simplification of "reality" as it is presented to our senses. This statement is true whether we consider simple perceptions or complex thoughts, and whether we look at science, art, sports, business or any other area of human interest. Imagine, for example, what the radio broadcast of a football game would sound like if it were presented by a society editor, or by the proud father of one of the players, or by a foreigner studying American customs. The society editor might spend all her time describing the lovely uniforms and discussing the family backgrounds of the players; the proud father might report only what his own son was doing; and the foreigner might be much more interested in the cheers and card stunts than in the progress of the game. Each of these three descriptions could be perfectly true and valid as far as it went, but what football fan would accept any of them as an adequate report of the game? Each description, including the professional sportcaster's, would deal with only some aspects of the "real game"; each would reflect not only what "really happened" but also the interests and biases and vocabulary of the reporter.

In effect, there is no such thing as pure reality; there is only reality as described and interpreted and reacted to by someone. Some descriptions are more accurate or more detailed than others, but no description is complete. Even if someone were ambitious enough to collect descriptions of a football game from everyone who was there, check them with other kinds of evidence, spend years sifting and combining these accounts, and give a final report of the game many volumes long, there would still be details that were omitted. The report would still be only an abstract, even though a very detailed one, of what happened at the game. In any case, no one would read the report, since each possible reader would be interested in those aspects of the game that he considered interesting or important, not in the most detailed account that human patience and ingenuity could devise. Hence, any useful report of the game would involve far more abstraction and organization and simplification than our imaginary multivolume monstrosity of a description.

This process of abstraction is carried even farther in scientific laws than in many other kinds of statements. In history, biography, and literature, as well as in everyday speech, we are often concerned with describing an event in as much rich detail as time and the limitations of language permit. Our several imaginary broadcasts of the football game, different as they were, were nevertheless all trying for such completeness within the limits of the reporters' interests. In science, however, we are always concerned with picking out certain aspects of the situation to be related to other aspects. In relating the period of a pendulum to its length, the physicist need not concern himself with what the pendulum is made of or with whether it is a clock pendulum, a plumb bob, or a museum display. Similarly, the psychologist's statement that removal of the reinforcer reduces the frequency of the response applies whether the reinforcer is food or praise and whether the response is pecking a key or studying spelling. The laws connecting independent and dependent variables are not descriptions of any particular event—they are statements about the conditions under which certain kinds of events occur. Scientific laws are not concerned specifically with the red sky in Chicago on June 10 or with the pendulum of John Jones's grandfather's clock, but with all red skies or all pendulums. Some laws may be quite narrow in the range of phenomena to which they refer, but even the narrowest always refers to certain kinds of events, never merely to a single unique event.

The Value of Scientific Laws

Scientific laws serve two main purposes. One purpose is practical—to provide man with the means of predicting and controlling events. Simply being able to predict what will happen and thus take measures to deal with it is of considerable value. Such prediction is what keeps the weather bureau and the various investment advisory services in business. It is even more useful, however, to be able to control events. An independent variable that we can manipulate gives us some degree of control over the dependent variable. This fact is the meaning of the saying that "knowledge is power." Only if we have a law about the conditions under which certain kinds of events happen can we set up the necessary conditions for one such event to happen when we want it to. It is not necessary, of course, for the law to be formally stated; much of our practical knowledge is very casual. However, the more complete and accurate our formulation of the laws is, the better able we are to control the world around us.

Scientific laws also have a less utilitarian value. Since earliest times man has sought to understand the world in which he lived. From the child trying to find out what makes the watch tick to the cosmologist trying to find out what makes the universe tick, man is constantly asking "what is it?" and "how does it work?" and "why?" No practical benefits are required to justify this curiosity; to gain the knowledge is benefit enough in itself. This benefit is the basis of pure science, the search for fundamental knowledge about the world.

Both of these purposes of science are exemplified in the study of the psychology of learning. The laws of learning are of crucial importance to education, to industrial, military, and other forms of training, to child rearing, to psychotherapy, and to a variety of other practical areas of work. They are also basic to an understanding of how individuals and societies come to be as they are, of how knowledge is obtained, indeed of how man acquires his unique humanness. Hence for both reasons an increase in our knowledge of the laws of learning is much to be desired.

THE NATURE OF THEORIES

Researchers are rarely satisfied, however, merely to collect more and more laws about learning or about anything else. To satisfy man's desire for understanding, knowledge must be organized. An encyclopedia full of laws relating each of a vast number of independent variables to each of a vast number of dependent variables might give its owner the emotional satisfaction of having a great deal of knowledge available, but it would not give the intellectual satisfaction of understanding the topics involved. Such satisfaction requires more general knowledge than that provided by this imaginary encyclopedia of laws. Even for practical purposes, such an encyclopedia would be cumbersome. It would be more convenient to have general principles from which the specific laws could be deduced. So, although the establishing of laws is in one sense the most basic activity of science, it is not the end of scientific activity. Much of the researcher's effort is dedicated toward establishing more general principles or interpretations. This effort takes him into the realm of scientific theory.

We have already seen that description represents some abstraction and organization and simplification of the events being described, and that the statement of laws represents a higher level of abstraction. With theory we come to a still higher level of abstraction. It differs in degree but not in kind from the lower levels. It is a serious mistake to think of a realm of theory that is separate and different from the realm of fact. When people speak of "facts," they are sometimes referring to descriptions of events ("It is a fact that John F. Kennedy became President of the United States in 1961.") and sometimes to laws ("It is a fact that hydrogen and oxygen will combine to form water."). As we have seen, both descriptions and laws represent organizations and simplifications of what is "really there" according to the language and the biases and the objectives of whoever is describing the event or stating the law. Theory exemplifies the same processes, but in still greater degree. It would be reasonable to say either that facts represent one kind of theory or that theories represent one kind of fact, but most reasonable to say that fact and theory represent different degrees of what is basically a single process.

What is a theory? This is not an easy question to answer, partly because there are a number of different opinions about what a theory should be like and what functions it should serve. It is really only through studying different theories—noting their similarities and differences and the purposes their creators had in mind—that one can get a general understanding of what theories are. In a sense, therefore, the rest of this book is an attempt to answer this question. In this chapter we can hope to get only a rough and general overview.

In the broadest sense, a theory is a systematic interpretation of an area of knowledge. In the psychology of learning, "system" or "systematic interpretation" is probably a better term than "theory," for theory is sometimes used in a narrower sense to refer to a kind of formal logical system. However, in this book we will use *theory, system,* and *systematic interpretation* as synonyms.

Three Functions of Theory

A theory of learning is usually three different but closely related things. First, it is an approach to the area of knowledge, a way of analyzing and talking about and doing research on learning. It represents the researcher's point of view about what aspects of learning are most worth studying, what independent variables should be manipulated and what dependent variables studied, what research techniques employed, and what language used to describe the findings. It focuses his attention on certain topics and helps him decide which of all the possible abstractions will be most useful. Thus theory serves as a guide and a source of stimulation for research and for scientific thought.

Second, a theory of learning is an attempt to summarize a large amount of knowledge about the laws of learning in a fairly small space. In this process of summarization, some exactness and detail are likely to be lost. In such precise and well-developed sciences as physics, theories do quite well in summarizing laws so that the same exact predictions can be made from the theories as from the much more detailed laws. Psychology, to date, has been less successful in finding such theories. Theories of learning, in attempting to summarize large amounts of knowledge, lose a good deal in completeness and precision. They are simplifications or skeletal outlines of the material with which they deal. As such, they represent a gain in breadth, in organization, and in simplicity, but also a loss in accuracy of detail.

Third, a theory of learning is a creative attempt to explain what learning is and why it works as it does. The laws give us the "how" of learning; the theories attempt to give us the "why." Thus they seek to provide that basic understanding which is one of the goals, not alone of science, but of all forms of scholarship. Theories represent man's best efforts to determine the underlying structure of the world in which he lives.

Intervening Variables

In most cases, theorists have sought this underlying structure in entities that were not visible to the observer. Theorists in the field of chemistry, for example, assumed the existence of molecules long before anyone had ever seen a molecule under the microscope. They did so because the laws of chemistry formed a simpler and more logical pattern if all substances were assumed to be made up of molecules. The laws of chemistry did not themselves deal with molecules, but with substances that could be seen and touched and weighed. The molecules were in effect invented by the theorists as an explanation for the laws. This invention was a creative guess that has received more and more support from later evidence and that has contributed immensely to the development of chemistry.

Let us consider a corresponding example, though admittedly a less striking one, from the psychology of learning. We might deprive an animal of water for a period of time, or reduce the animal's daily ration of water below the normal intake, or permit him to drink only for a limited time each day, or feed him a lot of dry food without water available, or inject a salt solution into his stomach. The extent to which we did any one of these things (e.g., how long he could drink per day or how much salt was injected) would be an independent variable. We would find that each of these independent variables was related in much the same way to each of several dependent variables. As any of these independent variables increased, the animal would become more active, would drink more water when water was available, would run faster to a place where he had found water in the past, and would be more reinforced by water if water was presented as a reward for making some response. These relationships constitute twenty laws, relating each of the five independent variables to each of the four dependent variables. We can, however, reduce this number to nine laws by saying that each of the five independent variables produces a state of thirst and that this thirst in turn produces changes in the four dependent variables. By hypothesizing this state of thirst, we have more than cut in half the number of laws required to describe the relationships involved.

So far this act of theoretical simplification is no more than what any layman does. It is so commonplace, indeed, that it is easy to overlook its importance. No one has ever seen or touched or weighed thirst. We have felt it in ourselves, but in anyone else we can only infer it. We have to infer someone else's thirst from what has happened to him (the independent variables) or from what he does (the dependent variables). If he tells us he is thirsty, his statement is only one of the possible dependent variables, and not necessarily the most reliable. When a child gets out of bed for the fourth time and tells his mother he is thirsty, she is understandably more likely to trust other evidence than what the child says.

Anyone who thinks it is possible to differentiate sharply between theory and fact should consider how much theory there is in the simple "factual" statement, "He is thirsty."

The psychologist's use of the concept "thirst" differs from the layman's in two respects. One is in precision. The psychologist is not satisfied with saying that certain manipulations will produce thirst and thirst will produce certain behaviors; he goes on to determine what degrees of the independent variables are related to what degrees of thirst and what degrees of thirst are related to what increases in the dependent variables. Thus the psychologist's use of the concept "thirst" allows for more complete and accurate detail than the layman's.

The other difference is that the psychologist is likely to go farther than the layman in relating this concept to others. Many theorists of learning have been struck with the similarities among hunger, thirst, pain, and a variety of other such hypothetical states (hypothetical because none of them can be directly observed). All of these tend to produce increases in activity and physiological changes characteristic of stress. Moreover, the termination of any of these is reinforcing. They have therefore often been classified together as *drives*. This concept of drive provides a higher level of theoretical integration, bringing together far more laws than the separate concepts of hunger, thirst, pain, and the like.

Theoretical concepts of the sort we have been discussing are often called *intervening variables*. This name reflects their place in the theoretical structure, intervening between the independent and the dependent variables and forming a link connecting them together. These intervening variables are states or conditions of the individual that are inferred from observations. *Habits, beliefs,* and *motives* are examples of intervening variables that are important in various theories of learning.

By this time the reader is very likely asking, "Are these intervening variables really there, waiting to be discovered, or are they invented by theorists as a matter of convenience?" In other words, is the theorist more like an explorer, discovering hidden truths, or is he more like an artist, creating views of the world that suit his own purposes? If the discussion so far has been vague on this question, it is because theorists are by no means agreed on the matter. Undoubtedly both discovery and creation enter into theory, as indeed into all scientific work. A theory must lead to valid predictions, must be consistent with well-established laws, otherwise it is worthless. This requirement sets limits on the theorist's creative freedom. On the other hand, the same laws can be interpreted in different ways, and these interpretations are not waiting around to be discovered—they must be created by an interpreter. Perhaps the theorist is less like either an explorer or an artist than like an architect, limited by his materials and by the demands of his job, but still working with originality and imagination to produce a new, useful, and beautiful structure.

This is admittedly not a very adequate answer to the question of whether the intervening variables are "really there." Some theorists talk as though they are really there and others as though it is merely convenient to pretend that they are there. It has been suggested that there should be two different terms, one for those that the theorist thinks he has discovered and the other for those that he thinks he has invented. Fortunately, we can leave this issue to the philosophers and concern ourselves only with the part that intervening variables play in the various theories we will be studying.

In any case, the element of creativity in theory construction explains why there are many theories of learning. Each theorist tries to find a way of structuring reality that will be useful and meaningful to him. The differences among the resulting theories reflect partly the differences in the topics that various theorists find most interesting to work with, and partly differences in the kinds of systematic structures that different theorists consider worth producing. All, however, reflect the efforts of thoughtful men to interpret the phenomena of learning in coherent and intellectually satisfying ways.

Kinds of Learning Theories

The currently important theories of learning can be classified in a number of ways. For our purposes, two main differences among these theories seem most significant. One of these is the difference between the *connectionist* and the *cognitive* theories. Connectionist interpretations of learning, however much they may differ among themselves, agree in treating learning as a matter of connections between stimuli and responses. (A response may be any item of behavior, while a stimulus may be any sensation. Connectionist theorists typically assume that all responses are elicited by stimuli.) These connections are called by a variety of names, such as habits, stimulus-response bonds, and conditioned responses. Always, however, there is a concentration on the responses that occur, on the stimuli (and perhaps other conditions) that elicit them, and on the ways that experience changes these relationships between stimuli and responses. Cognitive interpretations, on the other hand, are concerned with the cognitions (perceptions or attitudes or beliefs) that the individual has about his environment, and with the ways these cognitions determine his behavior. In these interpretations, learning is the study of the ways in which cognitions are modified by experience.

Common sense makes use of both kinds of interpretations. When discussing simple reactions or more complex physical skills, we are likely to say, "I guess it's just a bad habit I've learned," or "With all that practice, his reactions have become very fast and smooth." These are connectionist interpretations. On the other hand, when discussing matters that involve words or deliberate decisions, we often say things like, "He has acquired a lot of knowledge on that subject," or "You'll have to learn that people don't like to be treated that way," or "Now I really understand geometry!" These interpretations are all cognitive.

Whether a given psychologist will prefer a connectionist or a cognitive theory of learning depends partly on the kind of learning in which he is most interested. A specialist in the study of conditioning is likely to find a connectionist interpretation better suited to his needs, while a specialist in problem solving may find a cognitive interpretation more useful. However, each specialist will tend to believe that the theory he prefers is best, not only for his own field of study, but for the whole psychology of learning. This tendency reflects a desire for unity and simplicity that is one of the reasons why theories are developed in the first place. As a result, some people adopt general cognitive theories of learning and others adopt general connectionist ones.

In addition, philosophical differences bias people toward different interpretations. Connectionist theories lend themselves to greater precision and fit in better with an over-all scientific approach in which human learning is just one part of the natural world. Cognitive theories, on the other hand, make more allowance for the power and flexibility of man's intellectual processes and the ways in which he deals with complex problems. As a result, scientific psychologists have more often chosen connectionist interpretations, while applied psychologists (including those in education) have been more inclined toward cognitive interpretations. This is by no means a hard and fast distinction, however, and there are signs that it may be breaking down further.

The other major difference is between formal and informal theories of learning. An informal theorist gives an interpretation of learning in words. It is a more systematic, more precise, and more thorough interpretation than the proverbial man in the street would give, but it is fundamentally of the same sort. It is an attempt to explain in everyday language what learning is, how it operates, and what is going on in the person when it occurs. A formal theorist, on the other hand, tries to make his theory a formal, logical structure. As compared with the informal theorist, he is likely to make greater use of mathematics and to distinguish his intervening variables more rigorously from his independent and dependent variables. His goal is to create a system of postulates and theorems somewhat like Euclid's geometry, in which a great many laws can be logically deduced from a small number of postulates. This formal procedure has the advantage of making clearer just what the theorist is doing. It makes the logic of theory construction more explicit and also makes sloppy thinking easier to detect. However, it also has the disadvantage of making the theoretical writings harder to read and farther removed from everyday ideas of what an interpretation of learning should be. In the history of learning theory, formal systems have tended to develop later, building on the informal systems that preceded them.

Needless to say, neither the connectionist-cognitive distinction nor the formal-informal distinction is an all-or-nothing matter. There are various middle positions between the cognitive and the connectionist, and there are varying degrees of formality. Nevertheless, these two 'distinctions form a convenient basis for classifying the interpretations of learning that we will be investigating here. We will look first at some informal connectionist theories, which will illustrate the ways psychologists typically interpret learning. Next we will consider some cognitive theories, varying in formality. These are less popular among psychologists of learning, but have been influential in social psychology and in education and have important implications for the future development of learning theory. Finally we will look at some formal theories primarily of the connectionist sort, and at some compromise positions. It is hoped that this survey will indicate what learning theories are, what they try to accomplish, how successful they are, and what they can contribute to our understanding of the learning process.

Chapter 2

Contiguity Theories in the
Connectionist Tradition

MAN'S INTEREST IN psychology has a long history. At least since
the time of the ancient Greeks, philosophers have been speculat-
ing about topics that are now considered part of psychology. How
do we think and feel and learn and know and make decisions and
act on them? Attempts to answer these questions make up a considerable part of the history of philosophy. It was not until the
nineteenth century, however, that attempts were made to study
these topics experimentally. The first psychological laboratory
was founded by Wilhelm Wundt in Germany in 1879. Although
research in psychology had been going on before then, this date
marks the point at which modern scientific psychology was placed
on a definite institutional footing.

Wundt and his colleagues in early scientific psychology, like the
philosophers from whom they drew much of their inspiration,
were largely interested in conscious experience. They wanted to
understand man's' sensations and thoughts and feelings. They
wanted to take the continuous flux of conscious awareness and
analyze it into its basic components. Are memory images the
same as sensations? Are feelings a special kind of sensation or are
they something radically different? How is the intensity of a sensation related to the intensity of the physical stimulus that produces
it? These were the sorts of questions that the early experimental
psychologists studied.

This kind of psychology, developed in Germany, became to a
great extent the standard for the rest of Europe and for America.
The research in psychological laboratories and the discussion in

31

textbooks of psychology were principally based on this approach. Its acceptance, however, was never complete. In the United States, for example, there was always a considerable trend toward the study of objective behavior as well as of conscious experience. American psychologists were interested in what people did as well as in what they thought and felt. Along with this went an un-European interest in applied psychology, in the practical uses to which psychological knowledge could be put. So although American psychology developed largely within the German mold, it had its own individual features as well.

WATSON AND BEHAVIORISM

Early in the twentieth century, these features of American psychology came more and more into conflict with the German tradition. Pressure increased to break the traditional mold and to develop a psychology that was frankly oriented toward objective behavior and toward practical usefulness. To varying degrees, psychologists were taking up the cry, "Enough of studying what people think and feel; let's begin studying what people do!" This movement found its most vocal spokesman in John B. Watson (1878-1958). It was through his vigorous attacks on traditional psychology and his attempts to build a radically different system that American theoretical psychology came into its own.

In 1900 Watson received the first doctorate of philosophy in psychology granted by the University of Chicago. His dissertation was a study of maze learning by rats, and this concern with animal behavior was typical of his early interests. He was impressed by the fact that in studying animal behavior it is possible to dispense with consciousness and simply study what the animal does. Why, he asked, can't we do the same with humans? Behavior is real and objective and practical, while consciousness belongs to the realm of fantasy. Let's abolish consciousness from our discussions and study behavior! Watson's professors at Chicago agreed with many of his objections to traditional psychology, but considered his solution too radical. Perhaps they thought that, like so many young rebels, he would become more conservative with age and responsibility. In Watson's case, however, this change did not occur. After joining the faculty at the Johns Hopkins University in 1904, he became all the more convinced that his extreme position was the answer to psychology's problems. In 1913 he published the first formal statement of his position, an article entitled *Psychology as the Behaviorist Views It,* and the psychological revolution known as behaviorism was under way.

The reason for the name "behaviorism" is clear enough. Watson was interested only in behavior, not in conscious experience. Human behavior was to be studied as objectively as was the behavior of machines. Consciousness was not objective; therefore it was not scientifically valid and could not be meaningfully studied. And by "behavior" Watson meant nothing more abstruse than the movements of muscles. What is speech? Movements of the muscles of the throat. What is thought? Subvocal speech, talking silently to oneself. What are feeling and emotion? Movements of the muscles of the gut. Thus did Watson dispose of mentalism in favor of a purely objective science of behavior.

It is easy to satirize such a position. (Estes, for example, has suggested that a behaviorist might change the familiar motto from "Think!" to "Behave!" and finally to "Twitch!") But we must not overlook the tremendous importance of this position for the development of modern psychological science. Though much objective study of behavior antedated Watson, he stands out as the great popularizer, the man who turned this sort of study into a national movement and philosophy.

Watson's opposition to admitting anything subjective into psychology led him to reject much more than the study of consciousness. Another of his targets was the analysis of motivation in terms of instincts. At the time Watson's career began, it was common to explain almost any form of behavior as due to a particular instinct. Sociability was attributed to an instinct of gregariousness, fighting to an instinct of pugnacity, and so forth. These were assumed to be innate and to determine in considerable measure what behavior people would show. These instincts were too mentalistic for Watson. He asserted that our behavior is, on the contrary, a matter of conditioned reflexes, that is, of responses learned by what is now called classical conditioning. We do not show sociability or aggression because we are born with an instinct to do so, but because we have learned to do so through conditioning.

Watson's demolition of theories extended not only to instincts but to other supposedly innate mental characteristics of man. He denied that we are born with any particular mental abilities or traits or predispositions. All we inherit is our bodies and a few reflexes; differences in ability and in personality are simply differences in learned behavior. Thus Watson was in several respects a strong exponent of environment as against heredity in the familiar nature-nurture controversy. What we are depends entirely (except for clearly anatomical differences) on what we have learned. And since what has been learned can be unlearned, this contention meant that human nature, either in general or in a particular person, was greatly subject to change. There was practically no limit to what man, properly conditioned, might become.

This combination of objectivity with faith in the power of learning swept American psychology and captured the popular imagination. Combined with some more specific ideas about learning, it had great implications for child rearing, education, advertising, and social organization. When we consider how well Watson's ideas fitted with the American belief in equality of opportunity, emphasis on unemotional practicality, and faith in progress, it is no surprise that behaviorism came to occupy the center of the American psychological stage.

We cannot, of course, picture Watson as suddenly presenting behaviorism and having it promptly and universally adopted. When Watson published *Psychology as the Behaviorist Views It* the trends to objectivity and to environmentalism were already under way. The demolition of instinct doctrine was more the work of L. L. Bernard and of Z. Y. Kuo than of Watson. Moreover, Watson owed many of his ideas to sources as diverse as the philosophy of John Locke in England and the physiological psychology of Ivan Pavlov in Russia. Finally, alternative points of view continued to be defended, and Watson faced much opposition. Nevertheless, there was a marked change in American psychology during this period, and Watson was the keynote speaker around

whom any discussion of the change is likely to center. He gave behaviorism its name, its loudest voice, and its sense of mission.

Watson's Interpretation of Learning

What, then, was Watson's interpretation of learning? We have
already seen that he regarded all learning as classical conditioning. We are born with certain stimulus-response connections
called reflexes. Examples are sneezing in response to an irritation
of the nose and the knee-jerk response to a sharp tap on the knee.
These reflexes, according to Watson, are the entire behavioral
repertoire that we inherit. However, we can build a multiplicity
of new stimulus-response connections by the process of conditioning. If a new stimulus occurs along with the stimulus for the reflex response, after several such pairings the new stimulus alone
will produce the response. This conditioning process, first described by Pavlov, makes it possible for each response in the original repertoire of reflexes to be elicited by a great variety of new
stimuli in addition to the ones that originally elicited it. This, according to Watson, is how we learn to respond to new situations.

Such conditioning, however, is only part of the learning process.
We must not only learn to respond to new situations; we must also
learn new responses. Sneezes, knee jerks, and the like would not
carry us very far in dealing with complex situations. How can complex new habits be learned? The answer, according to Watson,
is by building up series of reflexes. Walking, for example, is a sequence of many responses, such as putting the weight on one foot,
swinging the other foot forward, bringing it down, thrusting the
weight forward from one foot to the other, and so forth. All these
responses occurring in proper order constitute the skilled performance of walking. The building up of such a sequence is possible because each response produces muscular sensations that
become stimuli for the next response. Thus new and complex behavior is acquired through the serial combination of simple reflexes.

Let us look at this kind of learning in more detail. Consider one
response in the sequence, such as swinging the leg forward. Originally the stimulus for this response is, perhaps, the sight of the

place toward which one is walking. However, the person can swing his leg forward only if his weight is on the other foot. Hence, whenever he swings his leg forward, he does so in the presence of those sensations from his own body that result from having his weight on the other foot. Those sensations thus are paired with the response of swinging the leg, and through repeated pairings they come to elicit leg swinging. Hence, in the well-learned habit of walking, the sensation of having weight on one foot automatically elicits the conditioned response of swinging the other leg forward. This response merges with the others in the sequence, each providing the stimulus for the next response. The sequence eventually becomes so well integrated that for practical purposes we can speak of the whole process of walking from one place to another as a single response, even though it is actually a complex sequence of stimulus-response connections.

A reader of the above discussion is very likely dissatisfied with Watson's explanation of complex learning. What, one may fairly ask, determines that this particular sequence of stimulus-response connections will be formed? Why does the sensation of weight on one foot elicit the response of swinging the other leg forward? Reading between the lines in Watson's last book (*Behaviorism*, first published in 1924), one gets the feeling that he was still seeking the answer to this problem. He had two different answers, neither completely adequate, and the relation between the two was still unclear. One answer was to say that the stimulus-response connections that make up the skilled act are conditioned reflexes. Each response produces sensations that become conditioned stimuli for the next response, and thus the whole sequence of conditioned stimulus-response connections is formed. This formulation gave Watson the satisfaction of having reduced complex habits to their simple building blocks, conditioned reflexes. Now, he said, we can turn to the physiologists to explain why conditioning occurs; we as behaviorists have done our job. However, Watson never really carried the analysis through in detail. If feeling one's weight on the left foot is the conditioned stimulus and swinging the right leg forward is the response, what is the unconditioned stimulus which always guarantees that the response will occur so that conditioning can take place? To this crucial question, Watson had no answer. As a result, his reduction of complex behavior patterns to sequences of conditioned reflexes is more apparent than real.

Watson's other explanation of this form of learning is in terms of two principles: *frequency* and *recency.* The principle of frequency states that the more frequently we have made a given response to a given stimulus, the more likely we are to make that response to that stimulus again. Similarly, the principle of recency states that the more recently we have made a given response to a given stimulus, the more likely we are to make it again.

Watson illustrates these principles with the example of a three-year-old child learning to open a puzzle box with candy inside. The child turns the box around, pounds it on the floor, and makes a variety of other useless responses. Finally, by chance, he presses a button on the box, which is the one response that will release the lid so he can open the box and obtain the candy. Since the box is now open and the candy obtained, the child is no longer in the presence of the stimuli that kept him working at the box. The last response he made in the presence of those stimuli was the response of pressing the button. The next time his father puts candy in the box and closes the lid, the child will go through much the same sequence of trial and error as before. However, by chance, he will try some new responses and leave out some of those from last time. Again, however, the last response he makes will be that of pressing the button, since that is the one which changes the stimulus situation. Every time he works with the box, pressing the button occurs, whereas other responses may or may not. Thus in the long run button-pushing gains a lead in frequency. Since it is always the last response, it always has a lead in recency. As a result, button pushing occurs sooner and sooner on successive experiences with the box. Since button pushing solves the problem, other responses have less and less chance to occur on successive experiences with the box. Button pushing as a response to the stimulus of the closed box has been learned.

This illustration shows only how a single response, pressing a button, is learned. The problem might, however, have required the child to make a series of several successive responses to open the box, with each response changing the situation so that the next

C

response could be made. Pressing the button, for example, might have opened an outer lid and revealed a lever that had to be moved sideways in order to open the inner lid. In this case both button pushing and lever moving would be learned in the same way, since each would change the stimulus and thus become the last response to the old stimulus. Such a series of responses could be extended indefinitely.

Why, then, does one particular response rather than others occur to the stimulus at a given place in a complex sequence? Watson's answer is that during learning many different responses occur to the stimulus, but that through the process described above, most of them drop out. The response that changes the situation gains in frequency and recency until it comes to occur as soon as the stimulus is presented. That particular stimulus-response unit in the sequence is then complete.

All of these statements about the learning of new responses are left rather undeveloped in Watson's treatment. How are conditioning, the principle of frequency, and the principle of recency related? How does the fact that the learner may at first make some wrong response much oftener than the right one, yet still eventually learn the right one, fit in with the principle of frequency? Watson does not tell us. He was confident that complex learning could be explained by simple principles, but his attempted explanations were tentative and were never organized into a clear and consistent theory.

Special Kinds of Learning

What about the learning of emotional reactions? Here Watson makes a small concession to heredity, since he recognizes three innate patterns of emotional reaction. In principle these reaction patterns are the same as reflexes, for we can state what movements (including those of the internal organs) they involve and what stimuli will produce them. However, they are more complicated than what is usually meant by a reflex. The three emotional reaction patterns may for convenience be labeled as fear, rage, and love. We must note, however, says Watson, that these labels refer to patterns of movement, not to conscious feelings. If we bang a gong close to a child, and he starts to cry, we may describe this event by saying that the stimulus of a loud noise has produced the emotion of fear. However, we are simply giving a name to the behavior we see, not commenting on the child's feelings.

Emotional learning involves the conditioning of these three patterns of emotional response to new stimuli. The above example of innate fear was taken from a famous experiment of Watson's, which can also be used to illustrate conditioned fear. Little Albert, aged 11 months, was permitted to play with a white rat, which he did happily and with no sign of fear. A metal bar was then hit with a hammer close behind him. He started and fell sideways. This sudden loud noise was repeated a number of times just as the rat was presented to him, and each time he reacted in the same way, sometimes also whimpering. These responses indicate that the noise was an unconditioned stimulus for fear. After this training, the rat was presented without the noise. Albert fell over, cried, and crawled away from the rat as fast as he could. This change indicates that through the training procedure the rat had become a conditioned stimulus for fear. According to Watson, such conditioned and unconditioned responses account for all of our emotions.

What about the acquisition of knowledge? Can conditioning be used to explain how one learns, for example, the facts of history? Certainly, says Watson, for this knowledge consists simply of saying certain words, aloud or to oneself. The response sequence involved in saying "William the Conqueror defeated Harold the Saxon at Hastings in 1066" is in principle no different from that involved in walking across a room. A question, such as "How did the Norman conquest occur?" elicits the statement, which is itself a sequence of words with each word a conditioned stimulus for the next one. Acquiring knowledge is a process of learning to give the proper sequence of words in response to a question or other conditioned stimulus.

All of our behavior, says Watson, tends to involve the whole body. When we think, we may pace the floor or furrow our brows. We announce our opinions with smiles or waves of the arm as well as with words. We cannot therefore really say that emotions are responses of the gut or that thinking is made up of vocal responses.

These are the dominant but by no means the only responses involved. Everything we think, feel, say, or do involves activity of, to varying degrees, the entire body. This is probably the most fundamental credo of behaviorism.

Evaluation of Watson

Watson's great contribution to the development of psychology was his rejection of the distinction between body and mind and his emphasis on the study of objective behavior. This battle was so effectively won that most of the learning theory in America today is, in the broader sense of the word, behaviorist. In this book we will see a number of theoretical systems that represent different variations on the behaviorist theme. All of them have in common a concern with objective behavior, a strong interest in animal studies, a preference for stimulus-response analysis, and a concentration on learning as the central topic in psychology. This fact makes Watson in some ways the intellectual father or grandfather of a large portion of the systems we will be considering here.

On the other hand, Watson was much less thorough than he might have been in dealing with the detailed problems of learning. We have already seen the incompleteness and inconsistency in his treatment of complex learning.

In his eagerness to build an objective psychology, he was somewhat cavalier with the matter of logical thoroughness. Perhaps if he had worked on his theory longer (after the 1920's he stopped publishing and devoted himself exclusively to applied psychology) he would have extended his system to deal with some of these problems. More likely, however, his zeal for freeing psychology from subjectivism and nativism was incompatible with laborious theoretical completeness. In any case, Watson is now admired mainly for his philosophical trail blazing rather than for his detailed system building. It has remained for others to try to build, within the behaviorist framework, a more complete theory of learning.

GUTHRIE'S INTERPRETATION OF LEARNING

Of those who have continued in the behaviorist tradition in recent years, the one who has remained closest to Watson's original

position is Edwin R. Guthrie (1886-1959). From 1914 until his
retirement in 1956, Guthrie was a professor at the University of
Washington. His university teaching career thus began only ten
years later than Watson's, and he himself never studied with Watson. His graduate education was more in philosophy than in psychology. Nevertheless, his interpretation of learning sounds much
like what Watson's might have been if he had had another decade
to work on the topic. His definitive work, *The Psychology of
Learning,* was published in 1935 and revised in 1952, and his
final theoretical statement was published in 1959. Thus Guthrie
can be regarded as a contemporary theorist in a sense that Watson cannot.

Among theories of learning, Guthrie's is one of the easiest to
read in his own words, but nonetheless hard for someone else
to discuss. It is easy to read because he wrote in an easy, informal
style, making his points with homely anecdotes rather than with
technical terms and mathematical equations. It is hard to write
about because his casual presentation contains the germ of
a highly technical, deductive theory of learning. Reading Guthrie
is like reading an exciting novel that contains a difficult allegory,
so that it can be read on an easy or a hard level. At the heart of
his system is one basic principle of learning. Interpreted loosely,
this principle is a source both of entertaining interpretations of
learning and of valuable advice about the management of
learning situations. Interpreted rigorously, it becomes the chief
postulate of a deductive theory. This theory, so deceptively simple
at first glance but so maddeningly complex on closer investigation, stands as a challenge to students of learning. Has Guthrie actually succeeded in summing up the whole field of learning in one
key postulate?

The Basic Principle of Learning

Guthrie's basic principle of learning is similar to the conditioning principle that was basic for Watson, but it is stated in a still
more general form. It says, "A combination of stimuli which has
accompanied a movement will on its recurrence tend to be followed by that movement." (Guthrie, 1952, p. 23) The principle
may be paraphrased as, "If you do something in a given situation,

the next time you are in that situation you will tend to do the same thing again." This principle is more general than the principle of classical conditioning, in that it says nothing about an unconditioned stimulus. It says only that if a response accompanies a given stimulus once, it is likely to follow that stimulus again. In classical conditioning, the response occurs with the (conditioned) stimulus during training because the unconditioned stimulus elicits it. This sequence of course fulfills Guthrie's conditions for learning. However, it does not matter to Guthrie whether the response is elicited during training by an unconditioned stimulus or in some other way. As long as the (conditioned) stimulus and the response occur together, learning will occur.

In claiming to sum up the whole field of learning in that one statement, Guthrie was inevitably challenging others to find inadequacies in the summary, and psychologists have been quick to answer the challenge. The first difficulty with this principle is that one often does many different things in the same situation. Which one will occur next time? This challenge is no problem for Guthrie; he simply replies, "The last one." A person struggling with a mechanical puzzle tries many responses. If he finally makes the correct response, he will tend to make this same response when next confronted with the puzzle. We say, then, that he has learned how to do the puzzle. Suppose, however, that he finally gives up and puts the puzzle aside unsolved. The next time he sees the puzzle he will tend to do what he did last, namely put it aside. In that case we do not say that he has learned how to do the puzzle, but he has still learned something. In both cases he was presented with a combination of stimuli from the puzzle. In each case there was a movement that removed the stimuli. To the observer, one of these movements represented success and the other failure, but to Guthrie they both represented responses that removed the stimuli of the unsolved puzzle and that therefore became more likely to occur again. In both cases a response was learned, and in both cases it was by the same principle, contiguous conditioning.

This aspect of Guthrie's system sounds much like Watson's principle of recency, since the last thing that occurred in a situation is the one that will occur again. However, Guthrie does not use Watson's other principle, frequency. Whereas for Watson a stimulus-response connection is something that varies in strength and grows stronger with practice, for Guthrie it is an all-or-nothing bond. The connection is either present or absent, with no intermediate variation in strength. Hence the conditioning of a movement to a combination of stimuli takes place completely in one experience, and further practice adds nothing to the strength of the connection.

At first glance this assumption seems contrary to well-known laws of learning. While practice may not make perfect, it usually does produce gradual improvement. How can Guthrie say that all the improvement takes place in a single experience? We must beware, replies Guthrie, of treating a "movement" as the same thing as an act or an accomplishment. Guthrie is referring in his principle of learning to specific small movements of particular muscles. It takes many such movements working together to make up a skilled act. Moreover, competent performance involves not just one but many skilled acts, each in response to a particular combination of stimuli. Hence learning how to do something involves learning an enormous number of specific stimulus-movement connections. Improvement in the skill is gradual even though the learning of each minute part occurs suddenly.

Consider a particular skill, such as riding a bicycle. For each possible position of the bicycle, a different motion is required in order to keep it upright. Each of these motions, in turn, is made up of movements of the arms, torso, and legs. A particular movement of the left arm to help correct a particular kind and degree of tilt may be learned in one experience, but it certainly does not follow that the whole skill of balancing the bicycle will be learned so quickly. If we also consider all the other aspects of bicycle riding, the distinction between learning a movement and gradually mastering a skill becomes evident. This illustration does not show that Guthrie is necessarily correct when he says that a movement is learned in one trial, but it does make this interpretation more plausible.

This explanation, however, introduces some ambiguity into Guthrie's theory. In many cases "the last thing one did in a situation" refers to an act, such as lighting a cigarette or making a remark. These, however, are skilled performances made up of many specific movements. Why does Guthrie treat them as if they were single movements which could be conditioned in one trial? Presumably what is needed here is an analysis in terms of hierarchies of complexity. Lighting a cigarette is a skill made up of many stimulus-movement connections that must be conditioned. However, once learned, this whole act behaves like a single movement and can be conditioned as such to combinations of stimuli. Guthrie does not concern himself with this relationship, but applies his principle of learning sometimes to movements and sometimes to acts, depending on the point he wants to make. Fortunately, this ambiguity is unimportant in most situations.

Guthrie's Substitute for Reinforcement

The aspect of Guthrie's theory that has been most attacked is his lack of concern with success and failure, with learning to do the "right" thing. Whatever one did last in the situation, right or wrong, is what one will do again. Guthrie makes no use of the concept of reinforcement. He does not say that we learn to make those responses that work, or that obtain reward. Whether or not something we do becomes learned as a response to the situation depends only on whether it changes the situation into a different situation, so that it becomes the last thing done in the old situation. Success has this result, since a solution changes a problem situation into a situation without a problem. Thus the successful act is the last one that occurs in the problem situation, and it will tend to occur if the problem is presented again. However, if the individual can somehow escape from the situation without solving the problem, the escape response will be learned. Inefficient methods may be learned and retained as well as efficient ones, since both get the person out of the situation. Mistakes may be repeated over and over again. We learn, not by success or by reinforcement, but simply by doing.

A number of testable predictions follow from this position. As an example, consider a hungry rat that can obtain food by pressing a lever. The rat learns to press the lever more and more rapidly. According to Guthrie, the rat learns because the food changes the situation through its effect on hunger and on the sensations in the mouth. Thus pressing the lever becomes the last thing the animal did in the old situation, and it becomes increasingly likely to occur. Suppose instead of getting food after each pressing of the lever the rat was simply taken out of the box as soon as it pressed the lever. This would change the situation even more than food did, so the rat should be even more likely to press the lever on his next opportunity than if it had been fed. This experiment has been done, and the results did not confirm the prediction. (Seward, 1942) The rats receiving food showed far more lever pressing than those removed from the box, contrary to what would be expected from Guthrie's theory. This experiment and others like it cast doubt on Guthrie's view that reward has nothing to do with learning.

It may be, however, that our interpretation of this experiment is not altogether fair to Guthrie. Although the food produced less change in the total stimulus combination than did removal from the box, the food did produce a marked change in certain particularly important stimuli. These were the *maintaining stimuli*— those stimuli that kept the rat active in the situation. In this particular case the maintaining stimuli were those resulting from food deprivation—in other words, the stimuli of hunger. In other situations they might be the stimuli of thirst or pain or sexual arousal or anger or fear. At some places in his writings Guthrie suggests that it is changes in the maintaining stimuli that are crucial for learning. If a response removes the maintaining stimuli, by definition it solves the problem and thus becomes the last response in the problem situation. If it fails to remove the maintaining stimuli, then no matter what other changes it may produce it cannot be the last response in the problem situation. By this interpretation, we can see why food might be expected in Guthrie's theory to produce more learning than removal from the box.

However, this interpretation also raises other problems. In some cases responses are learned that do not remove the maintaining stimuli. A softball player learns those responses that produce successful batting and fielding, even though a base hit or a good catch does not reduce the competitive excitement that provides the maintaining stimuli for playing. A rat in a maze learns the correct turn at each choice point, even though only the last turn is followed by any change in the maintaining stimuli. In both cases, however, the response does change the over-all stimulus combination, so that it is in one sense the last response in the situation. Thus we are faced with the problem that sometimes only changes in the maintaining stimuli are crucial, while at other times changes in other stimuli are important. How do we know which times are which? Guthrie does not tell us. By sometimes considering all stimuli and sometimes only maintaining stimuli, Guthrie can explain any case of learning after it has occurred, but he cannot do so well at predicting what learning will take place.

By now the reader can see more clearly why Guthrie's system is difficult to treat as a formal logical theory. When are we talking about movements and when about acts? When should we look at all stimulus changes and when only at changes in the maintaining stimuli? Because he concentrates on presenting simple, entertaining interpretations of learning, Guthrie never gives clear answers to these awkward questions. As a result, his theory, which at first glance seemed so direct and precise, turns out to be discouragingly vague. His attempt to reduce all learning to one basic principle is, in any precise sense, inadequate.

His loose, anecdotal approach reflects the fact that Guthrie was more interested in the undergraduate teaching of psychology than in detailed research. He himself produced only one major experiment bearing on his theory, a demonstration of the stereotyped behavior of cats in escaping from a cage. Perhaps because of this lack of emphasis on research he has had many sympathizers but few active followers. There has never been a long and active tradition of research within the framework of Guthrie's theory (though Fred Sheffield, at Yale, did make a start toward one). On the other hand, many psychologists have found that, once they stop treating Guthrie's system as a formal deductive theory and concentrate on its informal implications, its basic principle of learning turns out to be quite useful. In any situation, says Guthrie, if you want to know what an individual will learn, look at what he does. What he does, right or wrong, is what he will learn. As a formal postulate, this statement is inadequate, but as an informal source of advice, it turns our attention to aspects of learning that we would otherwise be very likely to neglect. We can best appreciate Guthrie's contribution by looking at his discussions of some practical learning situations.

The Breaking of Habits

Perhaps the best known of these applications is in Guthrie's three methods for changing a bad habit. All three methods depend on finding out what stimuli evoke the undesirable response and then finding a way of making some other response occur in the presence of those stimuli. This other response should then occur again the next time the stimuli are presented. The emphasis is on the exact stimulus and the exact response that are connected. Guthrie gives the example of a ten-year-old girl who, whenever she came in the door of her house, threw her hat and coat on the floor. Time and again her mother scolded her and made her go back and hang them up, but to no avail. Finally the mother realized that the stimulus for the girl to hang up her wraps was the mother's nagging. The next time the girl threw down her wraps, her mother insisted that she put them on again, go outside, come in the door again, and hang up her coat and hat at once. After a few trials of this procedure the girl learned to hang up her wraps. The desired response had been attached to the stimuli of coming in the door, and the habit of throwing down the wraps had thus been replaced by the habit of hanging them up. This procedure worked where the previous nagging had failed because this time the mother saw to it that the girl hung up her wraps in the presence of the particular stimuli (those resulting from having just come through the door) that had previously led to the response of throwing the wraps down.

The first method, which may be called the _threshold_ method, involves presenting the stimuli so faintly or weakly that the undesirable response does not occur. (The stimulus is then said to be below the threshold intensity for the response, hence the name.) The stimuli are then increased in strength so gradually on successive occasions that the response never occurs. These repeated experiences with the weak stimuli raise the threshold so that stronger stimuli will also be below threshold. Eventually the stimuli can be presented at full strength without eliciting the undesired response, since the individual has been making some other response repeatedly in the presence of the stimuli. This method is useful mainly for emotional responses, involving anger, fear, or the like. Guthrie gives the example of the old cavalry method of training saddle horses. If an untrained horse is saddled and ridden, it will buck wildly. This reaction can be avoided by employing the method of thresholds to replace the bucking response with a response of standing quietly. First a blanket is put on the horse's back. This pressure on its back is the sort of stimulus that induces bucking, but the blanket alone is too weak a stimulus to have this effect. After some experience with the blanket the horse is saddled. Prior to experience with the blanket, the saddle might have produced bucking, but now it doesn't. Eventually, after the horse's experience with the saddle, a rider can mount without producing bucking, though the horse would certainly have bucked if mounted before the training with blanket and saddle. The experience of not bucking while successively heavier weights were placed on its back has eventually resulted in the horse's standing still even for the weight of a rider.

The second method may be called the method of *fatigue*. The response to be eliminated is elicited again and again, until the individual is so tired that he stops making the response and does something else (if only resting) instead. This other response is then the one likely to occur when the stimuli are presented again. Again Guthrie has an example of a disobedient small girl, though we are not told whether it is the same one who wouldn't hang up her clothes. This girl had a habit of lighting matches. After scolding and punishment failed, her worried mother finally eliminated the habit by making the girl light a whole box of matches in quick succession. Long after the girl was thoroughly tired of lighting matches, her mother insisted that she continue. Eventually she began actively resisting, throwing the box of matches down and pushing it away. At this point new responses, incompatible with match lighting, had been attached to the stimuli from the match box. The next time she had a chance to light matches, the girl showed no inclination to do so. This method illustrates in extreme degree Guthrie's reliance on his version of the law of recency (doing again what one did last in a given situation) and his rejection of the law of frequency. The girl had lighted matches more frequently at the end of this experience than at the beginning, but the last thing she did was to push the match box away. Pushing it away was therefore what she tended to do when she next encountered a match box.

In the third method, which we may call the method of *incompatible stimuli,* the stimuli for the undesired response are presented along with other stimuli that can be counted on to produce a different, incompatible response. The original stimuli then become attached to the new responses. Guthrie illustrates this method with the case of a woman college student who could not study because of the distracting noise. She solved this problem by spending a period of time reading absorbing mystery novels instead of studying. These stories held her attention so well that she ignored the distracting noises. The stimuli of noise thus occurred along with the responses of reading and became attached to these responses. When she then changed back (however reluctantly) from reading mysteries to reading textbooks, she found that the noises no longer distracted her, for they were now attached to reading responses instead of listening responses.

It is noteworthy that there is no reference to punishment in any of these methods. Someone might suggest that it was punishing for the one little girl to go out of the house, come in again, and hang up her clothes, and also punishing for the other girl to light so many matches at once. True, says Guthrie, but remember that other forms of punishment had previously failed. The important question is not whether these experiences were punishing but what they led the individuals to do. Inflicting pain on someone, says Guthrie, cannot be expected to change his habits if the pain does not occur in the presence of the stimuli that produce the behavior. Scolding the one girl after her clothes were already on the floor, or slapping the other girl after she had finished with the matches, would be irrelevant to the habits in question. Only when the punishment resulted in a new response to the same stimuli was it effective. Moreover, as the threshold method indicates, absence of punishment may be just as good a way of producing new responses as is punishment.

This attitude is characteristic of Guthrie's interpretation of punishment. Always look at what punishment makes the individual do. If punishment succeeds in changing the punished habit, it is because it elicits behavior incompatible with it. If punishment fails, it is because the behavior elicited by the punishment is not incompatible with the punished behavior. Thus, if you want to stop a dog from chasing cars, slapping his nose as he runs is likely to work, whereas slapping his rear is not. The two blows may be equally painful, but the one on the nose tends to make him stop and jump backward, whereas the one on the rear tends to make him continue forward all the more vigorously. Hence the blow on the nose, by eliciting behavior incompatible with running after the car, makes this nonrunning more likely to occur next time. The blow on the rear, however, has no such effect; it may even strengthen the chasing. Punishment works, when it does work, not because it hurts the individual but because it changes the way he responds to certain stimuli.

If one wants to use these methods of Guthrie's as cure-alls for bad habits, a problem at once arises. In order to obtain different behavior from the individual, one has to change the stimuli in some way. For the little girl, coming in the door and taking off her wraps was not the same when she had just been sent out the door by her mother as when she had just come in after a long time outside. For the Army horse, not bucking to a blanket was different from not bucking to a rider. There was a considerable difference between the stimulus situation when lighting a fiftieth match under a mother's prodding and when lighting a first match for fun. Now, when the original stimulus situation is restored, how do we know whether the two situations are enough alike so that the last response in one will occur in the other? For example, will the dog that jumped back when presented with the stimulus of moving-car-plus-blow-on-the-nose also jump back when presented with moving-car-alone? The answer in all of these cases seems to be: try it and see. This difficulty weakens the general usefulness of Guthrie's advice, not to mention the problem of relating the advice clearly to the theory. However, we can scarcely expect to get advice that will work infallibly in every situation without any ingenuity on the part of the person taking it. Guthrie's interpretation of punishment and his methods for changing habits are valuable tools for interpreting situations as well as useful suggestions for dealing with them. A theorist who can give us this much need not be ashamed of his practical contributions.

Some Special Topics

Guthrie's emphasis on responses to stimuli and the ways of changing them shows up in other contexts, too. What of extinction? Since Guthrie does not talk about reinforcement, he cannot talk about extinction as resulting from the removal of reinforcement. Instead, he says that extinction is simply learning to do something else. The response was learned because it changed the stimulus situation into a different one, thus becoming the last thing that was done in the original situation. If, now, the learned response no longer produces this change, the individual will go on doing various things in the situation until some other response does change the situation. That new response will then be the one that tends to occur next time. If this new response consistently terminates the situation, it will replace the old response. If, however, there is no longer any consistency in what response will terminate the situation, behavior will be variable from time to time. No particular new response will be learned, but the old response will still be replaced by new responses, in this case, many new ones. If a dog has learned to get out of his yard by crawling through a hole in the fence, and if this hole is now mended, he may or may not discover some other mode of escape. In any case, however, the response of going to the place where the hole was will be replaced by some other response.

Guthrie's interpretation of forgetting is similar. Habits do not weaken with disuse; they are replaced by other habits. If we forget the German vocabulary we have learned, it is because the English words as stimuli have become attached to other responses than the German words. If we lose our skill at horseback riding, it is because we have practiced other, competing responses in situations that were somewhat similar to being on horseback (such as being on a bicycle). In most cases the details of the relearning process are obscure, and it would be difficult to predict with much accuracy how much of some knowledge or skill one would forget under a given set of circumstances. However, this interpretation of forgetting does provide a good starting point for studying the factors that influence forgetting. Even this start is more than many theorists have provided for this topic.

Forgetting, like acquisition, is usually gradual because of the many specific stimulus-response connections that make up a complex habit. If the correct responses have been attached to many different stimuli, it will take longer for new responses to get attached to all of these stimuli. Hence it is possible to make one definite prediction from Guthrie's interpretation of forgetting. We can predict that a habit will be better retained if it has been practiced in a number of different situations (i.e., in the presence of a number of different stimulus combinations). In the course of forgetting, new responses may replace the old, correct ones quickly in any one of these situations, but the old response will still be conditioned to many other stimulus combinations. On another occasion when the stimulus combination is different, the old response is likely to reappear. Forgetting, like learning, is specific to the situation, and what is forgotten in one situation may well be remembered in another. The "forgotten" response to the changed stimulus will occur only, however, if the response in question was originally learned to a variety of different stimulus combinations. Hence we can increase the resistance of a habit to forgetting (including those verbal habits that we call knowledge) not only by practicing it more but by practicing it in a variety of situations.

The impression one gets from most of Guthrie's writing is that human behavior is a very mechanistic matter. Behavior is rigidly controlled by stimuli, and changes in the stimulus-response connections follow simple mechanical laws. However, Guthrie has been more receptive than Watson to such concepts as desire and purpose. He recognizes that much behavior has a goal-directed character. Rather than ignoring this, as Watson was inclined to do, he attempts to interpret it in rigorously physical terms.

What does it mean to say that someone has a desire, a purpose, or an intention to do something? Guthrie recognizes four components: (1) a complex of maintaining stimuli that keeps the organism active, (2) something that blocks any simple, direct action that would remove the maintaining stimuli at once, (3) muscular readiness to make certain responses, and (4) muscular readiness for the consequences of this action. Consider a person in a burning building who has the intention of jumping to safety. In this case the four components are: (1) heat from the fire, choking sensations from the smoke, and fear, (2) the fire and the height that block him from simply running away, (3) the bracing of his muscles for the jump, and (4) the preparation of his body for the shock of the fall. These four components, says Guthrie, are all that we need to describe an intention.

If someone suggested to Guthrie that the intention is something mental, over and above these four physical components, he might have replied with his story about a strange murder case. A man resolved to shoot his neighbor, and hid outside the neighbor's house with a rifle pointed at the door and his finger on the trigger. While sitting there, he began to think better of his plan. He was about to get up and go away when the neighbor came out the door. He pulled the trigger and the neighbor fell. At his trial, the question rose as to whether or not he fired intentionally. According to Guthrie, this is a meaningless question. That part of his intention which took the form of words to himself had changed, but the part that involved a ready trigger finger had not changed. There was no one intention, only a variety of bodily adjustments which did or did not prepare him to shoot.

What is attention? A variety of responses that orient the sense receptors toward certain stimuli, as in looking or listening. There may even be scanning, involving searching movements that end when a certain stimulus is perceived. This formulation of attention makes it possible for Guthrie to reword his basic principle of learning in the form: "What is being noticed becomes a signal for what is being done." (Guthrie, 1959)

In all of these interpretations, Guthrie is insisting that the processes involved, though they may be called by subjective terms, refer to objective physical movements. They may be hard to observe, but they are there just as surely as any other movements. Guthrie particularly emphasizes the role of *movement-produced stimuli,* the sensations produced by our own movements. These play an important part in thought, purpose, the coordination of sequences of behavior, and responses to stimuli that are no longer present. Though they often function like intervening variables in his system (since they are often impractical to observe directly), he hesitates to call them intervening variables since for him they are just as objectively present as the independent and the dependent variables.

Guthrie's final theoretical statement (Guthrie, 1959), written shortly before his death, is both more technical and more tentative than most of his earlier work. He seems to be trying to clarify both his own ideas and his relationships to other theorists. In this statement he is concerned both with the concept of attention and with the formal structure of his theory. However, it is likely that Guthrie will be remembered not so much for his attempts, successful or not, at formal theory building as for his informal contributions to our thinking about the learning process.

In trying to understand or to control any learning situation, Guthrie reminds us to look at the particular response that is being made and the particular stimuli that are eliciting it. He warns us not to rely on vague exhortations, not to look for magic in the administration of rewards and punishments, but to concentrate on eliciting particular patterns of behavior in particular situations. Though he tends to draw his examples largely from child rearing and animal training, Guthrie has much that is useful to offer adult human learners as well. College students often complain that they know the material they have studied but that they somehow cannot present it on examinations. A familiarity with Guthrie's thinking would lead one to say, "If the behavior you want to produce is the behavior of writing essays about certain topics, practice writing essays, and practice in a situation as close as possible to that of an exam." A similar example is seen in military training, where studies of combat effectiveness have resulted in training situations being made more and more like combat. As a result, infantrymen in training spend less time practicing exact marksmanship with bullseye targets on the Known-Distance Range and more time practicing rough and ready marksmanship with silhouette targets that pop up to confront the trainee as he advances. Though we cannot say that these examples represent Guthrie's direct influence on the applied psychology of learning, we can say that Guthrie more than any other major theorist has emphasized the importance of such precise analysis of stimuli and responses.

Guthrie's approach can stand one in good stead in many learning situations.

SUMMARY OF CONTIGUITY THEORY

Watson and Guthrie of course have in common all the characteristics of behaviorism in the general sense of that term. In addition, there is one respect in which the two of them differ from the other behavioristic theorists we will be discussing, namely, in that they make no use of the concept of reinforcement. Watson ridiculed the idea that reward could determine what was learned, regarding it as a magical notion unfit for a scientific explanation. (Pavlov spoke of the unconditioned stimulus as a reinforcer for the conditioned response, but Watson ignored this aspect of conditioning.) Guthrie similarly avoided making any reference to the reinforcing effects of rewards. In their systems, learning is assumed to depend only on the contiguity of stimulus and response, in other words, on the fact that they occur together. Hence Watson and Guthrie are called *contiguity theorists*.

In taking this position, Watson and Guthrie stand in contrast to another group of behavioristic theorists, known as *reinforcement theorists*. This latter group are just as dedicated to objectivity and just as much attached to the stimulus-response language in describing learning. They do not, however, see any objection to recognizing the reinforcing effect of reward in their theories; in fact they consider this effect essential to the analysis of learning. It is to this group of connectionist theorists that we turn in the next chapter.

Chapter 3

Reinforcement Theories in the Connectionist Tradition

THE IDEA THAT pleasure and pain as consequences of our acts are important determiners of behavior has a distinguished history in psychology. It forms the basis of the theory of psychological hedonism that was developed by Jeremy Bentham and adopted by a number of other British philosophers. According to this view, we all do those things that give us pleasure and avoid those that give us pain. However, it remained for Edward L. Thorndike (1874-1949) to make a similar view central to the psychology of learning.

THORNDIKE'S EARLY CONNECTIONISM

Thorndike was a pioneer in experimental animal psychology. Instead of relying on stories about the intelligent feats of this or that animal, he took animals into the laboratory, presented them with standardized problems, and made careful observations of how they solved the problems. His monograph, *Animal Intelligence,* published in 1898, is one of the most renowned classics in the field. His most widely quoted study was with cats in a problem box. A hungry cat was confined in a cage with a tempting morsel of fish outside. The cat could open the door by pulling a loop of string hanging inside the cage. Usually a cat went through a long process of walking around, clawing the sides of the cage, and other responses before it pulled the loop of string and was able to leave the cage. On successive tests in the cage, animals took shorter and shorter times to pull the string. However, this improvement was very gradual. Even after several experiences of opening the door by pulling the string, animals on a given trial would still spend considerable time in other behavior before pulling the string. This led Thorndike to conclude that the cat's learning to pull the string involved not an "intelligent" understanding of a relation between string pulling and door opening but a gradual "stamping in" of the stimulus-response connection between seeing the string and pulling it.

At the time Thorndike published these studies, they were radical in two respects: their careful observation of animal behavior under controlled conditions and their concern with the gradual strengthening of stimulus-response bonds. They were Thorndike's answer to the argument about whether animals solve problems by reasoning or by instinct. By neither, said Thorndike, but rather by the gradual learning of the correct response.

In relation to Watson and Guthrie, however, another point is noteworthy. Whereas both Watson and Guthrie were contiguity theorists, Thorndike was a reinforcement theorist. Watson's laws of frequency and recency and Guthrie's basic law of learning both state that stimulus-response bonds are strengthened simply by the response occurring in the presence of the stimuli. Thorndike did not completely reject this view, which he summarized as the *law of exercise*. His primary law of learning, however, was the *law of effect*. This stated that the stamping in of stimulus-response connections depended, not simply on the fact that the stimulus and response occurred together, but on the effects that followed the response. If a stimulus was followed by a response and then by a *satisfier,* the stimulus-response connection was strengthened. If, however, a stimulus was followed by a response and then by an *annoyer,* the stimulus-response connection was weakened. Thus satisfying and annoying effects of responses determined whether the stimulus-response connections would be stamped in or stamped out.

The terms "satisfier" and "annoyer" sound startlingly subjective for a theory concerned with the mechanical stamping in and stamping out of stimulus-response bonds. This language is much more like that of the hedonistic philosophers than like that of the behaviorist psychologists. Thorndike was, indeed, criticized by behaviorists for this way of talking about learning. Actually, however, he defined these terms in a quite objective way: "By a satisfying state of affairs is meant one which the animal does nothing to avoid, often doing things which maintain or renew it. By an annoying state of affairs is meant one which the animal does nothing to preserve, often doing things which put an end to it." (Thorndike, 1913, p. 2) Thorndike says nothing here about the animal's feelings, only about what the animal does. Thus he adheres to the concern of behaviorism with what individuals do. His language may sound subjective, but his meaning is as objective as Watson's. Working at the height of the behaviorist movement, Thorndike had his disagreements with its extreme supporters, but actually he and they were close together in interests and objectives. In the broader sense of the term, Thorndike was certainly himself a behaviorist.

Later in his career, Thorndike modified the law of effect to make satisfiers much more important than annoyers. Reward, he decided, strengthens connections, but punishment does not directly weaken them. If punishment is effective at all in weakening the tendency to do something, it is because it produces variable behavior and thus gives some new response a chance to be rewarded. This position, except for the emphasis on reward, sounds much like Guthrie's. With this modification, the law of effect became simply the now familiar statement (but not at all familiar when Thorndike presented it) that satisfying consequences serve to reinforce stimulus-response bonds.

Thorndike was a man of practical interests, and he took a special interest in the psychology of education. For many years he served on the faculty of Teachers College, Columbia University. Throughout his professional life, his studies on the "pure" psychology of learning with both human and animal subjects were interspersed with studies on the applied psychology of education. His emphasis on specificity in learning and on the mechanical stamping in of stimulus-response connections has been both praised and condemned by educators over the years. (It is to him, indeed, that we owe the term "connectionism.") For our purposes, however, these aspects of Thorndike's work are too similar to Watson's and Guthrie's to require further comment here. Thorndike was no less a pioneer of objective psychology than Watson; indeed his original contributions were quite likely more important than Watson's. However, our concern here is that he incorporated within his objective psychology of learning the law of effect, and thus became the first real reinforcement theorist.

SKINNER'S INTERPRETATION OF LEARNING

Thorndike was not a particularly systematic theorist. He stated many principles of learning, but he did so in a rather casual way. His voluminous writings show little attempt at consistency in the details of formulation. For our purposes it will be more profitable, rather than studying Thorndike in detail, to look at a quite similar contemporary viewpoint, that of B. F. Skinner (b. 1904). Of a later generation than Thorndike, Skinner received his doctorate of philosophy in psychology from Harvard in 1931 and after teaching at the Universities of Minnesota and Indiana, returned to Harvard as a professor in 1948. His relation to Thorndike is somewhat like that of Guthrie to Watson: not by any means a disciple, but a contemporary thinker whose views are somewhat similar to those of a great pioneer. Skinner never studied under Thorndike, he developed his system independently, and there are definite differences between them. Nevertheless, Thorndike and Skinner are alike in being connectionist theorists who emphasize reinforcement as a basic factor in learning, who take a keen interest in problems of education, and who de-emphasize theory. This lack of interest in high-level theorizing was only implicit in Thorndike's writings, but Skinner has made it quite explicit in his system. It distinguishes both Thorndike and Skinner from some other connectionist reinforcement theorists, such as Hull, who will be considered later.

The Two Kinds of Learning

In contrast to the other theorists we have discussed so far, Skinner recognizes two different kinds of learning. They are different because each involves a separate kind of behavior. *Respondent* behavior is elicited by specific stimuli. Given the stimulus, the response occurs automatically. Respondent behavior is made up of such specific stimulus-response connections, called reflexes. We are born with a number of reflexes, and we acquire others through the process of conditioning. This learning of respondent behavior follows the pattern that we have referred to earlier as classical conditioning, though Skinner does not use that term. A new stimulus is paired with the one that already elicits the response, and after a number of such pairings the new stimulus comes to elicit the response. The knee-jerk reflex is an example. The presentation of the old (unconditioned) stimulus during training may be considered the reinforcer, since without it learning will not occur. Thus the learning of respondent behavior in Skinner's system is the same kind of learning that Watson assumed made up all learning. The only difference is that Skinner emphasizes the reinforcing role of the unconditioned stimulus.

Skinner maintains, however, that most behavior is of a different sort. This kind he refers to as *operant* behavior. Whereas the distinctive characteristic of respondent behavior is that it is in response to stimuli, the characteristic of operant behavior is that it operates on the environment. There is no particular stimulus that will consistently elicit an operant response. Skinner speaks of operant behavior as being emitted by the organism rather than elicited by stimuli. Most behavior is of this sort; walking, talking, working, and playing are all made up of operant responses.

Skinner does not mean to say that operant behavior is not influenced by stimuli. Much of his analysis of behavior is concerned with ways in which operant behavior is brought under the control of stimuli. However, such control is only partial and conditional. The operant response of reaching for food is not simply elicited by the sight of food; it also depends on hunger, social circumstances, and a variety of other stimulus conditions. In these respects it is in contrast to the respondent knee-jerk response, which is regularly elicited by a tap on the knee almost without regard to other conditions. Because of this distinction, Skinner does not consider it useful to think of operant behavior as made up of specific stimulus-response connections in the sense that respondent behavior is. Whereas Guthrie analyzes every bit of behavior in terms of the stimuli that produce it, Skinner prefers to think of most behavior (the operant kind) as emitted by the organism, without bothering to consider the multitude of stimuli that have something to do with its occurrence. The difference between Guthrie and Skinner on this point is one of emphasis and convenience rather than of direct disagreement. Both agree that behavior depends on the total pattern of stimuli, external and internal, that are present when it occurs, but Guthrie prefers to emphasize this point for all responses, whereas Skinner prefers to ignore it in those cases where no one particular stimulus is crucial to the occurrence of the response.

The learning of operant behavior is also known as conditioning, but it is different from the conditioning of reflexes. Operant conditioning is the same sort of learning that Thorndike described. Because for Skinner this is by far the more important kind of learning, this topic is one on which he and Thorndike are close together. If an operant response (often called simply an operant) occurs and is followed by reinforcement, its probability of occurring again increases. Whereas for reflexes the reinforcer is an unconditioned stimulus, for operants it is a reward (or, as Thorndike would say, a satisfier). Thus we may say that reward following an operant makes that response more likely to occur again. (Even though the stimulus for an operant is unknown, Skinner still often refers to the operant behavior as a response.) This is the pattern of operant learning, which is to say, of most of the learning discussed by Skinner.

Positive and Negative Reinforcers

Although Skinner is largely concerned with *positive reinforcers,* he also recognizes the existence of *negative reinforcers.* Negative reinforcers are aversive stimuli, ones that the individual commonly seeks to avoid. Whereas reinforcement results from the *occurrence* of a positive reinforcer, it results from the *termination* of a negative reinforcer. Electric shock, for example, is a negative reinforcer because the termination of the shock is reinforcing. Thus a response can be reinforced either by presenting a positive reinforcer or by removing a negative reinforcer.

An important point about reinforcers, both positive and negative, is that they can be conditioned. If a stimulus occurs repeatedly with a positive reinforcer, it tends itself to acquire the capacity to reinforce behavior. It is then called a conditioned positive reinforcer. A sign reading "Restaurant" will serve as a conditioned positive reinforcer for a hungry man in a strange city, because such signs have been associated with food in the past. Similarly, a stimulus that occurs with a negative reinforcer tends to become a conditioned negative reinforcer, as in the familiar case of the burnt child who learns to avoid the stove even when it is cold.

The topic of negative reinforcement is obviously related to punishment, but the exact relation is not obvious. Negative reinforcement results from the removal of a negative reinforcer, whereas punishment involves the presentation of a negative reinforcer. What effects does punishment have, and how are these effects produced? Skinner points out that punishment is not a very reliable way of preventing responses from occurring. Reinforcement increases the probability of a response, but punishment does not necessarily reduce the probability. When it does, the reduction may result from any of three reasons.

First, the aversive stimulus used as punishment is likely to have emotional effects. These emotional effects are respondents that are elicited by the aversive stimulus. These respondents are likely to be incompatible with the punished response, so that they reduce its probability of occurrence. For example, if scolding a child for eating forbidden candy makes him cry, it is likely also to stop his eating, since it is difficult to eat and cry at the same time. This effect, however, is temporary. When the aversive stimulus is removed the emotional effects soon dissipate. The punished behavior then occurs again, often at an even higher rate than before punishment. So, although this effect of punishment is often useful in stopping undesirable behavior, it is not useful in keeping it from happening again.

The second effect of punishment is an extension of the first. When a neutral stimulus is paired with an aversive stimulus that elicits a respondent, this is a conditioning situation. Whatever stimuli are present when punishment occurs thus have a chance to become conditioned stimuli for the emotional responses to punishment. These conditioned stimuli would then produce emotional respondents in the absence of the original punishment. As a result, the previously punished response would tend to be replaced by these competing responses, much as if punishment were still being presented. In our previous example, the child would tend to be frightened (make emotional responses) as soon as he touched the forbidden candy that had previously been paired with punishment. This fear would inhibit his eating responses. This effect of punishment, though basically similar to the first, is thus more lasting in its effects.

The third effect of punishment is an application of negative reinforcement based on the conditioned aversive stimuli from the second effect. When the individual turns away from the conditioned aversive stimuli, this removes these stimuli and provides negative reinforcement. He is thus reinforced for making a response (turning away) that is incompatible with the punished response. As a result, he learns to turn away instead of making the punished response. Once stimuli from the forbidden candy became aversive to the child, he was reinforced for anything that got him away from these stimuli. Since getting away from these stimuli is incompatible with approaching them, he was learning not to eat the forbidden candy. This process, somewhat similar to Guthrie's interpretation of punishment, is what disciplinarians usually hope to accomplish by punishment. However, this effect, like the second one, lasts only until the conditioned aversiveness of the stimuli extinguishes. To maintain this effect, the disciplinarian must be prepared to give further punishments as needed to maintain the new behavior.

In general, Skinner regards punishment as a poor method of controlling behavior. For one thing, it is deceptive, since the first of its three effects often makes it appear dramatically successful when in fact it has produced only a temporary effect. For another thing, the emotional behavior it produces is likely to be undesirable from other points of view. Replacing misbehavior with crying or anger is seldom a good solution. Finally, the emotional responses may become conditioned to stimuli other than the ones the punisher wishes, including the stimuli of the punisher himself. Thus punishment is both a rather unreliable technique for controlling behavior and a technique that is likely to have unfortunate side effects.

The Role of Stimuli

Although stimuli do not elicit operants in the sense that they elicit respondents, they may determine whether or not any given operant will occur. A stimulus acquires this influence through the process of discrimination. If an operant is reinforced in the presence of one stimulus but not reinforced when it occurs in the presence of a different stimulus, the tendency to respond when the second stimulus is present gradually becomes extinguished, and a discrimination is formed. The operant will then occur in the presence of the first stimulus but not of the second. Skinner refers to the first stimulus as an S^D and to the second as an S^Δ (S delta). With regard to any operant, an S^D is a stimulus in the presence of which the individual has learned to make the response and an S^Δ is a stimulus in the presence of which he has learned not to respond. However, the operant is still not elicited by the S^D as a respondent is elicited, since occurrence of the operant depends on factors other than the S^D. For example, a pigeon can be taught to peck a key when it is red (S^D) but not when it is green (S^Δ) by reinforcing with food the pecks of the red key but not those of the green key. However, the pigeon will show little tendency to peck the red key when completely satiated for food. The S^D is a major determinant of the operant pecking response, but it does not produce it in the automatic way that a stimulus elicits a reflex. Under these conditions the operant is said to be under stimulus control.

Skinner is militantly opposed to those aspects of theory that involve assumptions about entities or processes that cannot be observed. He denies, in fact, that his systematic treatment of behavior is a theory at all. Although Watson and Guthrie proudly claim to be talking only about what is physically real, Skinner points out that we cannot actually observe a habit or a movement-produced stimulus. Hence, for Skinner, such concepts are inadmissible. Here he even diverges from Thorndike, since a stimulus-response bond is something invisible assumed to exist inside the body. Skinner's insistence on talking only about behavior and its external determinants, not about what may be going on inside the body, has led to the statement that Skinner studies an "empty organism"; not empty in fact, of course, but empty so far as Skinner's interpretations are concerned.

Instead of talking about stimulus-response connections (except in the case of respondents), Skinner speaks of the rate at which a given operant is emitted under a given set of conditions. This language puts primary emphasis on the response, with the stimuli being of importance only as they set conditions for the response to occur. Moreover, stimuli constitute only one of the factors that influence the emission of operants; such factors as food deprivation (which Skinner does not regard as a stimulus) must also be considered. This language raises some question as to whether it is proper to call Skinner a connectionist, since he does not actually speak of connections being formed between stimuli and responses. However, his concern with specific responses, stimulus control, and reinforcement makes it more appropriate to discuss him as a connectionist reinforcement theorist than under any other heading.

The Scheduling of Reinforcers

Skinner's antitheoretical bias makes it difficult to discuss his system apart from his research and its applications (a fact of which Skinner would be proud). His research has been conducted almost entirely in one version or another of an apparatus that has become known as the *Skinner box*. This varies in size and form according to the organism being studied, but basically it is simply a box (or, from the subject's point of view, a room) containing a simple *manipulandum* (i.e., something the subject can manipulate) and a device for delivering reinforcers. The manipulandum may be a lever for rats to press, a key for pigeons to peck, a vending-machine plunger for humans to pull, or anything else appropriate for the kind of subject using it. The mechanism for providing reinforcers is typically some sort of feeder, delivering food pellets to rats, grain to pigeons, or candy bars to humans. Other sorts of reinforcers may be used, however, from drops of water for thirsty rats to peep shows for monkeys and humans. In some cases escape from electric shock to the feet is used as the reinforcer, in which case no separate reinforcement dispenser is required.

The basic principle on which the box operates is that responses to the manipulandum produce reinforcers. These responses are called *free operants,* since the subject is free to emit them at his own speed. The rate at which the free operant is emitted is the response measure. Whereas other experimenters may study speed of running, number of correct choices, or other aspects of operant behavior, Skinner and his followers study only the rate of emission of free operants. Whatever variable they manipulate, they study its effects in terms of this measure. However, as we have seen, there are many different free operants that can be studied. The important thing, says Skinner, is to find an appropriate operant for the kind of individual one wants to study, that is, an operant that the subject can emit conveniently and fairly rapidly. If this condition is met, the particular operant chosen makes little difference to the laws that will be found. We use levers for rats and keys for pigeons rather than *vice versa* because these manipulanda suit the response capacities of these animals, but we find similar laws for rats and for pigeons when each learns an operant appropriate for its own capacities.

The rate at which the free operant is emitted (the dependent variable) can be related to a great variety of independent variables. In practice, however, Skinner and his followers have concentrated largely on one independent variable, the *schedule of reinforcement*. This term refers to the particular pattern according to which reinforcers follow responses. The simplest schedule is *continuous reinforcement*, in which a reinforcer is given for every response to the manipulandum. This schedule is generally used when the subject is first being trained to use the manipulandum. After the response is learned, the schedule is usually shifted to some form of *intermittent reinforcement*, in which only part of the responses are followed by reinforcement. Skinner has collaborated with Charles Ferster on a large book, *Schedules of Reinforcement*, describing different schedules of intermittent reinforcement and their effects, but fortunately for the student they tend to represent variations on two basic patterns. If the frequency with which reinforcers are presented depends on the rate at which responses are emitted, this is called a *ratio* schedule; if it depends simply on the passage of time, it is called an *interval* schedule. In addition, each of these two kinds of schedule may be either *fixed* or *variable*. Combining these two bases of classification gives four main kinds of schedule.

In a *fixed-ratio* schedule, the subject is reinforced after every so many reponses. Thus a reinforcer may be delivered after every fourth or every tenth or every twentieth response. A *variable-ratio* schedule differs from a fixed-ratio schedule in that the reinforcer, instead of being presented consistently after every so many responses, is presented after a different number of responses on different occasions. In this case the ratio is the average number of responses per reinforcer. Thus on a variable-ratio five schedule, reinforcers are delivered on the average after every five responses, but on one occasion two successive responses might be reinforced, while on another occasion the individual might have to make as many as ten responses after getting one reinforcer before getting another.

On a *fixed-interval* schedule, a fixed interval of time has to elapse after one reinforcer is delivered before another can be obtained. Once this interval has elapsed, the first response will be reinforced. Thus on a fixed-interval one-minute schedule, the subject cannot obtain reinforcers oftener than one a minute regardless of how fast he responds. He can obtain one a minute equally well by responding rapidly all the time or by responding only once a minute. If he waits for awhile after the minute has elapsed before making the response, the reinforcement will be correspondingly delayed. A *variable-interval* schedule makes it possible to obtain a reinforcer sometimes sooner and sometimes longer after the previous one. Thus on a variable-interval two-minute schedule, the average time after presentation of one reinforcer when another would become available would be two minutes, but on any particular occasion the interval might be considerably shorter or longer. Hence the only way to be sure of getting all available reinforcers as soon as possible would be to respond continuously.

How do these schedules differ in the patterns of responding that they produce? First, ratio schedules typically give higher rates of responding than interval schedules. This difference is not surprising, since fast responding on a ratio schedule increases the number of reinforcements in a given period of time, whereas fast responding on an interval schedule only serves to obtain each reinforcement a little sooner. Second, both kinds of fixed schedules produce a "scalloping" effect, in which responding is slow after a reinforcement and gets progressively faster until the next reinforcer is delivered. The reason is that responses immediately after a reinforcement are never reinforced. Intuitively this effect is easier to appreciate in the fixed-interval schedule, since the individual has nothing to gain from responses during the interval. On a fixed-ratio schedule we might expect the individual to respond just as rapidly after a reinforcement as at any other time, since he has to make a certain number of responses before the next reinforcement regardless of when he makes them. This expectation, however, reflects a view of the organism as figuring out the most profitable strategy and acting accordingly. According to Skinner, we must simply look at the reinforcement contingencies. On a fixed-ratio schedule, the first responses after a reinforcement are never reinforced as quickly as the later ones, hence they occur at a slower rate. Finally, this scalloping does not occur with variable schedules. Since all responses, early or late, have a chance of being reinforced on a variable schedule, responding is at a constant rate except for the brief period that may be required for actually consuming the reinforcer.

In general, organisms will make more responses per reinforcer on any kind of intermittent schedule than on continuous reinforcement. If reinforcement is finally terminated altogether, resistance to extinction is also greater after intermittent than after continuous reinforcement. To obtain rapid steady responding and high resistance to extinction, the variable-ratio schedule is the most effective. It is possible, in fact, to get animals to work for food reinforcement on ratios so high that they are actually operating at a biological loss: the energy expended in operating the manipulandum is greater than that obtained from the occasional food reward, so that an animal can literally work itself to death.

These schedules differ in their sensitivity to various disrupting factors. This fact has been of particular interest in connection with

D

the effects of various drugs, and pharmaceutical companies have found it useful to test new drugs on animals responding to different schedules of reinforcement. One generalization which emerges from many studies is that interval schedules are more easily disrupted by a variety of drugs than are ratio schedules. Doses that will make responding on an interval schedule quite erratic will leave a ratio schedule largely unaffected. Apparently the rat's counting mechanism is more stable or less vulnerable than its timing mechanism. Though Skinner is pleased that his experimental techniques have been found useful for studying drugs, it is characteristic of his approach that he makes no attempt to draw inferences about what these drugs are doing to the animal's body. There is a lawful relationship between what drug goes into the body and what behavior comes out; what goes on between these two is no concern of Skinner's.

It should be noted that studies of different schedules of reinforcement are not concerned with how the response is originally learned. Ordinarily the subject is well trained to use the manipulandum before any form of intermittent reinforcement is introduced. Thereafter a given individual can adapt fairly readily to one schedule after another, changing his behavior to suit each new schedule. Thus Skinner's formal research has been largely concerned with a short-run aspect of learning, the rapid shifts in performance level to match shifts in reinforcement conditions. (Some writers, in fact, consider such shifts too short-run to be called learning at all, and refer to them simply as changes in performance.) These studies are concerned not with an individual's learning how to respond, but with his learning how rapidly to respond under a new set of reward conditions.

Shaping

We should not conclude from this emphasis, however, that Skinner has been uninterested in the process of learning how to perform complex tasks. Much of his less formal work has been concerned with this problem, and he has given striking demonstrations of training techniques. Though many experimental psychologists study animal learning, Skinner is almost unique in his concern with animal training. The technique by which he trains animals to perform complex acts that are outside their normal range of behavior is known as *shaping*. The behavior is shaped through a series of successive approximations, each made possible by selectively reinforcing certain responses and not others. Thus behavior is gradually brought closer and closer to the desired pattern.

Suppose you want to train a rat to press a lever to obtain a marble, carry the marble to the other side of the cage, drop it in a hole, and then run to a third place in the cage to get food. If left to its own devices, the rat might never go through this particular sequence of operations, and if it did the process would probably take so long that the food reinforcement at the end would have little effect on the initial bar-pressing response. If you tried to train the rat by simply waiting until it went through the whole sequence spontaneously often enough to learn it, in principle you might succeed, but the process would almost certainly exceed the span of your patience and might even exceed the life span of the rat. Yet this sequence is by no means at the limits of a rat's learning capacity; considerably harder ones have been mastered by rats with proper training.

To accomplish this training Skinner would begin by depriving the rate of food to the point where it was at about 80% of its normal body weight. Then he would train the rat to eat from the food magazine. On a number of occasions a click or some other signal would be followed by the delivery of food from the magazine into a tray. This procedure would be continued until the click led the rat to go immediately to the food tray. This part of the procedure is called *magazine training*. Then the shaping could begin. At first the click might be sounded and the food delivered whenever the rat touched the lever. Soon the rat would be spending much of the time between food deliveries close to the lever, and touching it frequently. Then the procedure could be changed so that food was delivered only when the lever was pressed. After the rat learned to press it regularly, food would begin to follow lever presses only if the rat, immediately after pressing the lever, touched the marble. In successive stages of training, the rat would get fed only if it picked up the marble, then if it moved it toward the hole, then if it put it into the hole, at which point training would be complete. Each stage of this shaping process would change the distribution of the animal's total behavior in the box, making responses that were originally rare occur more and more frequently. These responses, being closer approximations to the final performance, could then be reinforced and all other responses nonreinforced. Only after the rat learned to press the lever frequently, for example, was it practical to give reinforcement only when lever pressing was followed by marble touching. This gradual changing of a subject's typical behavior to bring it closer and closer to what is desired makes up the process of shaping.

Skinner has given a number of striking demonstrations of the shaping of operant behavior. He has trained rats to go through sequences of behavior even more complex and less ratlike than that described above. He has trained pigeons to play a modified version of ping-pong, pecking a ball back and forth across a table. With less complex operant behaviors, he has carried out the entire shaping process during a class period, with students watching the animal's behavior gradually change under the influence of the reinforcement procedure. Such demonstrations of course require some degree of skill and experience in finding responses and reinforcers that are appropriate for the organism being trained and in deciding how fast to go. Skinner, however, emphasizes the mechanical aspect of the procedure, the extent to which a variety of behaviors can be shaped by an almost routine application of the principles of reinforcement. Such demonstrations have in fact been criticized as mere technological applications of simple principles, contributing nothing to our scientific understanding of the principles themselves. However, they serve to demonstrate the power of reinforcement in molding behavior, and this demonstration is Skinner's object.

Not all of these demonstrations have been with animals. A technique recently developed for showing the automatic effect of reinforcement on human behavior is called *verbal conditioning*. In the first experiment of this sort (Greenspoon, 1955), the subject was instructed simply to say words. The experimenter gave the subject no clue in his instructions as to what sorts of words were desired. However, whenever the subject said a noun in the plural form, the experimenter said "mmhm." There was an increase during the session in the frequency with which subjects said plural nouns. This increase occurred in spite of the fact that many subjects were quite unaware, so far as could be determined by questioning, either of the fact that they were saying more plural nouns or of any relation between the experimenter's behavior and their own. When the "mmhm" was discontinued, frequency of plural nouns declined (extinction).

In another less formal experiment (Verplanck, 1955) subjects were simply engaged in conversation without even being told that this was an experiment. The experimenter (who in this case might better be called the interviewer) expressed interest in and agreement with any of the subject's remarks that were presented as expressions of opinion (i.e., "I think . . . ," or "It seems to me . . ."). Other kinds of remarks produced no reaction from the interviewer. Expressions of opinion became more and more frequent during the conversation. In both of these verbal-conditioning studies, verbal behavior was modified by reinforcing a given kind of verbal response and no other. Like any technique of operant training, this one depends on finding a reinforcer that will be effective for the particular kind of individual being studied, but once one is found the principle of reinforcement seems to apply as well here as elsewhere.

An interesting sidelight on the shaping of behavior is the way in which reinforcement can produce not only behavior that the experimenter intends but also behavior of which he has no advance idea. Suppose a timer is arranged to deliver a reinforcer every 30 seconds regardless of what the subject does. (This schedule is not the same as a fixed-interval schedule, where he has to make a particular response after the interval is up in order to be reinforced.) Whatever the individual is doing when the reinforcement comes is more likely to occur again the next time. Purely on the basis of chance, he is more likely to be doing something at that moment which he commonly does than something that he does more rarely. Given the fact that this behavior occurs commonly to start with, plus the fact that it has now just been reinforced, it is all the more likely to be occurring when the next reinforcer is delivered. This reinforcement will strengthen it some more and make it even more likely to occur at the right time to receive the third reinforcement. Thus this particular behavior becomes more and more likely to occur because it is reinforced, even though the experimenter did not deliberately reinforce that response rather than others. Rather, the learning was the result of a vicious circle: because the response occurred frequently, it was reinforced, and because it was reinforced, it occurred more frequently. The experimenter did not know in advance which of the various responses that the individual made frequently would be learned in this way; that selection depended on chance. There might be a period during which several different responses were reinforced before any one gained enough of a lead to start the vicious circle going. Behavior might be too variable for any one response ever to get the necessary head start. However, when it occurs, this unplanned reinforcing effect is an impressive demonstration of the automatic operation of reinforcement.

Skinner refers to this kind of unplanned learning through "accidental" reinforcement as *superstitious* behavior. The justification for this term is that the subject acts as though a certain behavior produced reinforcement, when in fact there is no necessary connection between the behavior and the reinforcement. The response is commonly followed by reinforcement only because both behavior and reinforcement occur frequently and hence often occur at the same time. The most successful experimental demonstrations of superstitious behavior have been with pigeons, but applications to human learning are not difficult to see. If a student carries a rabbit's foot into an examination for good luck, and does well, this experience will make him more likely to carry it into the next examination. Repeated successes while carrying the rabbit's foot will make his adherence to the foot as a source of luck stronger and stronger, even though it contributed nothing to his success and he would have done just as well without it. (We overlook the possibility that the confidence the talisman gave the student may have increased his effectiveness in taking the examination.) Many of man's beliefs, not only in charms and magic, but also in medicine, mechanical skills, and administrative techniques probably depend on such superstitious learning. A public speaker who thinks he is successful because he knocks three times on the podium before starting to speak is generally recognized as superstitious, but a speaker who thinks he is successful because he starts each lecture with a funny story may be equally superstitious by Skinner's definition. In humans, such superstitions are probably oftener learned in the first place from other people than from chance occurrences. However, when people claim that their faith in them has been validated by experience, this experience often follows the learning pattern that Skinner has described and illustrated.

Some Applications

As the reader has doubtless already guessed, Skinner has shown much interest in the application of learning principles to complex practical situations. He has written a book analyzing language as a system of operant responses (Skinner, 1957b). He has trained withdrawn psychotic patients not only to respond more actively to their environment but to adjust their responding to social stimuli (Skinner, 1957a). He has pointed up the various forms of reinforcement used in political, social, and economic control (e.g., describing ordinary wages as fixed-interval and piecework as fixed-ratio schedules for the control of economic behavior) (Skinner, 1953). Most ambitiously, he has described a utopian community called Walden II (in honor of Thoreau, who might or might not feel himself honored), in which the principles of learning are used to create a more ideal form of social organization (Skinner, 1948). Some critics regard these interpretations as highly speculative oversimplifications. They ask why Skinner, though steadfastly refusing to make inferences from what a pigeon does to what is going on inside the pigeon, is quite willing to make inferences from what the pigeon does to what is going on in human social organization. It must be admitted that Skinner's interpretations run far beyond his data. Of the four applications mentioned above, only that dealing with psychotics has led to a program of research, and that is still in its early stages. Skinner is both an ingenious experimenter and a prophet of the application of science to human problems, but the gap between these two roles sometimes looms large.

One application, however, has definitely not been left at the stage of speculation. This is the study of programmed learning, best known through its use in teaching machines. Though Skinner was not the first to suggest this approach to teaching, he has given the idea its main impetus. His object was to treat classroom learning like any other situation in which certain behavior, in this case largely verbal behavior, is to be shaped. The student must progress gradually from familiar to unfamiliar material, must be given an opportunity to learn the necessary discriminations, and must be reinforced. The classroom situation has many disadvantages from this point of view. A rate of progress appropriate for one student is too fast or too slow for another. Opportunities for each individual to make the required responses are limited, and reinforcement is often greatly delayed. Individual tutoring could solve all of these problems, but in most cases this is out of the question except perhaps for occasional supplementary work. What, then, can be done to give students in school the same advantages that pigeons in boxes have? Skinner's answer to this question is the teaching machine.

The basic component of the machine is the program. This is a series of combined teaching and test items that carries the student gradually through the material to be learned. An item may or may not convey new information to the student, but in any case it calls for him to fill in a blank in a statement. He can then look at the correct answer. If it agrees with his answer, this agreement constitutes the reinforcement. If not, he can study the correct answer so as to increase his chance of being reinforced next time. However, Skinner prefers to make the learning requirements so gradual that the learner rarely if ever does make mistakes. If this effort is successful, then on every item the student makes a correct reponse and is reinforced, which in Skinner's view is the best possible arrangement for learning. Individual differences are then reflected in the rate at which the student proceeds through the program. For a discussion of the logic and the advantages of this approach to teaching, see Skinner, 1961.

At this point the reader may be wondering, "Where does the machine come in? This is just the old, familiar workbook method." To some extent this is a valid point. Teaching programs can be, in fact have been, published in workbook form. The student fills in a blank, then turns to another page to check his answer. However, these programmed workbooks differ from the more familiar type of workbook in that they do all teaching through the items in the program, rather than serving to supplement lectures and textbooks. The same series of items that calls forth the student's responses also provides the information necessary for making the responses. This arrangement, in turn, forces the author of the program to plan the sequence of items very carefully in terms of just what he wants the student to learn and just how it can best be presented. Whether the program is in a workbook or in a machine is of secondary importance. Machines have some advantages in speeding up the reinforcement and reducing the likelihood of cheating by the student. It is likely, however, that much of Skinner's preference for machine presentation results from two factors: (1) the novelty effect of the machine, which very likely makes its use more reinforcing to the student, and (2) Skinner's personal liking for mechanized procedures. Although the machine itself has sometimes been a bone of contention between those who favor increased classroom efficiency and those who fear the loss of more personal values in education, this is a misplaced emphasis. The pertinent question is about the value of programmed methods of instruction in whatever form, not about teaching machines as such.

It is too soon to judge how valuable programmed teaching, by machine or otherwise, will prove in the whole context of education. Many factors besides efficiency as a specific teaching device are involved. However, it seems highly likely that for efficient mastery of certain technical materials, this approach will prove quite useful. At any rate, it is striking evidence that Skinner's applications are not restricted to tricks of animal training and to speculations about the organization of society.

Skinner's Relation to Other Psychologists

It is interesting at this point to notice Skinner's relation to both Watson and Guthrie. He differs from both, of course, on the issue of reinforcement. He resembles them, however, in his practical emphasis. Like Guthrie, he is more at home analyzing particular situations of practical interest than discussing abstract issues of general theoretical significance. In analyzing a response, Guthrie's first question is, "What stimuli evoke it?" while Skinner's is, "What reinforcer sustains it?" Both of these, however, focus the emphasis on a specific, manipulable detail of the situation. Guthrie has gone farther in relating specific situations to a general statement of what learning is, while Skinner has gone farther in actually experimenting with the situations he analyzes. Their differences are substantial, but their similarities are nonetheless noteworthy.

As for Watson, he and Skinner have in common a missionary zeal about what psychology should be and what it should contribute to human affairs. Both react vigorously against what they regard as vague, overtheoretical interpretations of human nature and in favor of strictly scientific study of behavior. Both present systems that their friends regard as highly useful and their foes regard as highly oversimplified. (Both judgments may, of course, be valid, for oversimplifications can be useful for many purposes.) Both appear as prophets, seeking to purge the errors from psychology as it is and to proclaim the glories of psychology as it should be. Both have a vision of what man can become if guided by the proper application of the principles of learning.

Though Skinner has gone farther than either Watson or Guthrie in putting his ideas to the experimental test, he is still open to criticism for being too narrow in his interests, for concentrating on the application of a few principles rather than on a more general understanding of behavior. For example, he has concentrated on rate of emission of simple, free operants practically to the exclusion of other response measures. He has used as reinforcers whatever worked, without asking what it is that makes a reinforcer reinforcing. He has refused to consider what it is inside the organism that makes possible all the complex learnings of which the human (and even the lower animal) is capable. To Skinner himself, these statements are not criticisms but compliments; they indicate how far he has gone in clearing away nonessentials and getting down to business. To many others, however, they imply that Skinner has failed to provide the sort of understanding that is one of the functions of theory. Whether Skinner is to be praised or condemned for these features of his work is a matter of one's own values, but at any rate the disagreement suggests that there is a need for other approaches.

Skinner has also been criticized on another basis. His experiments have typically been conducted on one or a very few subjects. Skinner believes that only by looking at the behavior of a single individual can one find the lawfulness in behavior. Many psychologists, however, take the contrary view: that stable, general laws can be obtained only by averaging the behavior of many individuals. Only thus, they say, can individual differences and accidental fluctuations be ruled out so that the widely applicable, general laws remain. The arguments on both sides of this question are too complex to consider here, but they point up another reason why many psychologists are dissatisfied with Skinner's system. They fear that Skinner substitutes ingenuity as a teacher for thoroughness as a scientist, and that he magnifies peculiarities of individuals into what he claims are general laws of behavior. Again we see, not necessarily a weakness in Skinner, but a reason why other psychologists have chosen other paths.

As an experimenter, Skinner has made important contributions to the psychology of learning. Free operant behavior, schedules of reinforcement, shaping, superstitions, and the Skinner box are among these contributions. He makes no claim to be a theorist, important or otherwise. Nevertheless, he has made contributions in this area also. We may note, for example, the distinction between respondent and operant behavior and the emphasis on precise control of behavior in the individual case. Not all of these contributions are regarded favorably by everyone, as we have seen. There is, however, no question about the importance of Skinner's contributions to both the pure and the applied psychology of learning.

MILLER'S INTERPRETATION OF LEARNING

We turn now to another connectionist reinforcement position, that of Neal Miller (b. 1909), professor of psychology at Yale. In principle Miller's system is not very different from Skinner's. It does, however, differ considerably in both vocabulary and experimental techniques. It is also more theoretical than Skinner's. Actually it represents to a great extent a simplification of the theory of Clark Hull, which will be considered in detail later. Treating Miller before Hull, though it reverses the natural chronological sequence, may serve as an introduction to the highly technical study of Hull's system.

Much of Miller's importance as a theorist comes from the applications of his theory to topics in personality, social, and abnormal psychology. These applications were worked out jointly by Miller and John Dollard (b. 1900). Miller's background in experimental psychology and Dollard's in clinical psychology and the social sciences made possible a very fruitful collaboration on these topics. The theoretical analysis of learning is primarily Miller's, with a heavy debt to Hull, but the applications are largely Dollard's. This formulation of the principles of learning is perhaps the most widely known of the current connectionist theories of learning.

The Four Elements of Learning

Whereas Skinner makes the concept of reinforcement central to his interpretation of learning, Miller does the same with *drive*. A drive is an aroused state of the organism, one that goads the individual into action. For Miller, a drive always involves a strong stimulus; moreover, any stimulus, if strong enough, acts as a drive. The drive stimulus may be either external or internal. Pain is an example of a drive produced by an external stimulus, while hunger and thirst are drives produced by internal stimuli. Some drives are produced by stimuli from an individual's own emotional responses. When we are angry or afraid, physiological changes take place in our bodies. Some of these produce strong internal stimuli, which are responsible for the drives of anger and fear. Whatever its source, a drive arouses the individual and keeps him active. Drive is thus the basis of motivation.

In an infant, or in an older individual in a highly unfamiliar situation, the activity produced by the drive has little direction. All sorts of different responses are made. It may happen that one of these responses serves to reduce the strength of the drive. If the drive is hunger, eating food will reduce it. If the drive is pain from electric shock, moving away from the electrically charged conductor will reduce it. When the drive is reduced (which often but not always, means that it is completely removed), the individual becomes less active. Thus one thing we say about drive is that a strong stimulus increases activity and the removal of the strong stimulus decreases activity.

So far this is only a statement about motivation, not about learning. However, a reduction in the strength of a drive has a very important property: it reinforces whatever response came just before. Thus whatever response serves to reduce the drive is reinforced and therefore tends to be learned. As a result, the behavior produced by drive in a familiar situation is quite different from the "trial and error" in an unfamiliar situation. The individual now quickly makes the learned response that has reduced the drive in the past and thus immediately reduces it again. Drive reduction is thus the basic operation in learning.

So far we have a drive, a response, and a resultant reduction in drive. One more element needs to be added: the collection of stimuli that guides the response. One does not simply learn a response to reduce a given drive whenever or wherever the drive occurs; the response depends on conditions. Under some conditions one reduces hunger by going to a restaurant, under others by cooking a meal. The stimuli that guide the response and that determine which response will occur are known as *cues*. Finally, the drive reduction that ends the learning sequence may of course be called a *reward*. This is the fourth of the elements in learning that Miller and Dollard have made famous: *drive, cue, response,* and *reward*. In Thorndike's puzzle box, for example, the drive was hunger (plus, very likely, exploration), the most important cue was the loop of string, the response was pulling the string, and the reward was escape and food.

This position might be regarded as a combination of Guthrie on the one hand and Thorndike and Skinner on the other. A strong (drive) stimulus acts as a maintaining stimulus, in Guthrie's terms. Its removal, however, acts as a reinforcer. Miller has used the term "drive" to include what Skinner would consider three different concepts. One of these is the negative reinforcer. Miller's definition of a drive is close to Skinner's definition of a negative reinforcer, since both are noxious and both provide reinforcement by their removal. The second concept is that of the *maintenance schedule*. The effectiveness of food as a reinforcer depends on the subject's recent feeding schedule; if he has been deprived of food, food will be more reinforcing than if he has not. Maintenance, for Miller, is another aspect of drive. The third concept is that of *arousal*. A number of stimuli will produce the respondent behaviors, such as acceleration of the heart and tensing of the muscles, that we call physiological arousal. For Miller, arousal is still another aspect of drive. Thus Miller has either advanced theory or confused the issue, depending on your point of view, by treating such diverse entities as hunger, pain, and emotional excitement under the single heading *drive*.

Imitation

In their first book, *Social Learning and Imitation,* Miller and Dollard state their basic interpretation and then proceed to apply it to a variety of complex situations. They note that much human learning behavior involves imitation. In a great many situations people solve problems, not by trying one response after another until one is rewarded, but by doing what they see someone else doing. How does this behavior fit into the simple Miller-Dollard model of learning? The answer is that the tendency to imitate is itself learned. When an individual makes a response, he often does so in the presence of cues produced by the behavior of others. His own response may be either like or unlike that of another individual. If the response is like that of someone else, and if the response is followed by drive reduction, the individual has been rewarded for using the cues from another individual to model his response after the other's. If the response is different and is not followed by drive reduction, the tendency to behave differently from the other is not rewarded and starts to extinguish. Thus imitative behavior is rewarded and other behavior not, so that the individual learns to do what he sees the other do.

Miller and Dollard give an example of two little boys, aged six and three, playing a game with their father. The father hid a piece of candy for each and then the two boys looked for them. Wherever the older boy looked, his younger brother tagged along and looked also. When the older boy found his candy and stopped looking, the little one had no idea where to look next. The only strategy he knew in this game was to imitate his brother exactly.

How had this pattern of imitation, so self-defeating in this case, been built up? Miller and Dollard refer to an earlier incident in the life of these brothers. On one occasion, the older boy heard his father's step and ran to greet the father as he came home from work. The younger boy happened to be running in the same direction at the same time. The father met both boys with presents of candy. Since the younger boy had not learned to distinguish his father's step, he was not running to greet his father; the fact that he was running was purely coincidental. Nevertheless, he was rewarded for the running. Naturally, there had been many times in the past when he had run and not been rewarded for it. The cue that made this time distinctive was the sight of his brother running. Thus there was a learning situation for the younger boy, with hunger as the drive, the sight of his brother running as the cue, running as the response, and candy as the reward. It was through this incident and many others like it, Miller and Dollard decided, that the little boy eventually learned to imitate his brother. Having often been rewarded for imitating his brother, he did so even in situations such as the hiding game where it was useless.

It is easy to think of such situations in which people are rewarded for imitating others. Miller and Dollard were not satisfied, however, merely to cite such examples. They went on to do experiments in which both humans and animals were taught to imitate. In one such experiment, the subject (a first-grade child) could get candy from a machine sometimes by turning the handle and sometimes by pressing it down. If the child made the wrong motion, he got no candy on that trial. Paired with each child was another person, who took a turn at the machine just before the subject did. Sometimes this other person was another child and sometimes an adult. If the adult turned the handle, turning the handle would also be correct for the child. If the other child turned the handle, however, only pressing the handle would work for the subject. In other words, in this situation the children were rewarded for imitating adults but not for imitating other children. The children not only learned to imitate the adult and not the other child, they also generalized this behavior to other adults and other children. Some other children were rewarded for imitating children but not adults, and they too learned. This one experiment illustrates not only the learning of imitation, but also generalization of imitation from one person to another and discrimination between people to be imitated and people not to be.

Miller and Dollard go on to apply these principles to a variety of social situations. They point out, for example, that we learn to imitate high-prestige people more than those of low prestige. A child is likely to be rewarded for imitating "those nice (middle class) children" and not rewarded for acting like "those nasty (lower class) children from across the tracks." The results of such learning to imitate high-prestige people may be seen in adolescent girls who try to dress and act like movie stars and in adult men who buy cars beyond their means in order to keep up with the Joneses. Miller and Dollard also apply the principles of imitation to the behavior of crowds. Mobs, they suggest, consist of people imitating one another and thus stimulating one another to deeds that few of the people would ever commit as isolated individuals. This argument is illustrated with a gruesome story of a lynch mob.

Fear and Neurosis

In their second book, *Personality and Psychotherapy,* Miller and Dollard consider the learning of personality and particularly the learning and unlearning of neuroses. They begin by pointing out three characteristics of the neurotic person: that he is miserable because of his conflicts, that he is stupid about certain aspects of his life, and that he has symptoms. They then proceed to explain these three characteristics according to the neurotic's previous learning. The crucial element in this learning is the learned drive of fear. This drive is the basis of the conflict, the source of the misery, and the cause of the stupidity.

What is a learned drive? Skinner would call it a conditioned noxious stimulus. Miller and Dollard, however, go farther in analyzing what they think goes on when a drive is learned. They begin their discussion with an experimental demonstration involving rats. A rat is placed in a box with two compartments, one of which has white walls and a grid floor, the other black walls and a wooden floor. The rat explores both parts and shows little preference among them. Then it is placed in the white compartment and given strong electric shock through the grid floor. Most rats soon escape the shock by running into the black compartment. This sequence of shock in white and escape to black is repeated several times. Then the rat is placed in the white compartment without shock. It runs rapidly to the black compartment. Since there is no longer a pain drive to motivate this escape behavior, Miller and Dollard explain it on the ground that a secondary drive of fear has been conditioned to the cues of the white compartment.

What is the nature of this secondary drive? Like all drives, say Miller and Dollard, it involves strong stimulation. These strong stimuli are produced by the rat's own responses. When the rat was first shocked in the white compartment, it made a variety of responses to the shock, such as tensing the muscles, increasing the heart rate, and other such indicators of emotion. (These are not, of course, voluntary responses in either rats or humans. Skinner would call them respondents.) These in turn produced strong stimulation which was added to the drive produced by the pain of the shock. These strong stimuli produced by the emotional responses make up the drive of fear. These emotional responses became conditioned to the cues of the white compartment, owing to the fact that they occurred in the presence of those cues and were followed by drive reduction when the rat escaped the shock. Now when the cues of the white compartment are presented without shock, they produce the emotional responses which in turn produce stimuli of the fear drive.

The fact that fear is a drive can be demonstrated by using it as the basis of new learning. This demonstration was done by closing the door from the white to the black section and making it possible for the rat to open the door only by turning a wheel on the wall near the door. The animals learned to turn the wheel and then run into the black compartment, even though there was no shock in the white compartment. In this case fear was the drive, sight of the wheel the cue, turning the wheel the response, and escape from fear (by escaping from the white compartment) the reward. Then the situation was changed so that turning the wheel would not open the door but pressing a lever would. As a result, the wheel-turning response then extinguished and the lever-pressing response was acquired. Thus the secondary drive of fear operated like a primary drive to motivate learning.

How does this kind of learning occur when we go from experimental rats to neurotic humans? Let us consider a child who is severely punished for any kind of self-assertive behavior. Whenever he tries to get his own way, he is subjected to pain, which produces emotional responses, which produce the secondary drive of fear. These fear-producing responses become conditioned to the cues which are present at the time, including the cues that come from his own self-assertion. As a result, any self-assertive behavior comes to produce fear, while submissiveness reduces the fear. The child is then afraid of self-assertion in the same way that the rat is afraid of the white compartment, and the child's submissive behavior is an escape from this fear-provoking self-assertion just as the rat's running to the black compartment is an escape from the fear-provoking white compartment.

However, the child's problem is worse than the rat's. As long as the rat is able to run to the black compartment, his fear is brief and does not disrupt his life. The child, however, is often placed in positions where self-assertive behavior might get him things that he wants. These positions occur even more often after he becomes an adult. The fact that he is afraid to be self-assertive is a great handicap in such situations. He is placed in a conflict between his desire for something and his fear of the self-assertive behavior that would get it for him. This conflict, in which he loses no matter what he does, is a source of misery. If he recognized the great difference between his present situation and that in which he was punished for self-assertion, he might be able to relieve the fear and resolve the conflict. However, this course requires that he recognize his problem and think about it. But he cannot do either since he has become afraid not only of behaving self-assertively but even of saying (to others or to himself) that he would like to be self-assertive. It is this fear of saying or even thinking that he would like to be self-assertive that makes his behavior stupid. He cannot make the thinking responses that would help him to understand and to solve his problems. He can, however, obtain some relief in a variety of ways. He may, for example, become so dependent, perhaps through symptoms of apparent physical illness, that others will feel obliged to take care of him and provide him with some of the things he wants. This would not be a deliberately adopted policy but a response learned through its fear-reducing effects. The "illness" would be called a symptom. It is a partial solution to the problem posed by fear and conflict, but it is only a partial solution, and it interferes with finding a more effective solution. This individual has all the characteristics of the neurotic; he is miserable, in conflict, stupid about his troubles, and has symptoms.

How can the neurosis be eliminated through psychotherapy? Since fear is the crucial cause, extinguishing fear is the crucial element of the cure. If the rat is given enough experience in the white compartment without shock, its tendency to make the fear-producing responses will eventually extinguish. Similarly, if the neurotic can be persuaded to make self-assertive responses (or do whatever else it is that he is afraid of) under conditions where he will not be punished, his fear will extinguish. Since the cues for fear come from the individual's own responses, he must gradually be induced to make these responses, first in very weak and indirect form, later more directly and strongly. Thus in the early stages of therapy the neurotic may timidly say that he sometimes thinks he could make helpful suggestions to his boss, while in the later stages he may express a violent desire to tell the boss off with assorted insults. As the patient extinguishes his fear of making self-assertive statements, he becomes more able to think sensibly about his conflict. Since talking about an act and doing it are somewhat similar, he also becomes by stimulus generalization less afraid of overt self-assertive behavior. Thus Miller and Dollard, through a considerably different theoretical system, come to a practical conclusion very much like Guthrie's threshold method for the elimination of undesirable emotional habits.

SOME RELATIONS AMONG INTERPRETATIONS

We have now considered several theories of learning, all of which are parts of the behavioristic tradition in the broad sense. They have two things in common. One is that they are connectionist theories, concerned with the connections of stimuli with responses. (Skinner is to some extent an exception, but even though he does not regard stimuli as eliciting operant behavior, he does regard stimuli as important in controlling it.) The other similarity is that all are of a relatively simple, informal sort. This quality does not necessarily mean that they are easy to understand. It does mean, however, that they make little use of formal definitions, abstract symbols, or quantitative equations. They are stated in ordinary language, with few if any technical terms, rather than in the special languages of mathematics or symbolic logic. These two characteristics set them apart from the other theories that we will consider in later chapters.

In what ways do these theories differ from one another? One split is between the contiguity theorists (Watson and Guthrie) and the reinforcement theorists (Thorndike, Skinner, and Miller). However, this difference is not as clearcut as it may seem. When Guthrie says that we learn responses which take us away from the maintaining stimuli, and Miller says that we learn responses which reduce strong stimulation, it is hard to see much difference between them. Guthrie does not, however, say that changes in maintaining stimuli are the only stimulus changes that can result in learning, so there is still some difference between him and Miller. We might think of Guthrie's contiguity principle and Miller's drive-reduction principle as two different (but not completely different) attempts to explain why we tend to learn those responses that are rewarded. Thorndike and Skinner, on the other hand, are not concerned with such explanations; they simply accept the principle that rewards are reinforcing and go on from there. Miller concludes that all learning requires reward; Guthrie concludes that reward is probably not thus required, and that anyway it is more worthwhile to talk about contiguity than about reinforcement.

Another difference among these theories is in the extent to which they make statements about what is going on inside the body. Watson, Guthrie, and Miller explain all sorts of things in terms of the internal responses that individuals make and the stimuli that these responses produce. Thorndike and Skinner make little use of such explanations; Skinner in fact argues that all such explanations are inappropriate. The borderline is again difficult to draw, however. Skinner is quite willing to consider verbal responses, even when they are very quiet, and emotional respondent behavior, even when instruments are required to record it. Watson, Guthrie, and Miller consider the stimulus-producing responses that they talk about just as physically real as those that Skinner will admit. The difference is thus only that Skinner will not talk about these responses unless he can point to them, whereas Watson, Guthrie, and Miller are willing to assume that they are there even when they cannot say exactly where they are and what they look like.

On the whole, the similarities among these interpretations of learning are more marked than their differences. This will be more apparent when we consider a markedly different group of interpretations—the cognitive ones. It is to these that we turn in the next chapter.

Chapter 4

Cognitive Interpretations
of Learning

ONE YEAR BEFORE Watson published his first challenge to American psychology, Max Wertheimer (1880-1943) published a challenge to the established psychology of Germany. The orthodoxies against which these two revolts were directed were, as we noted in Chapter 2, much alike. Both the American and the German versions were largely concerned with the structure of the mind. They tried to analyze conscious thought into its fundamental units, such as sensations, images, and ideas. Particularly in America, there was some trend toward studying behavior for its own sake, but psychology was still regarded as primarily the study of conscious experience. Experimentation was directed toward a more complete analysis of the contents of consciousness.

The forms which these two revolts took, however, were strikingly different. Watson's objection was that psychology should not be concerned with consciousness, but with behavior. He wanted to abolish the discussion of images and ideas in favor of a discussion of stimuli and responses. He still agreed with the earlier position, however, in being interested in analysis. He still wanted to work with fundamental units, though they were now units of behavior instead of units of consciousness.

Wertheimer, on the other hand, objected to the concern with analysis. It seemed to him that breaking consciousness into its parts destroyed what was most meaningful about it. He had none of Watson's objection to the study of consciousness; indeed consciousness was his main concern. What he wanted to do was to study consciousness as it appears in wholes, rather than break it down into parts. To the traditional psychology, anything we look at is a mosaic of tiny patches of color. Only as all of these tiny patches are put together do they make up the scene we observe. Wertheimer challenged this view. We actually see the scene, he insisted, as a meaningful whole. Only by a very artificial process of analysis can we break down this whole into patches of different colors and shades. The same applies to thinking. The traditional psychology regarded all our thoughts as made up of images connected by a process of association. This breakdown, too, Wertheimer rejected. Our thoughts are whole meaningful perceptions, not associated collections of images.

Wertheimer's first publication in this revolt against analysis was concerned with the phenomenon of apparent movement. It is well known that we see a light as moving from one place to another when in fact what has happened is that a light in one place was turned off and one in another place immediately turned on. This illusion is the basis of the apparent movement in lighted advertising signs. Prior to Wertheimer, this phenomenon had been regarded as a minor curiosity of no theoretical importance. To Wertheimer, however, it was striking evidence of the futility of analyzing a whole into its parts. The components were two separate lights going on and off, but the resulting whole was an impression of movement. The observer does not see the two lights flashing and infer that something is moving; the impression of movement is immediate and direct. This phenomenon of apparent movement so impressed Wertheimer that he named it the *phi phenomenon* and began a series of studies on it.

EARLY GESTALT PSYCHOLOGY

The phi phenomenon was only the starting point of an intellectual movement within German psychology. This movement was primarily concerned with perception, but came to include learning and other topics as well. Its emphasis was on whole systems in which the parts are dynamically interrelated in such a way that the whole cannot be inferred from the parts taken separately. Wertheimer applied the German word *Gestalt,* which may be roughly translated as "form" or "pattern" or "configuration," to these dynamic wholes. Such *Gestalten* (the plural of *Gestalt*) are of many sorts, and they occur in physics as well as in psychology. We have already considered the phi phenomenon as one example. A melody is another, since it depends on the relation between the notes rather than the notes themselves. "Die Lorelei" (to take an appropriately German example) is still the same tune when transposed into another key so that every note is different. A whirlpool is a third example, since it is a whirlpool not because of the particular drops of water it contains but because of the way the motion of the water is patterned. Because of this concern with Gestalten, the movement that Wertheimer started came to be known as *Gestalt psychology*.

The emphasis of the gestalt (as an English word it needs no capitalization) psychologists on unified wholes does not mean that they never recognized separateness. Indeed, a gestalt may be referred to as a segregated whole. Of particular interest was the way that gestalten come to stand out as distinct entities separate from the background against which they appear. This interest was expressed in the concepts of figure and ground. The *figure* in any perception is the gestalt, the entity that stands out, the "thing" we perceive. The *ground* is the largely undifferentiated background against which the figure appears. A melody, for example, is a figure against a ground that includes many other sounds. What appears as figure at one moment may not at another. If the listener stops paying attention to the melody in order to hear what his friend is saying, his friend's speech becomes figure and the melody becomes part of the ground. Such changes in figure-ground relationships play a part not only in perception but in learning and thinking as well.

It is of course possible to analyze a gestalt figure into component parts. The fact that three black dots on a white page appear as a triangle does not keep them from still being three dots. However, the important thing to a gestalt psychologist is that what we see immediately is a triangle. Afterward we can analyze the triangle into three dots and study what it is that makes these three dots appear as a triangle when another three, differently placed, do not. We cannot say, however, that the triangle is nothing but three dots. The triangularity, which depends on the pattern of the dots rather than on the dots themselves, is the most essential aspect of what we see. The gestalt figure is more than just the sum of three dots. This relationship is the basis of one of the watchwords of gestalt psychology: "the whole is more than the sum of its parts."

It is evident that Wertheimer and Watson, though rebels against similar traditions at the same time, were moving in opposite directions. Each may be considered both a pioneer and an extreme prototype of a certain approach to psychology. Watson's was the mechanistic approach, concerned with the components of behavior and the connections between them. Wertheimer's was the dynamic approach, concerned with unified patterns in consciousness. Without judging their importance relative to that of other men, we can say that in terms of conspicuous intellectual movements, Watson was the outstanding pioneer of connectionist theory and Wertheimer the outstanding pioneer of cognitive theory.

From the first, however, Wertheimer shared the spotlight with two of his colleagues, Wolfgang Köhler (b. 1887) and Kurt Koffka (1886-1941), both of whom eventually surpassed Wertheimer as publicists for the new movement. These two men wrote a number of books on different aspects of gestalt theory. Together with Wertheimer, they formed the nucleus of a group that became known as the Berlin school. All three, however, eventually moved to the United States. Perception remained their primary interest, but learning was by no means neglected. Throughout, the emphasis was on organized wholes, separated from other wholes but united within themselves by their dynamic patterning.

The interpretations of learning presented by Wertheimer, Köhler, and Koffka tend to be presented in the terminology of perception. Instead of asking, "What has the individual learned to do?" the gestalt psychologist is likely to ask, "How has he learned to perceive the situation?" Gestalt interpretations thus make an interesting contrast with the connectionist interpretations we have discussed earlier. It is true that gestalt theorists speak of memory traces, which are the effects that experiences leave in the nervous system. However, these are different from the stimulus-response bonds discussed by connectionist theorists. The memory traces of the gestalt psychologists are not isolated elements, but organized wholes, in other words, gestalten. Consequently, learning is not rimarily a matter of adding new traces and subtracting old ones, ut of changing one gestalt into another. This change may occur through new experience, but it may also occur through thinkng or through the mere passage of time. The way in which these estructurings occur is the concern of gestalt learning theory.

tudies of Insight

The most important contribution of gestalt theory to our unerstanding of learning is in the study of *insight.* Often learning ccurs suddenly with a feeling that now one really understands. uch learning is likely to be especially resistant to forgetting and specially easy to transfer to new situations. We speak of uch learning as involving insight. In such cases the gestalt lanuage of perceptual reorganization is particularly applicable. The earner who has insight sees the whole situation in a new way, a ay which includes understanding of logical relationships or pereption of the connections between means and ends.

Such insight is by no means restricted to humans. During Vorld War I Köhler, technically interned in the Canary Islands, id extensive studies of insightful problem solving in apes. These re described in his book *The Mentality of Apes.* He presented pes with problems in which bananas were displayed out of reach nd could be obtained only by using techniques new in the apes' xperience. For example, a banana might be hung from the top f the animal's cage, with boxes elsewhere in the cage which could e piled under the banana so that the ape could climb up and get . Or a banana might be outside the cage, far enough away so that could be obtained only by pulling it in with a stick. Such arngements had the advantage, from the gestalt point of view, of aaking all the necessary elements of the solution visible to the annal, which is not the case in a puzzle box or maze. He found that ese problems not only were often solved suddenly, but freuently were solved immediately after a period of time during hich the ape was not actively trying to reach the banana. Somemes it appeared that the animal, having failed to obtain the baana by familiar methods, sat and thought about the problem and en suddenly saw the solution. Such incidents are well suited to description in terms of perceptual restructuring. Köhler could

say that an ape suddenly saw the boxes, for example, not as play
things to be tossed around but as supports to be climbed on.
saw the relationship between the boxes and the bananas. During
the time that it was not actively doing anything about the prob
lem, the ape was undergoing a process of restructuring which
when complete, made an immediate solution possible.

It should not be supposed, however, that only such dramatic
examples of sudden and complete insight can be explained in ge
stalt terms. Gradual learning by trial and error can be interprete
as a series of small, partial insights. Köhler's problems were so ar
ranged that the ape could see all the necessary elements of the so
lution at once. All that was necessary was for these parts to be
come organized into an appropriate gestalt. A rat in a maze, o
the other hand, cannot see any relation between the pattern c
turns and the food at the end until this relation has been discov
ered by experience. The rat's restructuring must therefore b
gradual and piecemeal, since the situation permits no other kind
Nevertheless, the discovery that a certain pattern of turns is th
way to food is no less a cognitive restructuring than the discover
that boxes piled on one another are the way to food. The sudden
ness of the restructuring depends on the problem and the way it i
presented to the subject, but the principle is the same.

Gestalt Laws of Learning and Forgetting

Insight requires that certain aspects of a situation be seen i
relation to one another, that they appear as a single gestalt. Wha
factors determine whether this event will occur? In his book
Principles of Gestalt Psychology, Koffka pointed out that the sam
principles could be used to answer this question both in comple
problem-solving situations and in very simple perceptual situa
tions. He suggested, therefore, that certain laws of perception pro
posed by Wertheimer should also be taken as laws of learning
We will consider two of these: the law of proximity and the law
of closure.

The *law of proximity*, as applied to perception, refers to th
way in which items tend to form groups according to the way the
are spaced, with the nearer ones being grouped together. For ex
ample, if a number of parallel lines are drawn on a sheet of paper

with alternate wide and narrow spaces between them, the pairs with narrow spaces between will be seen as groups of two (see Fig. 1, Part A). It is these that are seen together, rather than the pairs with wide spaces between, because of their closer proxim-

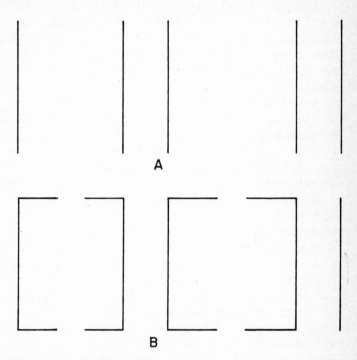

A

B

FIG. 1. *The laws of proximity and closure.* The parallel lines in part A form three sets of two, because of their proximity. In part B they form two sets of two with an extra one on each end, because of the closed figures formed by the middle pairs of lines.

ty to one another. This law also applies to spacing in time. Sounds close together tend to be heard as units. International Morse Code takes advantage of this principle by using intervals of silence of different lengths to separate letters and words, thus making these groups of sounds stand out as units. As applied to learning, the law of proximity may again refer to closeness either in space or in time. In reference to space, it would explain why it is easier for an ape to discover that he can reach a banana with a stick if the stick and the banana are on the same side of the cage (The reader may think that this is really an example from perception rather than learning, since the ape sees stick and banana as going together. If so, the reader has grasped part of the spirit of gestalt theory, in which perception and learning are inextricably tied up together.) In reference to time, it would explain why it is easier to remember recent events, which are closer to the present in time and hence more easily joined with the interests of the present in a common gestalt.

The *law of closure* states that closed areas more readily form units. Applied to perception, this fact can be seen by referring to the previous example of parallel lines. It is possible to change the grouping and make the more widely separated pairs of lines appear as groups. This change may be accomplished by connecting the ends of these lines so that they form two sides of a box. The connecting lines need not be complete; so long as the more widely separated pairs of lines appear to be parts of a figure that enclose space, they will tend to be seen together (Fig. 1, Part B). Applied to learning, the law of closure plays the same role in a cognitive theory of learning that reinforcement plays in a connectionist theory. As long as an individual is struggling with a problem, his perception of the situation is incomplete. A reward solves the problem and brings the hitherto separate parts of the situation together into a closed perceptual figure, consisting of the problem, the goal, and the means of obtaining the goal (Koffka, 1925). The emphasis is not on obtaining a reward but on completing an activity and bringing a number of parts into relation with one another. Thus this explanation is most convincing when applied to adult humans consciously working toward certain goals. The term "closure" has indeed been adopted informally by many nongestalt psychologists to refer to the sense of completion when a task is finished or a mystery solved. However, the relation between closure in this sense and closure of a geometric figure is somewhat forced. Perhaps it would be more accurate to say, not that Koffka has applied the law of closure in perception to learning, but that he has called a law about perception and a law about learning by the same name.

It is interesting to note that, for all the enormous difference between Guthrie's interpretation of learning and that of the gestalt psychologists, there is a certain similarity between Guthrie's primary law of conditioning and the gestalt psychologists' law of closure. Both regard reward as producing its effect by the way that it changes the situation for the learner. For Guthrie, the reward changes the situation so that the last response which occurred remains conditioned to the stimuli of the situation. For the gestalt theorists, reward changes the individual's perception of the situation so that the stimuli, the response, and the reward form a gestalt. From the point of view of a reinforcement theorist, this feature would justify classifying Guthrie's theory and gestalt theory together as contiguity (as opposed to reinforcement) theories.

The gestalt interpretation of forgetting, like that of learning, is concerned with perceptual changes. The memory trace tends to change spontaneously with time into a "better gestalt." The concept of a good gestalt is a rather difficult one to explain. It is the pattern of organization which a system tends to adopt, whether the system is a soap bubble or a perception. Thus, a soap bubble tends to adopt the form of a sphere; if forced into a different form, it will tend to become a sphere as soon as the force is removed. Similarly, perceptions tend to adopt certain forms as closely as the conditions of stimulation permit. Good gestalten tend to be simple and regular. In the case of physical gestalten, it is often possible to describe the characteristics of a good gestalt quite precisely with mathematical equations (for example, the formula for a sphere as applied to the soap bubble). As we move into the realm of perception, previous experience begins to play a part in determining what is a good gestalt. Familiar, meaningful forms tend to be better gestalten than unfamiliar, meaningless ones. Innate factors are still of major importance, however, in determining what constitutes a good perceptual gestalt. When we consider the topic of learning, we find experience still more important, but innate perceptual criteria still apply.

It is not surprising, in view of this interpretation, that the most famous study of forgetting by a gestalt psychologist (Wulf, 1922) was concerned with the forgetting of visual figures—simple line drawings. The subjects in this experiment were asked to look at the drawings and try to remember them, and then at various later times were asked to draw them from memory. Many differences appeared between the original drawings and the reproductions. In some cases the reproduction was simpler and more regular than the original; in other cases some salient detail of the original was accentuated in the reproduction; in still other cases the reproduction was more like some familiar object than the original had been. (None of the original drawings was clearly a picture of anything, but subjects saw many resemblances to familiar objects or patterns.) In all of these different kinds of changes, however, the experimenter saw a trend toward a clearer or more consistent figure, at least as it appeared to the particular person—in other words, a trend toward a better gestalt. In trying to remember the original figure accurately, the subjects actually succeeded in remembering an "improved" version of it. Forgetting was thus not simply a loss of detail, but rather a distortion of what was physically present in the original drawing into something else that constituted a better gestalt.

Insight in Education

Wertheimer's most noted contribution to the development of Gestalt psychology, once the enterprise that he started was under way, was in applications to education. He was concerned with insightful learning in school children. Whereas Köhler studied insight in apes for theoretical reasons, Wertheimer also had a very practical interest in the topic in school children. It seemed to him that teachers put far too much emphasis on rote memorizing at the expense of understanding. He therefore directed his studies toward finding ways in which learning could take place with greater insight on the part of the learner.

In his book *Productive Thinking*, Wertheimer makes a distinction between two types of attempted solutions to problems. Solutions of type A are those in which there is originality and insight; solutions of type B are those in which old rules are inappropriately applied, and hence are not really solutions at all. This distinction does not imply that B solutions depend on previous experience and A solutions do not. Both depend on previous experience; the difference lies in the original organization that characterizes A solutions.

Wertheimer found geometry an especially useful area in which to study different approaches to problems. One of his problems, which he presented to adults as well as children, required the subject to find the area of a parallelogram. Wertheimer would begin by showing the subject how to find the area of a rectangle, not simply the formula of length times height, but the reason why the formula works. He did so by dividing the rectangle up into small squares (Fig. 2, Part A) and showing that the area was the number of squares in a row times the number of rows. He then presented the subject with a parallelogram cut out of paper (Fig. 2, Part B) and the instruction to find its area. Some people replied that this was a new problem and they couldn't be expected to solve it without being told how. Some blindly repeated the now incorrect formula of multiplying one side times the other: a B type of solution. Other people attempted to find an original solution, but were unable to see the essential relationships. A few, however, came up with genuine A solutions. One child, noting that the two projecting ends were what made the problem difficult, asked for scissors, cut off one end, and fitted it against the other end, thus converting the parallelogram into a rectangle (Fig. 2, Part C). Another subject achieved the same goal by bending the parallelogram into a ring, so that the two ends fitted together, and then cutting the ring vertically to convert it into a rectangle. These two individuals showed a genuine understanding of the situation that made possible correct, original solutions.

If these individuals had applied the rule "base times *height*," which for rectangles is equivalent to the rule "one *side* times the other," the computation would have been correct, but nevertheless would have demonstrated no understanding. Thus it would have been much like a B solution, even though it would have happened to be correct. What they did, however, was to find an original way of converting this new problem into a familiar one, one that they knew how to solve. The final solution depended very much on previous experience, but it was previous experience organized in a novel way. The important thing about the solutions was the insight by which the new problem situation was restructured. From the solvers' point of view, they converted the parallelogram into a better gestalt, a rectangle.

Even when a solution is correct, it is important to distinguish

E

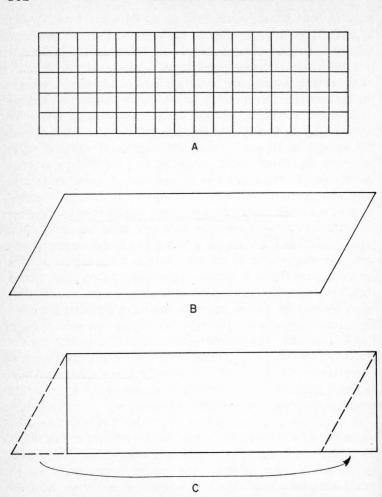

FIG. 2. *Wertheimer's parallelogram problem.* Part A shows Wertheimer's way of explaining why the area of a rectangle equals the product of length times width, in this case sixteen by five. Part B shows the parallelogram for which he asked subjects to find the area. Part C shows one person's solution to this problem by cutting off one end, moving it to the other end, and thus converting the parallelogram into a rectangle.

whether or not real understanding is involved. Understanding is not the same as logic. Both the inductive and the deductive methods of logic may be applied blindly. The inductive method, in which one reasons from particular instances to a general conclusion, is really just trial and error. Another person might have tried various possible formulas for the area of a parallelogram, found that base times altitude gave the same answer as the book in several cases, and concluded that this was the correct formula but without having any idea why. Though adequate for practical purposes, this would be a solution without understanding. Wertheimer enjoys giving examples of cases where such blind induction leads to absurdly wrong conclusions. The deductive method, in which one reasons logically from one principle to another, can also be applied blindly. A student may fumble around algebraically until he finds a valid proof that a certain equation is correct, but he may still not understand the equation in the sense that Wertheimer means. Understanding implies not merely logical correctness but a perception of the problem as an integrated whole, of the ways in which the means lead to the end. In going through an algebraic proof, for example, one should ask at each step not only "How does this follow logically from the previous step?" but also "How does this lead toward the solution I am looking for?" In Wertheimer's opinion, education should make such understanding, or perception of whole gestalten, its primary goal.

The value of creative problem solving is not restricted to such "purely intellectual" situations as the above. Wertheimer illustrates its value in social situations with an anecdote about two boys playing badminton. The older boy was so much better at the game than the younger that he won nearly every point, and the frustrated younger boy finally refused to play any more. Since this spoiled the fun for the older boy, it posed a problem for him. How could he get the younger boy to go on playing with him? He might have exhorted him to be a sport (probably in vain), or he might have offered a handicap (a better approach, but still not an answer to the fundamental problem posed by the one-sided competition). Seeing the competition as the crux of the problem, the older boy was able to propose a constructive solution. The competitive game of winning points was replaced by a cooperative game of seeing how long the two together could keep the bird going back and forth, and both were then able to enjoy playing. Again, understanding of the situation led to an insightful solution.

This book of Wertheimer's, set beside Guthrie's *Psychology of Learning*, points up the contrast between cognitive and connectionist views of learning in their extreme forms. Both books show a keen interest in the applied psychology of learning, especially as applied to children. Guthrie's emphasis is on training the child to make the right responses to the right stimuli. His question is always "What does the child do?" Wertheimer, on the other hand, is concerned with educating the child to have insights into the material. His question is "What does the child understand?" The difference is not irreconcilable, since Wertheimer is concerned with the ability to solve problems effectively and since Guthrie can talk about understanding in terms of movement-produced stimuli. Nevertheless, the difference in emphasis is tremendous. This emphasis on understanding, on the perception of relationships within an organized whole, is the great contribution of gestalt psychology to the interpretation of learning.

LEWIN'S SYSTEM

Among the gestalt psychologists who worked with Wertheimer, Köhler, and Koffka in Berlin was Kurt Lewin (1890-1947). Like the other leading gestalt psychologists, he eventually settled in the United States. His interests were different from theirs in a number of respects. Whereas they were mainly concerned with rather technical problems in perception, learning, and thinking, he was interested in motivation, personality, and social psychology. Gestalt psychology, in dealing with learning, tended to take the desire for certain goals for granted and to concentrate on the way the goals are obtained through cognitive restructuring. Lewin wanted to concentrate on the desires and the goals themselves, studying them in relation to the personality. The system he developed for conducting this study is not primarily a theory of learning, but it is a system of description within which learning, motivation, personality, and social behavior can all be discussed.

The Life Space

What Lewin wanted was a theoretical system for predicting the motivated behavior of a single individual. He found the answer in the concept of *life space.* This may be defined as the totality of facts which determine the behavior of a given individual at a given time. It is represented conceptually as a two-dimensional space in which the individual moves. This space contains the person himself, the goals he is seeking, the negative "goals" he is trying to avoid, the barriers that restrict his movements, and the paths he must follow to get what he wants.

This concept of life space is more complicated than is at first apparent. For one thing, it must not be confused with physical or geographical space. This is not the world of physical objects and real other people, but the world as it affects the individual. Hence an object of which he is unaware and which does not influence him would not appear in his life space, even though physically it may be close to him. Similarly, something he thinks is there and reacts to as if it were there is present in his life space even though physically absent. If a child thinks there is a tiger under his bed, the tiger is part of the child's life space, even if everyone else insists that the tiger is purely imaginary.

Can we say, then, that the life space is the person's environment as he himself perceives it? This is a hard question to answer, since it depends on just what we mean by "perceive." We cannot say that the life space is made up only of the things of which the person is consciously aware. An individual may be influenced by factors of which he is unconscious. For example, a certain high-school teacher would like to take an administrative position, and feels quite able to do so. Nevertheless, whenever an opportunity to apply for such a position comes along, he finds some excuse not to apply. After this has happened several times, his friends suspect that something is holding him back from seeking an administrative position, perhaps some deep-seated lack of confidence in his own ability. In Lewin's terms, there is a barrier in his life space between him and the goal of an administrative job. Yet he insists that he wants such a job and is going to apply as soon as just the right opportunity comes along. If we go by what he says, we would conclude that he does not perceive any important barrier between himself and the goal of an administrative job. If we go by what he does, we would conclude that he does perceive such a barrier, since he acts as if one is there. Which does he *really* perceive? This is a question we cannot answer, but fortunately we do not need to. If he acts as if the barrier is there, then it is there in his life space. It is from the way a person behaves that we know what is present in his life space. It is often convenient to speak of the life space as "the environment as the person views it," but we must keep in mind that what we really mean is "the environment as it affects his behavior."

The life space includes the person himself and his behavioral environment, which consists of everything that influences his behavior. Of particular importance in the life space are the goals the person is seeking, the things or situations he is trying to avoid, and the barriers that restrict his movement toward or away from them. Lewin represents the life space by two-dimensional diagrams (see Fig. 3). Any place, object, or situation that the individual wants to approach (strictly speaking, *acts as if* he wants to approach) is said to have *positive valence,* and is represented in the diagram by a plus sign. Any that the individual wants to avoid is said to have *negative valence* and is represented in the diagram by a minus sign. Barriers are represented by heavy lines separating one part of the life space from another.

These diagrams are of course highly schematic. They usually do not correspond to physical space. For example, a politician's life space might include the governorship of his state as a positive valence and the election as a barrier. The distances in the diagram between the politician, the election, and the governorship have no particular meaning in the life space that the diagram represents. What is important in the life space is the regions through which the politician must pass to reach his goal and the difficulties of getting from one region to another (i.e., the barriers). These considerations led Lewin to decide that the ordinary geometry of distances was not appropriate for picturing the life space. He therefore turned to the special kind of geometry known as *topology*. Topology is sometimes called "rubber-sheet geometry," since topological space can be stretched in any direction without making any difference. Topology is concerned only with the boundaries between regions, not with the sizes or shapes of the regions or the distances from one place to another. When an area is divided up topologically, all that matters is what regions separate one point

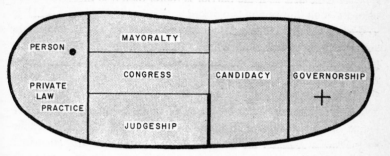

FIG. 3. *A topological diagram of a politician's life space.* At present the individual is practicing law. He sees three other regions available to him. From the mayorality or from Congress he could become a candidate for governor, but the boundary between the judgeship and candidacy appears to be impenetrable. The boundary between the region of candidacy and the positively-valenced region of the governorship also forms a barrier, indicating serious doubts as to whether he could win this election. Note that the sizes and shapes of the regions could be greatly changed without changing the meaning of the diagram, so long as the boundary relationships remained the same.

from another. Such topological space was much more convenient for Lewin's purposes than the space of ordinary geometry.

Whereas it is meaningless to ask the distance, in inches or miles, between a politician and his goal of being governor, it is meaningful to ask what regions he must pass through to get to the goal. Certainly the final region before the region of being governor is that of being a candidate. Before that there may be alternative paths—perhaps one by way of the mayoralty of a large city and another by way of Congress. These regions are not, of course, particular places in physical space, but they are meaningful parts of the life space. They are positions that the individual can occupy. Positive and negative valences are attributes of certain regions, as with the positive valence of the governorship. Barriers are boundaries between regions which are especially hard to penetrate. The barrier formed by the gubernatorial election, for example, is the boundary between the region of candidacy and the region of governorship. If a barrier is impenetrable for the person in question, he cannot enter the next region, and any path going to or through that region is blocked.

These topological diagrams can be used to represent all the significant elements in any life situation. Positive valences may be attached to regions as specific as "eating candy" or as vague as "maintaining social status." Negative valences may apply to situations as diverse as spanking for a child and guilt feelings for a criminal. Barriers may be physical (e.g., a locked door), intellectual (e.g., a difficult examination), or social (e.g., the exclusiveness of a positively valenced club). The regions through which a person must pass may be places, social statuses (e.g., child, adolescent, adult), activities (e.g., practicing tennis before becoming a star), or any other situations that necessarily occur to the individual as sequences. The diagrams of the life space can apply equally well to a child prevented from getting a cookie (positive valence) by a high cupboard (barrier) or to a student who must pass through the regions of college, medical school, and internship in order to become a doctor. In all of these cases we must remember that it is the situation as it influences the person, not the "objective" situation, with which we are concerned. If the politician were so sure he would lose the election that he declined to become a candidate, then the election would be an impenetrable barrier in his life space, even though his pessimism might actually be quite unjustified. (For a politician, such unjustified pessimism probably makes the example quite unrealistic.) In any case, it is subjective rather than objective reality that makes up the life space.

Predicting Behavior

The topological regions in a person's life space and the barriers between them indicate what paths it is (subjectively) possible for him to follow. The positive and negative valences of various regions suggest which of the possible paths he is actually likely to follow. However, Lewin also wanted to be able to indicate the relative strengths of tendencies to approach or to avoid different points in the life space. There are often a number of positive valences in the life space at a given time—which one will be approached? To answer this question, Lewin added *vectors* to his system. A vector is a force operating in a certain direction. It is represented by an arrow, with the direction of the arrow indicating the direction of the force and the length of the arrow indicating the strength of the force. Vector analysis has been most prominent in physics, where forces of different magnitudes operating in different directions play an important part. Lewin adopted only the idea of vectors, not the mathematical analysis that usually goes with them. In his diagrams, he indicated the tendency to approach a positive valence with a vector pointing from the person toward the valence, and the tendency to avoid a negative valence by a vector pointing from the person away from the valence. The length of the arrow indicates the strength of the tendency. This makes it possible to show which of the forces acting on an individual is the strongest.

Although the description of the life space provides a considerable basis for predicting an individual's behavior, a number of questions remain unanswered. When two or more paths toward a goal are available, which will be followed? When two or more vectors operate on an individual, will only the stronger be effective or will some compromise occur? If a barrier proves insurmountable, will some other goal be substituted for the inaccessible one? Lewin's reply is that topological psychology determines what behaviors are possible and what ones impossible. It does not tell us which one definitely will occur. However, the more we know about the details of a person's life space, the more we can narrow down the range of possibilities that are open to him. Thus more and more information will make our predictions better and better, until perhaps eventually they will become almost perfect.

Let us consider, as an example, a student who has a strong vector toward the region of being a teacher, and also a moderately strong vector toward the region of being well-to-do. We may suspect that this situation will lead to problems. However, if we know nothing about the topology of his life space, we cannot predict his behavior. If we know that in his life space these two positively valenced regions overlap (i.e., he perceives teachers as well to do) then there is no problem (regardless of what the objective situation may be). He will simply approach this goal of being a well-to-do teacher. If, instead, we know that in his life space the two regions are separate (i.e., teachers are not well-to-do), we are again unable to predict. He may simply react to the stronger vector, or he may find some compromise, or he may investigate the matter further and perhaps as a result restructure his life space (as by finding out that some teachers actually are well paid, which would make the two regions move together and overlap). However, if we can find out more about his life space, our chance of predicting successfully which of these things he will do will increase. If the region of being well-to-do includes a subregion similar to teaching (such as industrial training or school administration), this fact makes him more likely to approach that subregion as a compromise. If he has a vector toward further investigation of the possibilities, this increases the chance that he will get new information leading to a restructuring of the life space. As our knowledge of his life space increases, our ability to predict his behavior also increases.

As we include more of these complexities, the task of diagraming the life space becomes more difficult. Lewin tried hard to make his system complete enough to handle the great variety of human situations. He discussed the problems of regions, subregions, and boundaries. He searched for the best way to represent looking at something as distinguished from going to it. He extended his diagrams into additional dimensions in order to deal with plans for the future and with fantasies. As a result, his complete topological and vector analysis is rather complicated. Most of these technical details are treated in his book, *Principles of Topological Psychology*. In addition, much of the research which he and his (often devoted) students carried on was concerned with clarifying these problems. What effect do barriers have on valences? What determines whether a substitute goal will be acceptable to the person? These are the sorts of questions to which Lewin's research made important contributions.

In addition to his work on the life space, Lewin also developed theoretical interpretations of personality structure. These interpretations led to many experiments and applications, some of which are discussed in his book, *Dynamic Theory of Personality*. The only one of these that needs to be mentioned here is his concept of *tension*. Vectors result from tensions within the person. These tensions may be very similar to what Miller (and many others) refer to as drives. They may also, however, be of a less biological and more cognitive sort, such as the tension to complete a task once it is started.

Lewin's theoretical analyses of the person and the life space, along with the many experimental studies that he based on these analyses, made him famous as a psychologist of personality and of social behavior. He was always interested in the application of psychology to these areas. The organization of groups, the causes and cures of prejudice, and the effects of frustration are among the topics to which he made important contributions.

Lewin's Weakness in Predicting Learning

From the point of view of the psychology of learning, however, all of the above interests are pretty much beside the point. Lewin provided us with a system for describing and predicting behavior, but he did not give us a theory of learning. Much of the value of studying his system in this book lies in understanding why he did not. A knowledge of the life space as described by Lewin enables us to predict reasonably well what the individual will do. But how do we determine the structure of the life space? By observing the individual's behavior and inferring from it what the structure must be. Having observed someone's behavior, we figure out the structure of his life space. From this structure we predict what his behavior in the future will be. In order for this method to work, his life space must remain the same except for his own position in it. Learning, however, involves a change in the life space. How can we predict when and how such changes will occur? In some cases a knowledge of the life space (and the person in it) is enough, as for example when we predict that long exposure to a region of positive valence will produce satiation and make the valence less strongly positive. In most cases, however, we must take into account external, physical reality. If an individual comes to a door that he thought was unlocked, tries to open it, and finds it locked, the door changes in his life space from a permeable boundary to a barrier. How could we have predicted this change in the life space? Only by knowing that the door was, in fact, locked. But such questions of physical reality do not really enter into Lewin's system.

Lewin was, of course, aware of this problem, and he discussed the ways in which external events can produce changes in the life space. However, this part of his theory is very minor, and he never developed it in detail. In his research he showed a lively interest in finding out how best to change attitudes, but little of this practical interest found its way into his formal theorizing. In his theoretical work, for the most part, he was too busy examining the structure of the life space, the organization of the person, and the way these influence behavior to be concerned with the ways in which they are themselves changed by external events. As a result, his theoretical system is useful for stating the results of certain kinds of learning, but of little value in predicting what learning will occur under what conditions.

This lack of concern with learning as such reflects Lewin's philosophical view of science. He sees most psychologists as looking for statistical laws that apply more or less to people (or animals) in general, but not specifically to any given individual. He, however, wants to achieve such individual prediction. One way of doing so would be to find general laws for predicting how individuals will develop throughout their life histories. If we knew enough about the laws of heredity, of biological maturation, and of learning, and if we knew enough about an individual's ancestry and his lifetime of previous experiences, we could make quite accurate predictions of his present behavior. This is the approach that Guthrie or Skinner or Miller would have to take if he wanted to predict individual differences before doing any training. (Such prediction has not, however, been the goal of their work.) Lewin rejects this approach. So far as he is concerned, though it might be possible in principle it would be hopelessly cumbersome in practice. It would be especially cumbersome because the effect of each learning experience would depend on the way it was perceived, which in turn would depend on previous learning. Hence Lewin rejects attempts to explain present behavior by past circumstances, which would of course include previous learning. <u>Behavior at the present time depends on the life space at the present time, and explanations in terms of previous learning are inadequate and misleading</u>. With this bias, it is understandable that Lewin did not want to concentrate on problems of learning. However, in not doing so he left a serious gap in his theory. Without more information on how the life space can change, we are hard put to make long-term predictions and even more hard put to make recommendations about teaching, psychotherapy, or other problems in learning.

COGNITIVE AND CONNECTIONIST
THEORY COMPARED

At this point we may ask: why do some psychologists use the stimulus-response approach and others the cognitive approach? We saw some of the reasons for these different preferences in Chapter 1. Now, having considered some of the advantages and some of the disadvantages of both approaches, we may examine the question further. Let us consider two kinds of psychologist, each working toward certain objectives, and see why each chooses the theory that he does.

Let us look first at a psychologist working directly with individuals whose behavior he wants to predict. He might be, for example, a school counselor working with mildly disturbed children. He is concerned, not with children in general, but with each particular child that he sees. His job is to help this child by whatever means he can, regardless of whether he can explain the principles by which he does it. Usually the most effective thing for such a counselor to do is to find out as much as possible about this particular child and then use this information to reconstruct the child's life space. This method would be Lewin's. In using this method, he is not systematically applying laws, but is taking advantage of his own cultural background and playing whatever hunches he has. Cognitive theory is a more sophisticated description of what he regularly does.

Now let us look at another psychologist, this one doing research on learning. He wants to find laws of behavior, laws that have the same kind of generality as those in the natural sciences. He wants to explain man's behavior as part of the natural world, as the product of man's heredity and environment. To reconstruct the life space from behavior and then use it to predict new behavior is, for him, to miss the main point. He is not concerned with predicting one person's behavior by any means available; he wants to predict the behavior of people in general by means of precise laws. These laws should be applicable, not only to people whom the psychologist knows, but also to strangers whose life spaces he would have little basis for guessing.

Both of these psychologists recognize that each individual is unique. They differ in the place they give to this uniqueness in their systems. To the first, each person's unique nature is the starting point from which predictions are made and on which studies are based. To the second, a given person's uniqueness is the end result of the operation of many laws, something to be explained rather than something to be used as an explanation.

These considerations apply to all aspects of psychology, not just to learning. Are there any reasons why one or the other of these approaches is especially useful in the area of learning? On the one hand, we have already seen that the method of reasoning from behavior to the life space and then back to behavior is not by itself adequate for studying learning. This approach must be supplemented by some consideration of the relation between external events and the life space. Because Lewin largely ignored this topic, his approach in this respect is less adequate than those of the connectionists.

On the other hand, it is scarcely realistic to say that learning involves nothing but increases and decreases in the tendencies to make certain responses. The particular responses we make cannot generally be understood without reference to such concepts as beliefs and purposes. When our behavior changes as a result of something we are told, it seems more reasonable to attribute this behavior change to a change in our cognitions than to a change in our habits. As a result, the connectionist views we have looked at so far seem too narrowly mechanistic to deal with the complexities of human learning.

TOLMAN'S PURPOSIVE BEHAVIORISM

A number of attempts have been made to combine the advantages of cognitive and connectionist theory. Most of these have been extensions of connectionist theory to include some of the complexities with which cognitive theories commonly deal. One, however, was an attempt to give cognitive theory as close a connection with external stimuli and with learning as connectionist theory has. This was the system developed by Edward Chace Tolman (1886-1959), who for forty years was on the faculty of the University of California at Berkeley. Though Tolman's theory might well be regarded as an attempt to solve the difficulty of other theories we have discussed, it was actually developed earlier than many of them.

Tolman's major work, *Purposive Behavior in Animals and Men,* was published in 1932. Though his system has undergone a number of modifications since then, its essential spirit remains the same. Writing in the heyday of behaviorism, Tolman was impressed with behaviorism's objectivity, its concern with the precise measurement of behavior, and its faith in the improvability of man. At the same time he felt that behaviorism showed too little appreciation of the cognitive aspects of behavior. We do not simply respond to stimuli; we act on beliefs, express attitudes, and strive toward goals. What we need is a theory that recognizes these aspects of behavior without sacrificing objectivity. To fill this need, Tolman undertook to create what has been called a *purposive behaviorism*.

What is a purposive behaviorism like? Two of its characteristics are implied in the name. First, it is a form of behaviorism. As such, it is concerned with objective behavior, not with conscious experience. Moreover, it is concerned with the effect of external stimuli on behavior, not merely with a life space inferred from behavior. Thirdly, it is concerned with learning, with the way that behavior changes with changing experience of the external world.

However, this is a purposive behaviorism. Whereas Watson treated behavior as a matter of responses to immediately present stimuli, Tolman emphasized the relation of behavior to goals. Most of our behavior is not so much a response to stimuli as a striving toward some goal. Stimuli of course guide us toward the goal and determine at every step what means we will use to reach it, but the search for the goal is what gives unity and meaning to our behavior. We may shift from one approach to another as circumstances require, while still continuing to direct our efforts toward the same goal. As a result, it would be necessary for anyone who wanted to predict our behavior to know the goal we were seeking as well as the particular stimuli we were encountering along the way. Tolman's system is called a purposive behaviorism because it studies behavior as it is organized around purposes.

The behavior that Tolman wanted to study is _molar_ behavior. This term refers, not to the kind of behavior, but to the way in which it is analyzed. Molar behavior is behavior analyzed in fairly large, common-sense units, such as driving to work or cooking a meal. In practice, this is the way all theories of learning analyze behavior. However, some theories include an interest in _molecular_ behavior, which is behavior analyzed in terms of single movements of particular muscles. Walking a city block, for example, is a molar act made up of an enormous number of molecular movements—expansions and contractions of the various muscles of the legs and other parts of the body. Guthrie is an example of a theorist who puts a good deal of emphasis on molecular analysis. Tolman, on the the other hand, states explicitly that he is concerned only with molar behavior. The ways in which molecular movements work together to produce molar acts are of no concern to his system.

Cognitions as Intervening Variables

A given goal may be approached by a great variety of different acts, not only as sequences of responses but also as alternative possible ways of gaining the objective. Tolman's problem was to develop a theory for dealing with this complex variablity of molar behavior as it operates in search of goals. To do this, he considered it necessary to take account of the individual's cognitions, his perceptions of and beliefs about the world. These correspond to Lewin's life space. How could Tolman take them into account without sacrificing the objectivity of behaviorism? His answer was to make use of _intervening variables._ To appreciate the importance of this answer we must see it in historical context. The existing behaviorist theory regarded anything intervening between the stimulus and the response as itself a response, just as physical and potentially just as measurable as any other response. If the word "cognition" had any meaning at all for such behaviorists, it was either another name for tiny movements of the speech muscles or else a figment of some sloppy mentalistic theorist's imagination. Tolman objected to both these meanings of "cognition." He thought it should be possible to use the term "cognition" objectively without treating it as a physical, directly measurable movement. He therefore designated cognitions as in-tervening variables. In doing so he both made the concept of cognition more respectable in behaviorist circles and introduced the concept of intervening variables into psychology.

As an intervening variable, a cognition is not a thing. It is an abstraction defined by the theorist. While it is possible that physiologists may some day find some particular activity in the brain that corresponds to a cognition, this possibility is no concern of Tolman's. The meaning of the word "cognition" is determined by the definition that the theorist gives it. For Tolman, this definition is in terms both of stimuli and of responses, since it intervenes between them. Experience with certain stimuli results in the formation of certain cognitions.

In addition, certain needs produce *demands* for certain goal objects. (Deprivation of food, for example, produces a demand for food.) These demands are also intervening variables. Cognitions and demands work together to produce responses.

The difference between this system and the other cognitive theories we have discussed so far is mainly one of emphasis. For Lewin, the relation of the life space to external stimuli is to some extent a side issue. For Tolman, it is of central importance. He is a theorist of learning, and learning involves changes in cognitions resulting from experience with external stimuli. In this sense Tolman could be considered a stimulus-response theorist even though he is not a connectionist. However, the notion of life space fits easily into Tolman's system. He has, in fact, adopted large parts of Lewin's system into his own. Basically, Tolman's system is a cognitive theory, but with more emphasis than most on external stimuli.

Predictions from Tolman's Theory

How is Tolman's theory different from a connectionist one? Both attempt to predict behavior from stimuli and other antecedent conditions. Does the fact that Tolman uses cognitions as intervening variables make any real difference? Consider an individual who makes a certain response to certain stimuli and obtains a reward. What learning does this experience tend to produce? For Guthrie, Skinner, or Miller, it produces a tendency for those stimuli to be followed by that response, provided other conditions (such as drive, in Miller's case) are appropriate. For Tolman, it produces a cognition that making the response will lead to the reward. If he now has a demand for the reward, he will make the response. How are these two interpretations really different?

The answer to this question is that not all cognitions take the form, "If I do this, I will get that." We form many other kinds of cognitions about the way the environment is structured, about things that go together, about what paths lead to what places. These various sorts of cognitions can then be used when needed to help the individual achieve his goals. Cognitions from several different learning experiences may be put together so that the individual can respond adaptively to new situations. Attention to such combination makes it possible for Tolman's theory to deal with more original and flexible behavior than is covered by the connectionist interpretations of learning that we have discussed so far.

One example of this greater flexibility is in cognitions about what leads to what. Once an individual has learned how to get from one place to another, he can use this knowledge to obtain rewards quite different from the one he obtained while learning. A rat that has learned its way around a maze while satisfying its demand for exploration can use this knowledge later to obtain food. This changeover is illustrated in an experiment by Buxton. Rats were given several experiences of spending a night in a large maze. There was never any food in the maze, and the rats were taken out of the maze at different places on different occasions. This variation was designed to insure that no part of the maze or path through the maze would be rewarded more than any other. After this experience, the rats were fed in the goal box of the maze while they were 48 hours hungry and were then put in the start box of the maze. About half of the rats ran to the goal box without a single error on this first trial, a record far above that of a control group without the previous experience in the maze. Since the rats had never been reinforced with food (or, presumably, with anything else) for following this particular path, it is difficult for stimulus-response theories to deal with this experiment. For Tolman, however, it is simple enough; the rats had formed a cognition (or perhaps a group of cognitions) about how the maze was arranged. They did not make use of this knowledge until they were given a reason to do so. In other words, the learning about the layout of the maze remained latent until food was experienced in the goal box. Hence this study is said to demonstrate *latent learning.* Several different kinds of latent learning have been studied; this experiment illustrates one of them. Whenever learning goes on without its being evident in performance at the time, latent learning is taking place.

Another way in which Tolman's theory achieved greater flexibility than connectionist theories was through its emphasis on learning the location of reward. Once an individual has learned where a given kind of reward is located, he can often get to that location by means other than those he originally used. If a shopper finds an intriguing store while exploring the city on foot, he (or more likely she) can return later by car or bus. Similarly, a rat that has learned the location of food may, if the experimental arrangements permit, take a detour to get there faster. This is illustrated by another experiment (Tolman, Ritchie, and Kalish, 1946). Rats ran across a table top, through an enclosed alley, and then along a series of elevated pathways by a roundabout route to food (Fig. 4, Part A). After they had learned to use this route, the alley was blocked, but eighteen new pathways were made available, leading in various directions from the table top (Fig. 4, right side). The rats did not, as one might expect from the principle of generalization, choose the doors closest to the one they had previously used. Instead, they tended to choose the one which pointed approximately toward the location of the goal. In other words, they chose the one which appeared to be a short-cut to the goal rather than those close to the original path. They had not merely learned a route to food; they had also learned the location of the food in space.

The two above experiments are typical of many that were done by Tolman and his students or were done by others but quoted by Tolman in support of his position. Because of their importance for the controversy between cognitive and connectionist interpretations of learning, these studies were often criticized for various details of their procedures and were often repeated by both friends and foes of Tolman's ideas. In some cases it turned out

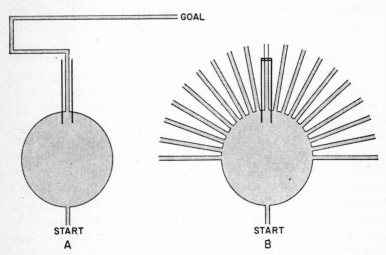

FIG. 4. *Learning the direction to a goal.* This is a top view of Tolman, Ritchie, and Kalish's apparatus. In part A, rats followed the roundabout route from the round table top to the goal, where they found food. In part B, the original route was blocked and 18 new paths were made available. The rats tended to choose the path pointing toward the goal.

that animals show the insightful behavior predicted by Tolman only under quite special conditions. However, whether or not rats behave according to Tolman's theory in any given situation, there is no doubt that this kind of flexible, insightful behavior does occur in some species (particularly man) under some conditions. The very fact that Tolman considered these experiments necessary shows how strong a hold connectionist interpretations of learning had on American psychology.

Tolman used a number of terms to refer to the cognitions that are learned in various situations. One popular term is *cognitive map*. It is easy to see how the two experiments discussed above can be interpreted by saying that the rats had cognitive maps of the areas they had explored. Those in the maze had a cognitive map of the various alleys, indicating which were blind and which led on to other choice points. Those in the roundabout path had a map that included not only the path but also the surrounding space with its possible shortcuts. If someone asks how it is possible to have maps in the brain when the brain is made up of nerve fibres that conduct impulses from one place to another, Tolman is not concerned. Cognitive maps are intervening variables, and if they explain learning Tolman does not care what connection they have with physiology.

Another of Tolman's terms, less popular but more impressive, is *sign-gestalt-expectation*. This is the individual's expectation that the world is organized in certain ways, that certain things lead to others. The inclusion of the word "sign" indicates that these expectations are mainly about stimuli which are signs of certain things, rather than about responses. The word "gestalt" emphasizes that the signs must be considered in context, that the whole pattern of stimulation is important. This term has become one of Tolman's trademarks; in fact his theory is sometimes called sign-gestalt theory.

These two terms point up the closeness of Tolman's formulation to those of the cognitive theorists we have already discussed. In many respects he was particularly close to Lewin, and he borrowed heavily from Lewin in later formulations of his theory. Tolman's later theoretical publications are full of diagrams of vectors and valences. He also added to Lewin's system of diagrams by making a distinction between *pragmatic performance vectors* and *identification performance vectors*. The pragmatic performance vectors refer to the tendencies actually to go to various places or to make other responses of acting on the environment. The identification performance vectors refer to the tendencies merely to observe things. They are concerned with exploring the situation, with observation of the environment. Thus Tolman distinguishes tendencies to observe the environment, either out of curiosity or in order to decide what to do about it, from tendencies to take action toward some part of the environment.

Six Kinds of Learning

We can see more of Tolman's relation to other theorists if we look at the six different kinds of learning that Tolman distinguished in one of his later theoretical articles (Tolman, 1949). While Skinner was disagreeing with Guthrie and Miller as to whether there are two basically different kinds of learning or whether there is only one, Tolman announced that there are six.

The first kind of learning is the formation of *cathexes* (singular, cathexis). This concept is taken from Freud's psychoanalytic theory of motivation. A cathexis, in Tolman's interpretation, is a tendency to seek certain goals rather than others when experiencing a certain drive. The drive resulting from food deprivation leads us to seek meat or candy but not to seek sawdust or ants. The difference is due to our previous experience of satisfying the drive of hunger by eating meat and candy but not by eating sawdust or ants. In cultures where ants are eaten, cathexes for ants are formed, and in cultures where meat is taboo, cathexes for meat are not formed. Whenever a given goal object satisfies a given drive, a cathexis of that demand on that goal object tends to be formed. The term "demand," which Tolman used in his earlier writing but later abandoned, might be viewed as a combination of a drive and a cathexis. Thus, the hunger drive plus the cathexis of this drive on some food would give rise to a demand for that food.

The second kind of learning involves *equivalence beliefs*. These are similar to Skinner's conditioned reinforcers. They are not merely beliefs that reward or punishment will be found in a certain situation, but cognitions that the situation is equivalent to the reward or punishment and hence in itself rewarding or punishing. The examples Tolman gives are of complex social learning, as when a child's receiving a gold star is equivalent for him to receiving love and admiration. Since we know so little about how equivalence beliefs are acquired, there is some question whether it was worth Tolman's trouble to separate this kind of learning from the forming of cathexes.

These first two forms of learning both depend on experiencing reward (or punishment). This feature is not present, however, in the third kind of learning. This is the formation of *field expectancies.* These are cognitions about the way the world is laid out, about what leads to what. They are essentially the same as what Tolman earlier called sign-gestalt-expectations. Nearly all of what we ordinarily call knowledge comes under this heading. When we learn the route from one place to another, or when we learn what tools can be used for what purposes, we are forming field expectancies. Cognitive maps are made up mostly of field expectancies. The paths and barriers of Lewin's life space represent field expectancies. These field expectancies develop through experience with the objective world. Demands and rewards may influence them indirectly by changing the individual's focus of attention, but they have no necessary connection with either demands or rewards. Thus we might say that Tolman is a reinforcement theorist with regard to cathexes and equivalence beliefs, but not with regard to field expectancies. It is in this third kind of learning that Tolman proclaims himself clearly as a cognitive theorist. It is thus the heart of his system.

The fourth kind of learning consists of *field cognition modes*. These are different from anything we have discussed so far, and Tolman does little more than suggest that they exist. Field cognition modes are ways of learning, or biases toward learning certain things more readily than others. To some extent, of course, these are innate, but they are also to some extent learned. Probably the most striking example of a field cognition mode is our tendency to use language in a tremendous variety of learning situations. If a human learns a maze in the laboratory, he is likely to learn it as a verbal sequence of lefts and rights. This use of language makes the process of maze learning different for humans from what it is for animals. The learning of the maze is itself a matter of forming field expectancies, whether the learning is animal or human. The way in which it is learned, however, depends on field cognition modes. The original learning of language as a means for learning other things was therefore the learning of a field cognition mode. The differences in IQ scores and in personality among people raised in different cultures are partly attributable to differences in field cognition modes, since these produce differences in what people will learn from the same (objectively speaking) experience.

The fifth variety of learning in Tolman's system is *drive discrimination*. This is the ability to distinguish among different drives. For example, there is some evidence that animals have to learn the difference between hunger and thirst. This learning is of course closely related to the learning of cathexes, in which demands are related to goal objects. This appears to be a rather trivial category, and there is some question as to why Tolman bothered to treat it as separate from other forms of learning.

The sixth and final kind of learning is *motor patterns*. This is essentially Tolman's concession to, of all people, Guthrie. Guthrie had criticized Tolman's system as concerned only with the individual's cognition that certain acts would obtain certain goals, not with the acts themselves. Guthrie satirized this aspect of Tolman's system as leaving a rat in a maze "buried in thought." He claimed that if the rat ever got to the food, this was the rat's business, not the business of Tolman's theory. Tolman, open to suggestions from his critics as well as from his supporters, took account of this objection in listing the different kinds of learning. The muscular skills by which one actually gets to goals were never of much concern to Tolman's study of molar behavior, but he granted that they would have to be considered in a complete theory of learning. How does one learn to ride a bicycle without falling, to fire a rifle accurately, or even to walk? Tolman is not really concerned with answering these questions, and does not feel obliged to fit the topic closely into his system. He suggests that Guthrie's analysis in terms of stimulus-response connections learned by contiguity may be appropriate for this kind of learning.

This list of the six kinds of learning shows Tolman's borrowing from Freud, Guthrie, and the reinforcement theorists. We have already referred to his use of Lewin's diagrams. This breadth is also reflected in the variety of variables that he took into account in explaining behavior. In addition to all the aspects of the situation, he listed four main kinds of individual-difference variables. Only

one of these, we may note, involves learning. The four are heredity, age, training, and endocrine, drug, or vitamin conditions.
Using the initial letters of these four, Tolman labeled them the
HATE variables. (One wonders how Tolman, a devout Quaker,
came to arrive at this particular set of initials.) The HATE variables help to illustrate the breadth of Tolman's concern with different aspects of behavior. Discussions of such diverse factors
as age and vitamin conditions are rare in learning theory. They are
valuable as a reminder that learning, for all its great importance,
is far from being the only determinant of behavior.

Of Rats and Men

Tolman is probably unique among cognitive theorists in having given more attention to the behavior of animals than of humans. (This was also Köhler's emphasis at one stage of his career,
but he also did extensive work in human perception.) To some
extent the preference reflects the same factors that have influenced
behaviorists in general toward animal work: the greater simplicity
of animals and the greater opportunity to control their environ-
ments. It probably also reflects Tolman's special concern to show
that a cognitive system could still be objective, that it need not depend at all on anything the individual says. Tolman himself, in the
tongue-in-cheek manner so characteristic of his writing, presented
a third possible explanation. He suggested that psychologists typically begin with an interest in solving the great problems of human
life, then become frightened by the awesome implications of
such a task and flee to safer aspects of the study of behavior, such
as learning in the rat. Certainly Tolman is right in saying that many
psychologists are aware of a conflict between their desire to at-
tack the great questions of life directly and their desire to concentrate on other questions that are less exciting but that they have
more chance of being able to solve. Tolman's own career reflects
this conflict clearly.

On the one hand, Tolman was a man of strong social conscience.
(He was one of the faculty members who left the University of
California rather than sign the controversial loyalty oath in 1950.)
In 1942 he published a small book called *Drives toward War,* in

which he analyzed the psychological causes of war and presented some suggestions for removing them. His analysis of the biological drives, social techniques, and psychological dynamisms leading to behavior, warlike or otherwise, combined experimental, clinical, and historical sources. On the basis of this analysis he suggested several fairly radical changes in our political, economic, and educational systems, changes which he thought would reduce the impetus toward war. Among these was a plan for a world state, along with some psychological suggestions for making this admittedly visionary idea a bit more practical.

On the other hand, Tolman had as his principal ambition the development of a schematic rat world, a system from which he could predict completely the behavior of rats in a laboratory environment. This is reflected in his whimiscal dedication of *Purposive Behavior* to *Mus norvegicus albinus,* the white rat. He wanted to include enough different variables and to have flexible enough constructs to achieve this goal completely. In the presence of the tremendously complex human social situations that the layman usually wants the psychologist to predict for, this seems like a very modest ambition. He did not, however, achieve his goal.

Evaluation of Tolman

If we consider how Tolman combined the best of both connectionist and cognitive theory, what a broad range of variables he took into account, and how early he anticipated later developments in the logic of theory building (the use of intervening variables), we could easily conclude that Tolman is the greatest learning theorist we have considered. In its conception, his theory may very well be the best there is. The conception, however, was never really carried into execution. Tolman discussed the kinds of laws psychology needs, but he did not develop these laws. He did experiments intended to show that cognitive formulations are better than connectionist ones, but he did not do experiments to make these cognitive formulations precise enough to be really useful for prediction. He pointed the way toward an extension of cognitive theory to include the best aspects of connectionist theory, but he did not carry the program through. He is therefore open to the ame criticism as the other cognitive theorists, that he does not give us a basis for predicting from objective stimuli to objective behavior. He gave us a cognitive framework (or perhaps we should say a gestalt) for interpreting learning, but he did not provide us either with detailed laws of learning like Skinner's or with a general principle of learning like Guthrie's. Thus his system is more a road sign or a pious hope than it is an accomplished fact.

This shortcoming is not really a failure on Tolman's part, however, for his attitude toward his own theorizing was always tentative and whimsical. He regarded theory-construction not as a serious business of building great intellectual edifices for the future but as a half playful trying out of different approaches. As a result he was constantly revising his theory, making suggestions and then abandoning them before he had time to explore their implications. His writings are a mixture of earnestness and whimsy, of high-flown theorizing constantly being pulled up short by a chuckle. His desire to construct a schematic rat world was thus partly an aspiration but also partly a joke. He wanted not so much to build a truly adequate theory as to explore the whole activity of theory building, both playing with it himself and puncturing the excessive claims of others. As a result, he has been widely respected and widely loved, but not widely followed.

Tolman died in the same year as Guthrie, and his final theoretical statement appeared in the same book as Guthrie's (Tolman, 1959). He ended his chapter with a statement of what he had tried to do in his theorizing, a statement that stands as a sort of final summary of his career in psychology. He admitted some doubt as to how well his work would stand up to the canons of scientific procedure, but indicated that standing up to canons was not what mattered most to him. He had followed "his own gleam and his own bent," which is the most that any scientist can do. And, most important, he had had fun.

Tolman's system, incorporating as it does ideas from many sources, is the outstanding attempt to develop a cognitive interpretation of learning that would have the virtues of connectionist theories without their limitations. Though it has much to recommend it as the outline for a complete theory of learning, it has failed to achieve a wide and lasting following. Tolman himself wondered, in his final statement, if the system might be too out of date to deserve such a careful reconsideration. MacCorquodale and Meehl (1953) had presented a more formal version of some aspects of Tolman's theory, but this attempt did little to provoke new research or theoretical work. For the currently active attempts to combine the best features of cognitive and connectionist theory, we must look elsewhere. These current attempts have come from connectionists trying to expand and liberalize their theories, rather than from primarily cognitive theorists. They have developed for the most part in connection with the formal connectionist theories, and should be considered in that context. It is to these formal connectionist theories and their relations to cognitive theory that we turn in the next two chapters.

Chapter 5

A Major Formal
Connectionist Theory

THE MOST AMBITIOUS and most famous of the formal connectionist learning theories is that of Clark L. Hull (1884-1952). Long a professor at Yale, Hull probably had more effect on the psychology of learning than any other theorist in the past thirty years. He was a behaviorist in the Watsonian tradition, but far more sophisticated than Watson in the philosophy of science. His early training, before he became a psychologist, was in engineering, and something of the engineer's outlook is evident in his desire to construct an elaborate, formal, precise structure of psychological theory.

The Postulational Method of Theory Construction

Hull's concept of the ideal theory was a logical structure of postulates and theorems, similar to Euclid's geometry. The postulates would be statements about various aspects of behavior. They would not be laws taken directly from experiments, but more general statements about the basic processes involved. Like the postulates of geometry, they would not themselves be proved but would be taken as the starting points for proofs. From these postulates, a great variety of other statements, called theorems, could be logically derived. Each theorem could be proved by arguing logically from some combination of postulates. These theorems would be in the form of laws of behavior.

So far, such a theory is simply a logical creation. We have said nothing about whether its statements are true or false, only about

how they hang together logically. When a theorem is proved, all
this means is that if the postulates are true, the theorem must also
be true. In order for the theory to have any value as a descrip
tion of the real world, it is necessary to compare the theorems with
actual laws of behavior as determined by experiments. In othe
words, after the theorist has determined by logic that the theorem:
follow from the postulates, he must then determine by experimen
whether they are true. If they are, the whole theory is supported
if not, the theory is weakened and requires revision.

To anyone not acquainted with the philosophy of science, thi
approach may seem backward. The theorist starts with postulate
that may or may not be true. He then proves logically that i
the postulates are true, certain theorems must also be true
Next he determines by experiments whether each theorem is in
fact true. Finally, he uses the truth or falsity of the theorem:
to argue indirectly about the truth or falsity of the postulates. I
a theorem turns out to be false, he knows that at least one of the
postulates from which he proved the theorem must also be false
since it led logically to a false conclusion. In consequence, som
postulate (the theorist may not yet know which one) must be
changed so that the theorems which follow from it will be true. If
instead, all the theorems turn out to be true, this verification in
creases his confidence that all the postulates are true. However
he can never be absolutely sure that the postulates are true, since
false postulates can sometimes lead to true theorems. As mor
and more theorems turn out to be true, he becomes more and mor
confident that the postulates are true, but there is always the pos
sibility that eventually a theorem derived from the postulates wil
turn out to be false.

Although this theoretical approach may sound both compli
cated and strange, it is actually rather similar to what w
do in many familiar situations. Consider a teacher who is con
cerned about the poor performance of a certain student, one sh
knows has a high IQ. She suspects that his difficulty may reflec
two factors: (1) a fear of competition, and (2) a tendency to reac
to fear by "freezing up" and being unable to act effectively. Thes
guesses are the equivalent of postulates. Either or both of them
may be true or may be false. They cannot be tested directly

since fear is not directly observable. They can, however, be tested indirectly. To test them, the teacher must first figure out how a student who had this fear and this reaction to fear would behave in certain situations. This is the process of deducing theorems from postulates. Thus, if the teacher's "postulates" about the student are true, it should also be true that: (1) he will do better on test items if they are presented to him casually in conversation than if they are part of a test, (2) if given an opportunity to compete for a prize, he will refuse, and (3) if offered a chance to give a talk to the class on some topic that interests him, he will accept. The teacher may try each of these approaches and see what happens. These, then, are three experiments, each designed to test one of the teacher's "theorems." (We assume the design is sound.) If in each case the student does what the teacher predicted, her confidence in her interpretation (i.e., in her "postulates") will increase. She cannot, however, rule out the possibility that all of his behavior is really due to some other combination of factors, and that eventually he will do something that does not fit at all with her interpretation. She can become more and more confident that her interpretation is correct, but she can never be absolutely sure of it.

If it turned out that her first two predictions were confirmed, but the third was not, she would know that her "postulates" were not entirely correct. She might decide, since he refused to address the class even when no competition was involved, that his fear was not merely of competition but of any situation in which he was threatened with failure or disapproval. She could then look for new situations in which to test this revised "postulate." In this way her interpretation of his behavior would be a self-correcting process of making and testing assumptions.

The teacher's thinking in this example and Hull's thinking in constructing a scientific theory are of course markedly different in scope and in logical formality. These are differences of degree, however, rather than of kind. The teacher was concerned with very narrow interpretations, involving the behavior of a single student, while Hull was concerned with very broad ones, involving the whole range of human and animal behavior. In addition, Hull wrote down his postulates in detailed form and tested the theorems in controlled experiments, whereas the teacher merely developed hunches and tested them in a rough-and-ready fashion. Nevertheless, the two cases are basically similar enough to show the kind of reasoning that Hull followed in building his theory.

It should be clear from the above that Hull did not regard his theory as a final statement about the nature of learning. Rather it was intended as a tentative formulation, always subject to revision to bring it in line with new data or new ideas. This tentativeness was a necessary characteristic of the kind of system he wanted to build. A set of postulates from which many laws of behavior are supposed to follow by strictly logical deduction has more chances of being wrong than does an informal system that makes fewer or less exact predictions. Watson's and Guthrie's theories are informal enough to leave considerable doubt as to just what they would predict in a particular situation. Skinner's and Tolman's systems are mainly systems of terms and methods for gathering and describing data. Hull, however, intended to create a theory specific enough so that it would be easy to see when it was contrary to the evidence. A theory of this sort is practically certain to be wrong in some respects when it is first formulated, hence it must be open to change as these errors are discovered.

It was Hull's plan to write three books expounding his theory. The first was to present and explain the postulate system. This appeared in 1943 as _Principles of Behavior_. Though various revisions of the postulate system have been published since then, this book remains the cornerstone of Hull's theoretical writing. The second book was to contain detailed derivations of individual behavior in a variety of situations. This was published in 1952 as _A Behavior System_. It contains 133 theorems with their derivations from the postulates and the evidence bearing on their correctness as laws of behavior. The topics with which these theorems deal are as diverse as discrimination learning, locomotion in space, and the acquisition of values. An invalid during the last few years of his life, Hull was barely able to finish this second major book. In the preface, he expressed his regret that the third book in the series, which was to present derivations of behavior in social interactions, would never be written. Four months later he died. Although his trilogy thus remains incomplete, it gives us a good picture both of the grandness of Hull's conception and of the many respects in which the actual system fell short of Hull's aspirations. It is possible that if Hull had lived longer and had been in better health during his last years, many of the shortcomings of his theory would have been corrected. As it is, we must judge both his successes and his failures by his works as they stand.

HULL'S BASIC POSTULATES

Hull does not make Skinner's distinction between respondent and operant behavior. For him, as for Watson, Guthrie, Thorndike, and Miller, all behavior involves stimulus-response connections. A response is never simply emitted; it is always a response *to* a stimulus. However, Hull is more explicit than any of the above four regarding all the factors other than the stimulus that influence the response. His postulates are concerned largely with the systematic presentation of these various other factors and their interrelationships. As might be expected, this system of postulates and theorems is much more complicated and technical than any of the other systems we have discussed so far. These qualities make it more difficult to capture the flavor of Hull's writing in a brief account. We shall begin with a relatively nontechnical account of Hull's system, followed by some examples of his attempts at precise deduction and quantification.

The Four-Stage Analysis

Like most theorists, Hull wanted to develop a system for predicting the dependent variables of behavior from various independent variables. Recognizing the variety of independent and dependent variables with which he had to deal, he tried to simplify the task of prediction by introducing intervening variables. We saw in Chapter 1 how the use of such intervening variables makes it possible to summarize a great many details with a small number of concepts. Hull organized his intervening variables into a four-stage predictive scheme. The first stage consisted of the independent variables from which he was predicting, the fourth stage of the dependent variables to which he was predicting, and the second and third stages of intervening variables connecting them. Knowing the values (amounts or degrees) of the independent variables, he could compute the values of the intervening variables at stage

F

2. From these he could in turn compute the value of the intervening variable at stage 3, and from that finally predict the values of the dependent variables. The general outline of this elaborate scheme is given in Fig. 5, which may serve as a guide to the explanation below.

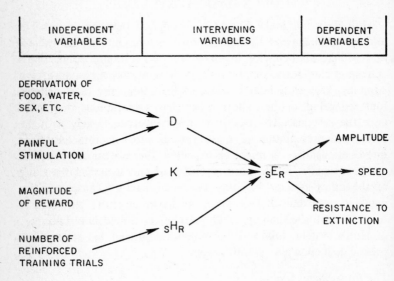

FIG. 5. *A schematic representation of Hull's basic system.* The independent variables influence the intervening variables, which in turn influence the dependent variables. Some elaborations of this simplified scheme are discussed later in the text.

The independent variables include all those that can be directly manipulated by an experimenter. These may be summarized briefly, since they are discussed in more detail in connection with the intervening variables. Some of the independent variables refer to the stimulation the learner is receiving at the moment, such as the brightness of a signal light or the intensity of electric shock. Others refer to immediately preceding events, such as the number of hours since his last meal or the amount of muscular effort he has recently put forth. Still others refer to previous experience in the same learning situation, such as the number of times he has previously made the response to be learned or the magnitude of the reward that he received the last time he made the response. The number of such independent variables that could be mentioned is endless; the important thing for our understanding of Hull is the way that he has organized them in his system.

Habit Strength and Drive

The second stage of the analysis introduces intervening variables. These are hypothetical states of the organism that cannot be observed but that are assumed to be directly controlled by the independent variables. The two most prominent ones, *habit strength* and *drive*, differ only in detail from the corresponding items in Miller's system of drive, cue, response, and reward. Habit strength refers to the strength of the learned connection between a cue or cues and a response, a connection built up through reinforced practice. Drive, for Hull as for Miller, is an activated state of the organism, and a reduction in drive serves as a reward.

Since Hull is a connectionist theorist, habit strength is a key concept in his system. It is the strength of the bond connecting a stimulus with a response. To indicate the nature of this connection, habit strength is abbreviated $_sH_R$ (pronounced S H R), the H standing for habit and the S and R subscripts standing for the stimulus and the response which the habit connects. This habit is a permanent connection, which can increase but cannot decrease in strength. All long-term learning involves the formation and strengthening of habits. Each time a response occurs in the presence of a stimulus and this event is quickly followed by reinforcement, the habit strength of this stimulus-response connection increases. In this assumption (Postulate 3 in the final version of his system), Hull resembles all other reinforcement theorists. Like Miller but unlike Skinner, he goes on to say that all reinforcement involves a reduction in the strength of a drive stimulus. The rate at which habit strength builds up with successive reinforced responses (given by an equation in Postulate 4) follows the well-known "law of diminishing returns," so that each successive reinforced response contributes less to $_sH_R$ than the previous one.

Eventually a point is reached at which additional reinforced responses contribute very little more to habit strength.

Drive is a temporary state of the organism, produced by deprivation of something the body needs or by painful stimulation. There are many different specific drive conditions, of which hunger, thirst, and pain are typical examples. Drives have two different functions. For one thing, each drive condition, such as hunger or thirst, produces a characteristic drive stimulus. This stimulus indicates the particular need from which the body is suffering. A rapid reduction in this drive stimulus is reinforcing. As a result, any response that occurs just before a reduction in a drive stimulus tends to be learned as a response to whatever stimuli are present. (We have already seen this relationship in connection with the postulate about the building up of habit strength.) The other function of drives is an activating or energizing one. All drive conditions combine to make up the total drive level of the organism. This total drive (abbreviated D) serves to raise the individual's activity level. This activating effect of D can be seen both in an increased level of general body activity and in the increased vigor with which all learned habits are performed. This analysis is essentially the same as Miller's (not surprisingly, since Miller based his on Hull's), but somewhat more detailed as well as more precisely stated.

Incentive Motivation

Unlike either Skinner or Miller, Hull was concerned with the size of the reward used as a reinforcer. We are all familiar with the law that people tend to work harder for a larger reward than for a smaller one. In other words, the level of performance is commonly higher when a larger reward is given after the response occurs. How should this law be handled by the theory? In his 1943 book, Hull treated the magnitude of the reward as one aspect of reinforcement. The larger the reward, the greater the reduction in drive, and hence the greater the increase in habit strength. However, this treatment proved not to be satisfactory. Experiments showed that changes in the magnitude of the reward produced very rapid changes in the level of performance, much faster than the slow growth of habit strength could explain. This difference was particularly difficult for Hull to explain when the change was from a larger to a smaller reward. If the reward was made smaller and performance became poorer, this result seemed to mean that the habit strength had become less. Yet habit strength involved a permanent bond, one that became stronger with reinforced practice but never became weaker. Here was a striking example of a discrepancy between theory and experiment. How would Hull deal with it?

Hull's answer, in the later versions of his theory, was to introduce a third intervening variable at the second stage of the analysis. Along with habit strength and drive he added *incentive motivation* (abbreviated K). The magnitude of the reward, in the new version, affects only K, not habit strength. The level of K depends on the size of the reward on the few immediately preceding trials. When the size of the reward is increased, at whatever stage of practice, K increases, and when the reward is decreased, K decreases. Incentive motivation thus refers, as the name implies, to the motivating effect of the incentive that is provided for making the response. The distinction between incentive motivation and reinforcement is subtle, since both depend on the reward, but the difference is none the less important. In order for a habit to increase in strength, the response must be followed by a reward that reduces a drive stimulus. The size of the reward makes no difference to the rate at which habit strength is built up; any reinforcement is as good as any other. The size of the reward does, however, affect the level of incentive motivation. Large rewards make for higher values of K, smaller rewards for lower values. When a rat learns to run down an alley for food, we see a gradual increase in its speed, an increase resulting from reinforced practice. However, over and above this slow increase in speed, we can increase or decrease the speed rapidly by changing the size of the food pellet we give at the end of each run. In the same way, it may be possible to increase a worker's output immediately by offering him more pay for each item produced (thus increasing K), whereas it would take much longer to increase his output by training him in better work methods (increasing habit strength).

Excitatory Potential

These three intervening variables, $_sH_R$, D, and K, work together to produce another intervening variable, which constitutes the third stage of the analysis. This is called *excitatory potential* and refers to the total tendency to make a given response to a given stimulus. It is abbreviated $_sE_R$, according to the same principle as $_sH_R$. It is equal to the product of the three other intervening variables; in other words, $_sE_R = {}_sH_R \times D \times K$. This equation means that the tendency to make a given response to a given stimulus depends on a habit built up through reinforced practice ($_sH_R$) and on two motivational factors, one depending on an internal state (D) and the other on an external incentive (K). For everyday purposes, one might refer to the $_sH_R$ for a given response as "knowing how to do it," to the K as "knowing what is to be gained by doing it," and to D as "wanting the thing that is to be gained." Hull, however, would not use this terminology, as he would consider it too vague and cognitive for an objective science of behavior. For Hull, $_sH_R$, D, and K are defined by the operations that produce them (reinforced practice for $_sH_R$, deprivation or painful stimulation for D, nutritive substance for K), not by any vague, everyday names that we might choose to give them.

The Dependent Variables

The fourth and final stage of Hull's analysis is made up of the dependent variables, the aspects of behavior that can actually be observed and measured. Hull relates three of these to excitatory potential ($_sE_R$): (1) the amplitude or size of the response, (2) the speed of the response, and (3) the total number of responses that will occur, after reinforcement is removed, before extinction is complete. As $_sE_R$ increases, amplitude, speed, and number of responses to complete extinction all increase.

What Fig. 5 shows, and what we have discussed, is only the barest outline of Hull's (1952) system. The final version of his theory had 17 postulates and 15 corollaries (theorems that follow immediately from a single postulate), which he hoped would cover the whole range of known behavioral phenomena. For example, he postulated the existence of unlearned stimulus-response connections, but did not elaborate the topic and rarely referred to such innate connections in his theorems. He discussed the effect of a delay between the response and the reinforcement in weakening the response tendency. He went into considerable detail about generalization and about the way generalized habit strengths combine (i.e., what happens when the same response is learned to two different but related stimuli). These details are beyond the scope of this book.

OTHER POSTULATES AND COROLLARIES

A number of elaborations, however, deserve fuller discussion here. One of these is the concept of *threshold*. This is a minimum value that excitatory potential ($_sE_R$) must reach before any observable response will occur. In other words, a very small value of $_sE_R$ for a given response will not result in a very weak or very slow response, but in no response at all. Only when the excitatory potential reaches a level greater than the threshold value will any response occur. Hull took the concept of threshold from the study of neurophysiology and of sensation and applied it to the field of learning. It implies that in many cases there will be an initial period of learning experience in which apparently no learning is taking place. Learning is occurring, but it is not yet apparent in behavior. This is because the combination of $_sH_R \times D \times K$ gives a value of $_sE_R$ smaller than the threshold value. An increase in either $_sH_R$ or D or K might be enough to raise $_sE_R$ above threshold. If so, the learned response would then occur on the next presentation of the stimulus.

A second concept is *oscillation*. This refers to the assumption Hull makes that any given amount of excitatory potential is not an exact value but the average of a random distribution of values. When $_sH_R$ and D and K have been multiplied together to give the value of $_sE_R$, we still cannot predict with certainty what the amplitude or speed of the response will be. The reason is that the oscillation of $_sE_R$ may have carried the excitatory potential momentarily above or below the value computed. The oscillation in the value of $_sE_R$ is rapid and random (following approximately a normal distribution). The fact that Hull found it necessary to introduce this concept shows that his system, for all its complexity, could not hope to achieve perfect prediction of behavior. An element of random, unpredictable variation had to be introduced to make the system at all realistic.

Oscillation implies that a given response may occur on one trial and not on the next, in spite of the fact that $_sE_R$ is greater (due to the one additional reinforcement) on the latter trial than on the former. The reason is that the oscillation of $_sE_R$ brought its momentary value lower (and below the threshold) on the latter trial than on the former, even though the average value of the possible range of oscillation was higher on the latter trial. Therefore it is possible in memorizing a series of items to get one right on an earlier trial and wrong on a later trial. Guthrie would explain the same phenomenon by pointing out that the exact stimulus situation varies from moment to moment, so that the response can reasonably be expected to vary also. Since these momentary stimulus changes are both too slight and too complex to measure practically, Hull prefers to talk about oscillation as a separate intervening variable rather than to assume that all oscillations in the response are caused by variations in the stimulus.

When two incompatible responses have been learned to the same stimulus, so that two $_sE_R$s are competing for expression, the principle of oscillation may be used to predict which will occur on any given trial. The oscillations of the two $_sE_R$s are not synchronized, so that when one $_sE_R$ is momentarily high the other may be high, medium, or low. If the ranges of oscillation of the two $_sE_R$s overlap, each response will occur on some trials. If the $_sE_R$ for one response is considerably stronger than that for the other, so that their ranges of oscillation overlap only slightly, the stronger will occur most of the time and the weaker only rarely. If the two are equally strong, so that their ranges of oscillation coincide, each will occur half of the time. All such situations involve the conflict between two response tendencies, and the degree of overlap of the two ranges of oscillation makes it possible to predict how often each of the two competing responses will occur.

Third, there is the concept of *reactive inhibition*. This is a tendency not to repeat a response that has just been made. The amount of reactive inhibition resulting from a response depends on the amount of effort required to make the response, so that reactive inhibition is roughly equivalent to fatigue. Since this tendency not to respond works against and tends to cancel the effects of excitatory potential ($_sE_R$), it is subtracted from $_sE_R$ to give the net excitatory potential used in predicting the amplitude and latency of responses. The abbreviation for reactive inhibition is I_R. The fact that there is no subscript S indicates that the inhibition is against any making of that response, regardless of the stimulus that produces it. The total amount of I_R against a given response increases each time the response occurs but decreases with the passage of time. It is for this reason that subjects usually perform better on a learning task involving a lot of effort if their practice is *distributed,* with short periods of practice separated by short periods of rest. These rest periods provide an opportunity for I_R to dissipate. Hull also uses reactive inhibition to explain why extinction occurs. Once reinforcement is removed, successive responses no longer build up $_sH_R$ but continue to build up I_R. As a result, inhibition gradually overcomes $_sE_R$ until no further responding occurs. However, after a period of time the I_R dissipates and the response again occurs, giving spontaneous recovery.

There is a derivative of reactive inhibition called *conditioned inhibition.* This is abbreviated $_sI_R$ to indicate that it is a kind of habit connecting stimulus and response. Conditioned inhibition may be thought of as a habit of nonresponding produced by reactive inhibition. We can think of I_R as a negative drive that can be reduced by not making the response. Whenever the individual who has been responding ceases to respond, this "response of stopping responding" is reinforced by the fact that I_R starts to dissipate. The habit of stopping responding that is learned in this way is $_sI_R$. This $_sI_R$ explains, among other things, why spontaneous recovery is not complete. The I_R built up during extinction dissipates with time, but the $_sI_R$ learned in the process remains. It is noteworthy that Hull does not treat I_R and $_sI_R$ consistently as a drive and a habit, respectively. In his equation he simply subtracts both I_R and $_sI_R$ from $_sE_R$.

A fourth elaboration of Hull's theory is found in two corollaries concerning *secondary reinforcement* and *secondary drive*. These are closely related to Skinner's concepts of conditioned positive reinforcers and conditioned negative reinforcers, respectively. When a neutral stimulus (one that does not act either as a drive or as a reinforcer) is paired with a sudden reduction in a drive stimulus, the neutral stimulus tends to acquire reinforcing properties. For example, if a rat is frequently fed in a white box, the box will become a secondary reinforcer. It can then be used, even without food, to reinforce some new response. If the rat, still hungry, is put in a situation where turning right will bring him to the empty white box and turning left will bring him to an empty black box, he will learn to turn right. The reinforcement for turning right is not drive reduction (primary reinforcement) but secondary reinforcement from the white box. Similarly, money becomes a secondary reinforcer for humans because, even though worthless as an object, it makes possible so many rewards.

Once a secondary reinforcer has been established through association with primary reinforcement, it is possible to use it to establish another neutral stimulus as a secondary reinforcer. In principle, this process can be continued indefinitely, with a primary reinforcer being used to condition a secondary reinforcer, that secondary reinforcer used to condition another, that one a third, and so on. In practice, however, this sequence is quite difficult to accomplish, since the reinforcing properties of secondary reinforcers tend to extinguish when primary reinforcement is no longer paired with them.

Secondary drive is already familiar from Miller and Dollard's discussion of the learning of fear. For once, Hull goes into less detail than they do. For Hull, secondary drive is simply the attachment of drive characteristics to a neutral stimulus through the pairing of the neutral stimulus with a drive stimulus. Once this learning process has occurred, the secondary drive stimulus has the same effects on learning as a primary drive stimulus. Its presentation contributes to the individual's total drive level (D) and its removal is reinforcing. The outstanding example of a secondary drive is fear. A neutral stimulus that is paired with pain soon acquires drive properties, and the drive it produces is called fear. According to Hull, however, a secondary drive can be learned through pairing a neutral stimulus with any primary drive.

Since Hull assumed that all learning involves reinforcement, either primary or secondary, he faced a problem in stating the corollary concerning secondary drive. If a secondary drive is learned through the pairing of a neutral stimulus with a primary drive, where is the reinforcement in that learning situation? Hull answered this question by specifying that the learning experience must include not only the neutral stimulus and a drive stimulus but also a sudden reduction in the drive stimulus. In other words, the learning of a secondary drive requires that three events happen in quick succession: presentation of a neutral stimulus, an increase in a primary drive stimulus, and then a decrease in the drive stimulus. This specification saved the principle that primary reinforcement always requires drive reduction, but raised other problems. It implies, for example, that a person will learn to fear a stimulus paired with a short stab of pain but not a stimulus paired with an equally intense long-lasting pain, since in the latter case there is no reduction in the pain for some time after the pairing. A number of studies have tested this and other such surprising predictions, generally with results unfavorable to Hull's assumption. The fact that Hull made such an implausible assumption rather than give up the principle that all learning involves reinforcement is an example of the difficulties that a concern with theoretical consistently can cause.

A final corollary that must be considered is concerned with the *fractional antedating goal reaction*. This imposing expression can best be understood by analyzing it in parts, starting at the end. A goal reaction is a response of consuming a reward, which by definition is at the goal of a sequence of responses. Thus, when a rat eats food in the goal box at the end of a maze, it is making a goal reaction. An antedating goal reaction is one that occurs before the individual gets to the goal and involves an anticipation of the goal. (In an earlier version of his theory Hull used the term "anticipatory goal response.") However, this antedating goal reaction obviously cannot be a complete goal reaction, since there is no food to be consumed until the goal is actually reached. The rat in the maze can anticipate the food by licking its chops and salivating, but cannot make the complete eating response until food is available. These parts of the goal reaction that can occur before the goal is reached are therefore called fractional antedating goal reactions.

The abbreviation for fractional antedating goal reaction is r_G.

This is usually read as "little r G," which is a sort of pun on the word "little." It indicates both that the written letter r is lowercase and that the goal reaction referred to is fractional and hence small.

How is the r_G acquired? Like any other responses, says Hull —by reinforced practice. When a rat eats food in the goal box of a maze, it is making goal responses that are reinforced by the drive reduction from the food. This goal reaction occurs in the presence of stimuli from the goal box, such as its color, smell, and floor texture, and thus is learned as a response to these stimuli. As a result there will be a tendency for the goal reaction to occur in response to these stimuli even in the absence of food. However, the stimuli in the rest of the maze are much like those of the goal box, so that there will also be a tendency for the goal reaction to occur to these stimuli while the rat is in the maze but not yet in the goal box. Since such an antedating goal reaction can only be fractional in the absence of food, it is the r_G.

Although Hull limited his formal consideration of r_G to such obvious examples as fractional eating responses, the concept can be applied to any goal response. In the case of humans, there might be fractional antedating reading responses, baseball-playing responses, or money-pocketing responses. These could be conditioned, respectively, to the stimuli of the library, the sand lot, and the pay envelope.

The important aspect of the r_G is that it produces stimuli which have a major role in guiding the individual's behavior. A stimulus produced by a r_G is called a s_G. The function of s_G in Hull's system is much like that of Guthrie's movement-produced stimuli. The chief difference is that the s_G in Hull's system has reinforcing properties, which would of course not be included in Guthrie's system. The reinforcing properties of s_G arise from the fact that these stimuli were closely paired with drive reduction during the original goal reaction (e.g., eating). This pairing resulted in their becoming secondary reinforcers. As a result, any stimulus that produces r_G, and hence also s_G, will have a secondary reinforcing effect.

DERIVATION OF THEOREMS

We have said that Hull's goal was to derive the laws of behavior logically from a simple system of postulates. After considering the number of concepts and assumptions that Hull packed into his 17 postulates, the reader may not think that there is anything simple about the system. However, its relative simplicity is more evident if we note that *A Behavior System* contains 133 theorems, some with several parts, all following from the 17 postulates. Moreover, these 133 represent the limitations of Hull's time and energy rather than the limitations of the theory—there could have been many more. There is no question that the system represents an accomplishment of major proportions.

Discrimination Learning

Many of the derivations of theorems are quite complex, requiring a careful working-through of mathematical relationships. For our purposes, however, a nonmathematical treatment of one of the simpler derivations will be enough to illustrate Hull's approach. Theorems 3 and 4 deal with a special case of discrimination learning. In general, discrimination learning requires that the individual learn to respond to one of two stimuli and not to the other. The discrimination might involve a pigeon learning to peck at a red key but not at a green one, or it might involve a teacher learning to be firm with her pupils but not with the school administrators. In the special case considered in Theorems 3 and 4, the tendency to respond to one stimulus is much stronger at the beginning of training than the tendency to respond to the other, but only responses to the latter stimulus are reinforced during training. Learning the discrimination means that the individual must learn to respond to the stimulus which at first has a weak excitatory potential and not to respond to the one which initially has a high excitatory potential. The theorems predict the shape of the learning curve in this situation.

The derivation of the theorems goes as follows: Each time the correct response occurs, its habit strength and hence its excitatory potential increase. Each time the incorrect response occurs, conditioned inhibition is built up (Hull ignores reactive inhibition here, assuming distributed practice) and the net excitatory potential ($_sE_R$ minus $_sI_R$) for that response is reduced. However, the two stimuli are somewhat similar (otherwise there would be no discrimination to learn), and generalization occurs between them.

When the individual is reinforced for responding to the correct stimulus, this reinforcement increases not only the habit strength for the response to that stimulus but also (to a much lesser extent) the habit strength for the response to the other stimulus. Similarly, when a response to the incorrect stimulus occurs and is not reinforced, some of the conditioned inhibition generalizes to the correct stimulus-response connection and the net excitatory potential for that connection is reduced.

It might seem at first glance that these two kinds of generalization would cancel each other out and make no difference. However, it is necessary to take into account the relative number of times that responses to the correct and the incorrect stimuli occur. Early in learning, since there is much more $_sE_R$ for responses to the incorrect stimulus, responses to that stimulus will be much more frequent. As a result, generalized inhibition from nonreinforced incorrect responses will weaken the incorrect tendency faster than reinforced correct responses can strengthen it. Consequently, while $_sE_R$ for responding to the incorrect stimulus is being rapidly weakened, $_sE_R$ for responding to the correct stimulus is also being weakened, though much more slowly. However, since the $_sE_R$ for the incorrect stimulus is being reduced more quickly, the tendency to respond to the correct stimulus is growing *relatively* stronger, so the probability (i.e., the relative frequency) of responding to the correct rather than the incorrect stimulus is increasing. The oftener the learner responds to the correct stimulus, the oftener he is reinforced for doing so and the more rapidly his $_sE_R$ for doing so increases. The less often he responds to the incorrect stimulus, the less $_sI_R$ generalizes from the incorrect stimulus to weaken the $_sE_R$ to the correct stimulus. For both of these reasons, $_sE_R$ for the correct stimulus increases at a faster rate as the learning goes on.

As the response to the correct stimulus gets stronger, three things happen. One is that habit strength for the correct stimulus begins to approach its upper limit, according to the principle of diminishing returns, and so the excitatory potential for response to that stimulus increases less and less rapidly. Second, more and more $_sE_R$ generalizes from the correct to the incorrect stimulus, since more responses are now to the correct than to the incorrect stimulus. Third, since there are fewer responses to the incorrect stimulus,

$_sI_R$ builds up less rapidly. The second and third of these events both serve to keep the excitatory potential for responses to the incorrect stimulus from getting any weaker. Since the correct tendency is increasing in strength more slowly and the incorrect tendency is no longer decreasing, the probability of responding to the correct stimulus now increases more slowly than before.

When we put all these considerations together, we can see that the probability of responding to the correct stimulus rather than the incorrect one increases slowly at first, then more rapidly, and then slowly again. This variation is shown graphically in the S-shaped *learning curve* in Fig. 6, which shows the strength of the response at each stage of learning. Learning curves with this shape are called *sigmoid,* from the Greek letter sigma. This sigmoid curve is different from the learning curve when the reinforced response is originally the stronger, and also different from the theoretical curve for the building up of habit strength for a single response, given in Postulate 4. Both of these other curves rise most rapidly at first and gradually slow down as learning progresses (Fig. 6). Thus the sigmoid learning curve is predicted for discrimination learning only in this special case where the correct connection is weaker in the beginning than the incorrect one, and it takes a fairly complicated line of reasoning to make the prediction. However, the prediction is consistent with experiments. In a number of different kinds of learning, it has been found that tasks on which learners do badly at first give sigmoid curves, whereas those on which the learners do fairly well at first give curves with rapid rises at the beginning. Thus Hull's prediction, specialized and technical though it is, is confirmed by experimental data.

In the derivation of Theorems 3 and 4, Hull did not merely present the verbal reasoning given here. He also worked through a numerical example, computing actual values of excitatory potential and conditioned inhibition and using these to determine the probability of a correct response for an average learner at each stage of practice. (Because of oscillation, he could not predict to any particular individual learner.) He was thus able to give, not merely the general shape of the learning curve, but exact probabilities for the particular values of $_sE_R$ that he used in his example.

Cognitive Predictions

In addition to numerical predictions like this one, Hull also derived less exact theorems dealing with more complex forms of learning. He was well aware of the challenge to connectionist theory that was posed by Tolman, Lewin, and other cognitive psy-

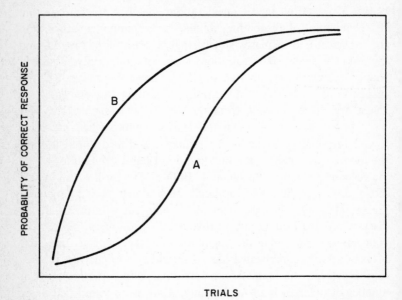

FIG. 6. *Two shapes of learning curves.* Curve A is sigmoid, the shape predicted by Hull for the case where the wrong choice has a greater $_sE_R$ at the beginning of training than the correct choice. Curve B is negatively accelerated, the shape Hull predicted for the case where the correct choice is initially the stronger. Curve B resembles the growth curve for the $_sE_R$ of a single response.

chologists, and he wanted to show that the kinds of behavior these cognitive psychologists studied could be shown to follow from his theory. He therefore derived a number of theorems dealing with movement in free space and with insightful problem solving. In deriving these, he made great use of the fractional antedating goal reaction (r_G). This proved to be a powerful tool for interpreting insightful behavior in connectionist terms. When Tolman says an individual has a cognition that food is to be found in a certain place, or when Lewin says that a certain region in the life space has positive valence because it contains food, Hull can say that the stimuli of this place elicit r_G for food. Fractional antedating goal reactions can thus be seen as cognitions about the location of goal objects. In making such interpretations, Hull was following the tradition of Watson and Guthrie, reducing ideas and expectations to small movements of parts of the body. However, he went into more detail than Watson or Guthrie, and in doing so reduced the gap between connectionist and cognitive interpretations of learning.

By using r_G, Hull could predict that an individual might approach a goal object by a route that he had never before used. Once the individual saw the goal object, or any stimuli commonly associated with it, r_G would be aroused by these stimuli. As a result, the individual would tend to approach the goal object, regardless of whether the route by which he had approached it was one he had ever before used for approaching that goal. His behavior would thus conform to Lewin's prediction, that he should tend to approach a region of positive valence from whatever direction and by whatever means the situation required. It would also fit Tolman's interpretation of behavior as a seeking of goals rather than a running off of habits. Approaching old goals by new techniques is thus one phenomenon, emphasized by cognitive psychologists, with which Hull is able to deal.

Closely related to new approaches is the matter of detours. Much of the emphasis in gestalt interpretations of learning is on finding new ways to reach goals when the old familiar ways are blocked. The new ways involve finding detours around barriers, either in physical space or in Lewin's topological life space. Gestaltists interpret such detour solutions as involving a restructuring of the life space, a realization that it is possible to get around the barrier. Hull concerns himself only with physical space and concentrates on the trial-and-error process by which the detour is discovered. The inexperienced individual, when confronted by a barrier, is likely to spend some time in futile attempts to penetrate the barrier and continue directly on his way to the goal. As reactive inhibition builds up and partially inhibits this direct response, says Hull, the oscillations of this and other responses occasionally make some other response momentarily stronger. Eventually this process results in the individual accidentally finding a route around the barrier. The response of taking this indirect route is reinforced and thus becomes more likely to occur if the individual again encounters that barrier on the way to that goal. Hull derived a number of theorems about the factors that would make such detour learning easier or more difficult. This kind of learning involves problem solving, but without insight.

For an individual experienced in free space, however, the situation is different. In the course of ordinary life, individuals often reach the same goal by different routes. Different habits leading to the same goal come to form a habit family. All members of the habit family have r_G for a certain goal in common. When one of these habits is blocked, another member of the habit family can readily take its place, so that progress toward the goal can continue. Those habits in the family that obtain the goal most quickly and easily are preferred, both because they involve less delay of reinforcement and because they result in less reactive and conditioned inhibition. The habits in the family are thus arranged in a hierarchy of preference, ranging from the most to the least preferred. A less preferred habit will ordinarily be used only if all the more preferred ones are blocked. This arrangement of habits is known as the *habit-family hierarchy*. We might think of the habit-family hierarchy as Hull's equivalent of a cognitive map. In making use of it to explain detour behavior, Hull is in effect saying that the ability to show cognitive behavior, to act as if one has a cognitive map, is the result of prior learning. He is reinterpreting cognitive behavior as a product of prior connectionist learning.

The addition of incentive motivation to Hull's system provided him with another convenient tool for reinterpreting insightful learning in his own terms. One of the points that Tolman emphasized was the distinction between learning how to get to a given place and learning whether to expect a reward there. In making K separate from $_sH_R$, Hull conceded this point. Learning how to get somewhere or do something is a matter of habit strength, which builds up slowly. Learning where reward is located is a matter of incentive motivation, which both increases and decreases rapidly. It is thus possible for $_sH_R$ to reach a high level while K remains very low. In such a situation, the introduction of a large reward would raise K and thus result in a sudden improvement in performance. This response would constitute latent learning, one of Tolman's favorite phenomena, but it would be consistent with the newer version of Hull's theory.

These applications of Hull's theory to complex, insightful phenomena of learning do not by any means close the gap between connectionist and cognitive interpretations. For one thing, some learning phenomena emphasized by cognitive psychologists are still largely beyond the reach of Hullian explanations. Buxton's latent learning experiment, described in our discussion of Tolman, is very difficult to explain in Hullian terms, even with the aid of habit-family hierarchies and fractional antedating goal responses. For another thing, these derivations of Hull's are less precise than many of his others, and there is room for some dispute as to how rigorously the theorems really follow from the postulates. Nevertheless, Hull has gone far enough in closing the gap between the two kinds of theory to point the way toward a possible eventual amalgamation, in which cognitive principles would be accepted as valid but would be interpreted as the result of prior learning of a connectionist sort. Such an amalgamation is still far off, but not as far off as it once appeared.

STRENGTHS AND WEAKNESSES OF THE SYSTEM

Hull saw the value of his theory not so much in the particular intervening variables it included as in its rigorous quantification. The postulates do not merely state that certain variables are related; they give equations by which one can be computed precisely from the other. For example, the postulate regarding habit formation contains the equation $_sH_R = 1 - 10^{-.0305\dot{N}}$, where $\dot{N}$ is the total number of reinforcements. Using this equation, one can state the exact level of habit strength for any given number of reinforcements. Similar equations are presented connecting the other second-stage intervening variables to the independent variables and also connecting excitatory potential to the dependent vari-

ables. The equation connecting the second-stage intervening variables to $_sE_R$, which involves simple multiplication, has already
been given.

Hull dedicated much of his effort in the last years of his life to
the problems of quantification. He wanted to develop a scale of
measurement for excitatory potential that would be applicable to
any response. How can $_sE_R$ for pressing a lever be made comparable to $_sE_R$ for running down an alley? Hull's answer (which
will be meaningful only to those readers who have studied
statistics) was to use the standard deviation of the oscillations of
$_sE_R$ as a measuring unit. This use of the standard deviation as a scaling unit is an idea Hull took over from the specialists in mental testing. He could then say that $_sE_R$ for a given response was two standard deviation units above zero, and this statement would have
the same meaning regardless of what response he was talking
about. This unit is also convenient for analyzing competition between responses, since knowing the $_sE_R$ for each response in standard deviation units also automatically tells how much their ranges
of oscillation overlap and hence how often each will occur. Hull
regarded the development of this scaling unit as one of the leading achievements of his life.

The evaluation of Hull's work by others has, however, been
rather different from his own evaluation. It is just on the matter of
quantitative rigor that he is most vulnerable to criticism. To some
extent the reason is that his attempts at quantification were premature. The exact values in his equations, such as the $-.0305$
in the equation for habit strength, were typically based on the results of a single experiment. He made the suggestion, but never
developed it, that the values in the equations might vary from individual to individual. Thus different people might have different
equations for the development of habit strength, with the specific
value being greater than $-.0305$ for fast learners and smaller
for slow learners. Moreover, when Hull came to derive theorems
from his postulates, he often used different values in his equations
from the ones given in the postulates. For all of these reasons,
it seems clear that these values were intended to be illustrative
rather than literally correct. What Hull attempted to present in his
books was the general outline of a rigorous theory together with

some suggestions as to how the outline could be developed into a full-scale, quantitatively exact system. He was still a long way from actually having such a system when he died.

Even if we leave aside the matter of precise, quantitative values, the system does not live up to the ideals that Hull set for it. In a system such as Hull's, it should be possible, given the values of the independent variables, to compute the values of the intervening variables and from these the dependent variables. Even if the precise numbers needed to make the computations are not available, it should be possible to explain how the computations would be made. In many of Hull's cases, however, it is not possible, because a given topic is either covered by two or more contradictory postulates or is not covered at all. An example of the latter kind of problem is the definition of incentive motivation (K) when the drive is a painful stimulus, such as electric shock. Presumably in that case K would be determined by the amount of pain reduction that a response produced, perhaps specified by the difference in volts between the shock received before the response and the smaller shock received afterward. However, since K is defined by the weight of food or other nutriment consumed, it is impossible to apply Hull's equations to the situation where painful stimulation is the drive.

How Do We Predict Extinction?

Let us consider in detail a case where several postulates can apply to the same situation and lead to conflicting predictions. Suppose we ask how many nonreinforced responses will occur before complete extinction, when $_sE_R$ is at a given level at the end of acquisition. There are three ways that we might do this. First, we might use Postulate 16, which relates excitatory potential to the number of nonreinforced trials necessary to produce complete extinction. To use this postulate, we would compute habit strength, drive, and incentive motivation at the end of acquisition and multiply them together to get the excitatory potential for the response at the beginning of extinction. We would then use the equation in Postulate 16 to compute how many trials to extinction would be produced by that level of $_sE_R$. This would be the most straightforward approach.

However, since Hull used reactive and conditioned inhibition as explanations of extinction, we might instead use these intervening variables to compute the number of trials to extinction. Knowing the general outline of Hull's system, we would expect to be able to compute the amounts of I_R and $_sI_R$ built up by any given number of nonreinforced trials requiring a given amount of effort. However, when we consulted Postulate 9, dealing with reactive inhibition, we would soon find that it is not stated in such a way as to make these computations possible. There is one equation relating amount of reactive inhibition to number of nonreinforced trials, and another equation relating amount of work to number of nonreinforced trials before complete extinction. Neither equation takes account of all the information we ought to have if we are to make full use of the intervening variables in the theory. We might use either of these incomplete equations to compute resistance to extinction, and in either case we would get a different answer from the one we obtained using Postulate 16.

Still a third alternative would be to use the postulate (unnumbered, since in his haste Hull left it out of the postulate set and had to add it later in a footnote) that discusses changes in incentive motivation (K). With no reward, K would rapidly approach zero. Since $_sE_R = {_sH_R} \times D \times K$, $_sE_R$ would also rapidly approach zero. Within a few trials, $_sE_R$ would be so small as to be below the threshold, and no response would occur. This approach thus gives an answer even more different from the other two than they were from each other. Whereas both other approaches at least lead to the prediction that extinction would be gradual, this approach predicts very rapid extinction. We are thus more than ever in doubt as to what Hull's theory really has to say about how long it will take to extinguish a given response.

The mere fact that these three ways of answering the question would give three quantitatively different answers is not in itself a crucial problem, since we have seen that the particular numerical values Hull used were mainly illustrative. However, the lack of internal consistency which this illustration points up is a serious weakness in the system, probably more so than any other flaw. When a theory makes incorrect predictions, it can be modified, as Hull intended that his theory should be. When a theory does not deal with a given issue at all, we can accept this limitation in its scope and hope that some day it may be expanded to include the neglected topic. However, when a theory is internally inconsistent, so that it makes conflicting predictions about a given issue, its worth as a rigorous theory is seriously compromised. To some extent we can blame Hull's failure in this regard on the revisions in his theory. For example, when the intervening variable K was added to the system in a later revision, this change called for a number of adjustments in other postulates, but some of these were never made. Racing against time in the last years of his life, Hull considered it more important to show what could be done with parts of his system than to make the system as a whole complete and consistent. Nevertheless, we must recognize that the theoretical system Hull actually created falls far short of the standards he himself set for theories.

Hull's Place in History

By the irony of history, it appears that Hull failed where he most wished to succeed and succeeded in the respect that interested him least. He wanted both to build a deductive theory, at once broad in scope and rigorous in detail, and to encourage others to carry on the same sort of theoretical work. We have seen how far he fell short of his first aspiration. Moreover, his failure has probably discouraged others from attempting such a task. Many observers have noted a trend in learning theory away from the sort of all-encompassing theories that we have been discussing so far, toward theories of smaller scope designed to explain only certain kinds of learning. This trend may well reflect in part Hull's failure. For many years, psychologists have dreamed of doing for their field what Newton did for physics—developing a theory that would be at once vast in its scope, precise in its applications, and elegant in its simplicity, a theory that would pull together the loose ends of psychology into one master system. In pushing so far toward this goal and yet falling so far short of it, Hull convinced many psychologists that the day of such a master theory in psychology is still far off.

Yet in his failure, Hull also achieved success beyond that of any other recent learning theorist. His terms, his interests, and his ways of formulating psychological questions have become more widespread than those of any other theorist. More experiments have probably been inspired by his work than by anyone else's in the past thirty years. His interpretations of drive, reinforcement, extinction, and generalization are standard starting points for discussion of these topics. He has been attacked, defended, and elaborated until to many people "learning theory" and "Hullian theory" have become synonyms. The system of terms that he introduced has been aptly referred to by Cotton as "the Esperanto of psychology." His outstanding position in the psychology of learning, as well as the complexity of his system, justifies devoting this chapter to him alone. In addition, there are various other interpretations of learning that owe much of their inspiration to Hull. We have already considered one of these, Miller's, and we will see more in the next chapter.

Chapter 6

Compromise and Emergent Theories

HULL OCCUPIES SUCH a focal position among the systematic interpretations of learning that there is a tendency to think of all other systems in relation to his. The three systems to be considered in this chapter differ markedly among themselves, and none of them fits neatly into the categories we have considered so far. Each, however, may be thought of as a logical development from Hull's work. The first, Spence's, is most clearly an extension of Hull's. The second, Mowrer's, illustrates a gradual transition away from Hullian thinking toward a more and more cognitive system. The third, Estes', is quite different from Hull's in detail but like it in being an ambitious attempt to build a formal model to describe learning.

SPENCE'S SYSTEM

Almost by definition, a system such as Hull's is never completely finished. As new laws are established by new experiments, the postulates are almost certain now and then to require some modification. Hull's system at his death was in a particularly unfinished state, however, since changes which Hull made in the last few years of his life had not yet been carried through to their logical conclusions. The system thus suffered, as we have already seen, from internal inconsistencies. The job of straightening out the inconsistencies and reaching the logical conclusions was undertaken by Kenneth W. Spence (b. 1907). Spence was a prize student of Hull's at Yale and afterwards became professor of psychology at the State University of Iowa. For two decades before

Hull's death, Spence was a major contributor to his thinking and a great producer of research relevant to the theory. When Hull died, Spence continued the tradition in which he had long been a major figure. His recent contributions to that tradition are presented in his book *Behavior Theory and Conditioning,* originally presented as a series of lectures at Yale.

In spite of their close connection, Hull and Spence differ somewhat in their approach to theory. Though Spence is a great exponent of theory construction, he is more cautious about it than Hull. His theory, though it can readily be seen as a revision of Hull's, is less elaborate, less formally stated, and more obviously tentative than Hull's. Even though Hull expected to keep modifying his theory in the light of new evidence, he stated it in the form of a formal, finished structure. Spence states his more casually, leaving more of the details to be settled by experiment. In particular, Spence regards Hull's inclusion of specific numerical equations in his postulates as highly premature. With our present information, or lack of it, he believes that such specific equations can only represent misleading pseudo precision. Spence is also more concerned than was Hull about the *boundary conditions* of a theory. These are the limits within which a theory is expected to operate. For example, a theory of education that worked well for explaining and predicting what happens in middle-class American schoolrooms might fail completely if applied to education among the Bushmen, because education among Bushmen is a topic outside the boundary conditions of the theory. Similarly, a theory intended to deal with learning by animals or human babies, where language does not enter in, might not be appropriate for learning by school children or adults. Therefore a theory should specify the conditions to which it is and is not intended to apply. Thus in various respects Spence does not set his aspirations for theory quite as high as Hull, but he is nonetheless a major advocate of theory construction as vital to the development of science.

The chief innovations in Spence's system as compared with Hull's are those concerned with K, the incentive motivation factor. At Hull's death this had still not been fully assimilated into his system. Spence undertook to clarify the status of K, and in doing so made radical changes in the whole basis of the theory.

The Relation of K to r_G

Hull intended to define all of his intervening variables in terms of the independent variables that produced them and the dependent variables that they influenced. Nevertheless, he was quite willing to speculate about what physiological changes inside the organism might be involved. Habit strength might be related to some change in the neural connections between the sense organ that receives a stimulus and the muscle or gland that makes a response. Drive might be related to a bodily need (as Hull himself suggested) or to a strong stimulus (as Hull suggested and Miller emphasized). But what of incentive motivation? Is there any bodily process to which this construct can be related? Yes, says Spence, there is the fractional antedating goal reaction. Hull never clarified the relationship between K and r_G, but it seemed to Spence that such a relationship existed and should be made explicit. The r_G is assumed to be a response, but one differing from other responses in that the sensations it produces are reinforcing. If an individual has eaten a large quantity of food several times in a certain place, the r_G of each will be strongly conditioned to the stimuli of that place. When he observes these stimuli, r_G will occur and produce s_G. If he had eaten only a little food on previous occasions in that place, the r_G and s_G would be only weakly evoked. If he had never eaten there at all, they would not be evoked at all. Note, however, that the same condition (amount of food) which determines the strength of r_G also determines the magnitude of K. Let us say, then, suggests Spence, that K is nothing more than the total strength of r_G and the associated s_G. By combining into one of these two concepts, K and r_G, we have simplified the theory and eliminated some of the uncertainty as to just where K fits.

This change, however, has implications beyond a mere simplification. For although K and r_G in Hull's system have so much in common, they differ in one important respect. For Hull, K is related to a stimulus-response connection: the greater the food reward for making a given response to a given stimulus, the greater the K for that stimulus-response connection. On the other hand, r_G is related only to a stimulus: the more the eating that has occurred in the presence of a stimulus, the greater the tendency to make r_G in response to that stimulus. By treating K as nothing more than r_G, Spence has related K purely to the stimulus. Thus the incentive component in the equation for excitatory potential is not the incentive for making a response but the incentive for getting to certain stimuli. If we should refer to these stimuli that evoke r_G as "signs that food is near," the similarity of this theory to Tolman's would be emphasized.

A closely related innovation in Spence's system is concerned with the building up of habit strength. Hull, in the final version of his theory, made habit strength a function of the total number of times that the response had occurred in the presence of the stimulus and been reinforced. The size of the reinforcement, however, made no difference. Is it reasonable, we may ask, to assume that there is no difference in this respect between a huge reward and a tiny one, but a very important difference between a tiny one and none at all? Spence solves this problem by assuming that H (he omits the subscripts) does not depend on reinforcement. Whenever a response is made in the presence of certain stimuli, he says, H increases. Thus H depends only on practice, not on reinforcement. Reward operates only through K (that is, r_G), not through H.

With these changes from Hull, what does Spence's system look like? As with Hull's, Spence's H, D and K combine to produce E. For reasons that need not concern us here, D and K are added together instead of multiplied, so that the equation becomes $E = H(D + K)$. As with Hull, various other components enter into the full equation, but this abbreviated form will be adequate for our purposes. In this formula, H depends only on the total number of times that the response has been made in the presence of the stimuli, while K depends on the extent to which goal responses have occurred previously in the presence of the stimuli. Thus drive reduction does not enter into the equation at all, and reinforcement enters only indirectly through r_G.

As a final complication, it must be pointed out that the above applies only to the learning of responses that lead to rewards which can be consumed. Where a response is rewarded by escape from a noxious stimulus (or is negatively reinforced, in Skinner's terms) different laws apply. As in Hull's theory, these have not been worked out as fully as those for positive reinforcement, but one point stands out: <u>drive reduction *is* more important in the learning of these responses</u>. The experiments by which Spence supports this interpretation are ingenious, but it is not necessary to report them here.

It is hoped that the astute reader will have noted the many resemblances between Spence's theory and those of a variety of other theorists we have discussed. Like Skinner's, Spence's system is in a practical sense a stimulus-response reinforcement theory. However, Spence attempts to analyze the nature of reinforcement, which Skinner does not, and in the process sounds much like Guthrie. Both H and K depend only on practice: in one case practice in making the instrumental response, in the other case practice in making r_G. In that sense, Spence's theory is as much a pure contiguity theory as Guthrie's. Moreover, r_G is an example of movement-produced stimuli contributing to the maintenance of goal direction, a thoroughly Guthrian notion. Finally, and most interestingly, Spence has a marked resemblance to the cognitive theorists, particularly Tolman. Though in his earlier years Spence was an outspoken critic of cognitive interpretations, his own work has led him over the years to a theory that lends itself well to cognitive purposes.

Spence's theory deals with phenomena of interest to cognitive psychologists in much the same way that Hull does, but his theory is even better adapted to doing so than Hull's, because Spence has eliminated reinforcement as a fundamental concept (at least so far as positive rewards are concerned). In place of reinforcement, he has the r_G mechanism, which can easily be regarded as the anticipation of reward. This reasoning completes the separation, begun by Hull, between learning about what paths lead where and learning about where reward is located. In accepting this distinction, which is central to Lewin and Tolman but absent in Skinner and only hinted at in Guthrie, Spence made a large stride toward <u>a more cognitive interpretation of learning</u>. Though often a critic of others' formulations, Spence has included elements of more other systems in his own system than has any other theorist of learning except perhaps Tolman.

MOWRER'S INTERPRETATIONS OF LEARNING

For all his similarities to cognitive theory, Spence sticks firmly to his connectionist terms and to his insistence that cognitive behavior is basically a matter of responses and stimuli. Another well-known theorist, who also began his work somewhat in the Hullian tradition, has moved toward cognitive interpretations in his terms as well as in his ideas. This is O. Hobart Mowrer (b. 1907) currently a professor at the University of Illinois. Originally noted, like Miller, for his applications of learning theory to personality, Mowrer has recently been best known for his concern with the place of sin in psychopathology. In addition, however Mowrer has attained note as a theorist of learning and of thinking. Beginning with attempts to resolve certain problems within connectionist theory, he has become more and more a cognitive theorist as he has proceeded.

Mowrer's Older Two-Factor Theory

The problem which Mowrer originally tried to solve was concerned with the nature of reinforcement. Is it, or is it not, a matter of drive reduction? Mowrer agreed with Hull and Miller that the answer is usually yes. The events that are reinforcing are the ones that relieve hunger or pain or fear or some other noxious state. However, Mowrer was particularly concerned with the learning of emotional reactions, and here the situation seemed to be different. When Miller's rats learned to be afraid of the white compartment, or when a burnt child learns to fear the fire, what is the reinforcement for this learning? A common-sense answer would be that the pain, of electric shock or of a burn, is the reinforcer. Hull and Miller did not accept this common-sense interpretation, but maintained instead that it was a reduction in pain immediately afterward that served as the reinforcer. We have already seen how Hull and Miller tried, by this interpretation, to maintain a consistent drive-reduction explanation of reinforcement. To Mowrer, however, the common-sense explanation seemed preferable. It seemed unreasonable to him that the emotional responses a rat or a person makes when hurt are reinforced by the termination of the pain. If that were true, brief punishment would reinforce any response, while lengthy punishment would have no effect on it. Everyday experience contradicts this idea, and Mowrer did a number of experiments that further contradicted it. These results led Mowrer to formulate a *two-factor* theory of reinforcement.

Mowrer's two-factor theory was much like Skinner's distinction between the conditioning of reflexes and the learning of operant behavior. Several people prior to Mowrer had, in fact, suggested that classical and instrumental conditioning are basically different kinds of learning. It remained for Mowrer, however, to sharpen the distinction and to emphasize its importance for the understanding of all learning situations.

Mowrer referred to his two forms of learning as *sign learning* and *solution learning*. The two are sharply demarcated in various ways. Sign learning involves classical conditioning of involuntary responses of the smooth muscles in the internal organs and of the glands. These are what we call emotional responses, and the most important example is fear. An unconditioned stimulus, such as pain, elicits these involuntary fear responses. Any stimulus that is paired with the unconditioned stimulus can then become a conditioned stimulus for the fear responses. Thus the unconditioned stimulus that elicits the emotional response is also the reinforcer in the conditioning of fear to new stimuli. This form of learning is called sign learning because the conditioned stimulus becomes a sign of danger and thus elicits an emotional response.

Solution learning is the instrumental conditioning of responses that reduce drives. It involves voluntary responses of the striped, skeletal muscles. The reinforcement for this form of learning is the reduction of the drive. It is called solution learning because the response solves the problem posed for the individual by the drive.

So far Mowrer seems to be adding very little to what Skinner had already said. He has substituted the terms *sign learning* for the conditioning of respondent behavior and *solution learning* for the learning of operant behavior. Also, he has restricted sign learning to the emotional responses of smooth muscles and glands. The importance of his contribution is in suggesting the relationship between these two kinds of learning. In a great many cases the drive that is reduced in solution learning is a secondary drive that was previously acquired by sign learning. The learning process thus has two stages. In the first, fear (or possibly some other emotional response) is conditioned to some stimulus by a process of sign learning. This fear response produces stimuli that act as a drive. In the second stage, an instrumental response that reduces the fear drive is learned by the process of solution learning. The instrumental response reduces the fear by getting the individual away from the conditioned stimulus that arouses the fear.

Consider as an example a child who is bitten by a dog. Since the unconditioned stimulus of pain from the bite produces emotional responses characteristic of fear, the sight of the dog becomes a conditioned stimulus for fear. This event is sign learning. On a later occasion, the sight of the dog (or perhaps, through generalization, the sight of any dog) produces fear, a secondary drive. If the child now runs away, thus escaping from the fear-producing sight of the dog, this running response will be reinforced by fear reduction. This event is solution learning. Both stages of the learning process must be considered in order to understand the child's reaction to the dog.

In principle, either stage of the process can occur without the other. In practice, however, it is doubtful if they ever occur independently. When a drive is conditioned (stage 1), there is usually some response available that will reduce it at least slightly (stage 2). Moreover, primary drives for which one learns an instrumental response (stage 2) are likely to have some component of secondary drive resulting from previous learning (stage 1). For example, when a person in the dentist's chair feels a slight pain, the resulting drive is due only partly to the pain itself, and partly to fear. The fear in turn results from the fact that in the past slight pain has sometimes been followed by greater pain and thus become a conditioned stimulus for fear appropriate to the greater pain. Thus pain combines with fear of pain to produce the total drive. A reassurance, such as the dentist's saying, "I'm almost done," can reduce the fear and hence reduce the total drive, even though it cannot reduce the actual pain.

This two-stage analysis of learning by Mowrer sounds very much like that presented by Miller and Dollard. However, by treating the acquisition of fear as sign learning, Mowrer avoids Miller and Dollard's problem of finding a drive-reducing reinforcer for the acquisition of the fear response. For Mowrer, it is the on-set of the drive, serving as an unconditioned stimulus, that re-inforces the fear response in stage 1, whereas Miller and Dollard would say that the end of the drive reinforces the fear response. Mowrer's view is more consistent both with common sense and with experimental evidence. On the other hand, such a sharp dis-tinction between two kinds of learning seems artificial to many people, especially in view of the fact that such principles as extinc-tion, generalization, and discrimination apply to both. However, as the reader can see by comparing the discussion of Miller and Dollard with the discussion of Mowrer, in most situations it makes little difference which assumption one makes. Although our under-standing of the learning process will be very incomplete until this issue (along with many others) is resolved, many practical appli-cations are possible without the answer to this theoretical question.

The Newer Sign-Learning Theory

Since the original presentation of his two-factor theory in 1947, Mowrer has modified it by pointing out that solution learning has many of the characteristics of sign learning. Suppose an in-dividual learns not to do something for which he has been punished. According to two-factor theory, in stage 1 of this learning the sen-sations produced by his own behavior became a conditioned stim-ulus for fear. In stage 2, the response of changing his behavior away from that which was punished was reinforced by reduction of the fear, and learned. In stage 1, sensations from his own behav-ior became danger signs. Why, asks the new Mowrer, should we not say the same thing about stage 2: that sensations from the in-dividual's own behavior became signs of hope? When the fearful person felt himself making the new, never punished response, he felt safer, because the sensations from this response had previously been followed by a reduction in fear. This new interpretation of Mowrer's replaces his older two-factor theory with a new, cog-nitive-sounding one-factor theory. All learning, in this new ver-sion, is sign learning.

Through learning, according to this theory, stimuli become

G

signs of fear or hope. Even the acquisition of bodily skills can be interpreted as sign learning. When we learn certain movements in riding a bicycle, for example, we are learning that certain sensations from our bodies mean we are doing it right, while other sensations indicate that we are about to tip over and must act quickly to keep our balance. The important thing about these stimuli is not that they elicit certain responses but that they have certain meanings, that they are signs of success or of impending failure in our attempt to ride. The history of Mowrer's thinking, in coming to this position, is covered in his recent book, *Learning Theory and Behavior*.

This new interpretation of learning makes Mowrer more cognitive than any of the other theorists we have discussed who developed their systems within the connectionist tradition. It is therefore interesting to compare him with Tolman, the cognitive theorist who is closest to the connectionists in his interests and objectives. The two are alike in one key respect: both regard all (or at least most) learning as sign learning. They are also alike in being more concerned than most cognitive theorists with the relationships between independent and dependent variables in the external world. In some respects, however, they differ. For one thing, Tolman goes farther than Mowrer in emphasizing cognitive patterning. Mowrer talks about sign learning but not, like Tolman, about sign-gestalt learning. Neither does Mowrer discuss the complex organizations of cognitions that Tolman calls cognitive maps. Mowrer's illustrations tend to be simple ones, with little concern about the organization of the life space. For another thing, Mowrer is still largely a reinforcement theorist. He is concerned with signs mainly as they point to increases or decreases in drive. The signs he talks about are signs of hope or fear or disappointment, not signs that path A leads to point B. For both of these reasons, Tolman's concept of the field expectancy has no real counterpart in Mowrer's system. Instead, Mowrer is concerned with a fire alarm as a sign of danger, or with the jingle of money in one's pocket as a sign of hope, or the like, not with the signs that provide our complex cognitive orientations. Thus Mowrer is less cognitive than Tolman, but the difference seems to be more one of emphasis than of real disagreement.

ESTES' STATISTICAL MODEL

We have seen so far in this and the previous chapter that attempts to make connectionist theory elaborate, formal, and precise have often gone along with tendencies to make it more like cognitive theory. This tendency is seen in the work of Hull and of others, such as Spence and Mowrer (though not Miller), working more or less in the Hullian tradition. In striking contrast to this trend is another line of approach to the formalization of connectionist theory, an approach far removed from cognitive theory. This is the recent development of *statistical learning theories*.

Attempts to describe learning mathematically are nothing new in psychology. Hull, as we have noted, put many of his postulates in the form of mathematical equations and used specific (even if only illustrative) quantities in a number of his derivations. Various other theorists have described learning as a function of several quantifiable variables. Beginning in 1950, however, there has been a burst of interest in this approach. It resembles Hull's approach in its attempt to derive behavior logically from assumptions, but tends to be narrower in its scope and hence less likely to become involved in contradictions. However, it looks as though the statistical learning theorists are growing more ambitious as their theories become better established, so that their general approach to theory construction may turn out not to be very different from Hull's.

A number of people have contributed to the development of statistical learning theory. The statistical approach was developed independently by William K. Estes (b. 1919) in 1950 and by Robert Bush and Frederick Mosteller working together in 1951. Since Bush was trained in physics and Mosteller in statistics, it is not surprising that their approach put greater emphasis on the purely mathematical aspects of the method than did Estes'. Since these two original publications, these three men and a number of others have worked, often together, on further development of this kind of theory. However, we may treat Estes as the most representative theorist in the group, both because he has probably contributed more than any one other person to the development of statistical learning theory and because the outstanding trends in this area have tended to become incorporated into his own publications. The same book that contains Guthrie's and Tolman's final statements also contains an up-to-date statement of Estes' views (Estes, 1959).

Estes studied with Skinner during the period that Skinner was at the University of Minnesota, and he took his doctor-of-philosophy degree there in 1943. His work with Skinner on the effects of punishment was an important contribution to Skinner's thinking on that topic. However, his interest in building mathematical models of learning is of course a departure from Skinner's antitheoretical bias. Moreover, the assumptions in Estes' theory seem to show the influence of Guthrie, with whom he did not study, more than of Skinner.

Estes' system may be spoken of as a _model_ of learning because, at least at the beginning, it makes no attempt to be a complete, all-encompassing theory. In this respect it is more modest than Guthrie's, Skinner's, or Hull's, and perhaps reflects some of the same concern about boundary conditions that Spence expresses. Rather the model is a very simplified statement of assumptions from which a few aspects of learning can be predicted with (hopefully) a good deal of accuracy. It is a model in the same sense as a three-dimensional model of an atom, with wooden balls for electrons, protons, and neutrons. No one claims that such a classroom model is a complete and accurate representation of an atom; we know very well that electrons are different from wooden balls and that their orbits have little in common with pieces of wire. Nevertheless there are certain respects in which the model and the real atom are alike. Given these similarities, the model enables us to predict certain things about the way the atom itself will behave. To the extent that a model enables us to predict some aspect of reality, it is useful. We need not argue whether or not it is true, since at best it is never more than a partial representation. This is much the same logic of theory construction that Hull used, but Estes carries it farther, beginning with a simple model and expanding it gradually at the same time that he is testing its usefulness.

One way to look at Estes' model is as an attempt to make certain ideas of Guthrie's more precise, to turn a part of Guthrie's broad, practically oriented theory into a model appropriate for laboratory study. The reader will remember that Guthrie regarded the learning of a skill as the conditioning of a great many particular stimulus-response connections. Estes simplified this suggestion by grouping all possible responses into two categories: those that produce a given outcome and those that do not. Thus, in Guthrie's terms, he is concerned with acts rather than movements. Estes would record, for example, only whether a basketball player successfully shoots a basket or not, without regard to the innumerable muscle contractions that go to make up either outcome. Similarly, a circus dog either jumps through the hoop or does not, regardless of whether the jump is graceful or clumsy and regardless of whether not jumping through involves jumping and missing, sitting quietly, or running away. In this way Guthrie's concern with what the learner does is changed into a concern with what he accomplishes, with the successful and unsuccessful outcomes of his behavior. (Note, however, that success is defined by the observer, not necessarily by any purpose of the learner's.) We may call these two classes of responses (or, strictly speaking, of response outcomes) A1 and A2.

Stimulus Elements

Having simplified the matter of responses, Estes is prepared to face the complexity of stimuli. He regards any stimulus situation as made up of many small stimulus elements. In principle, such an assumption is clearly realistic. At any given moment we are being bombarded by a great number and variety of stimuli. As we read a book, we may be stimulated by the words on the page, the pressure of the book on our hands, the furniture around us, and the sound of a passing car, to give only a very incomplete list. Altogether these make up the stimulus complex that influences our behavior. However, if we try to analyze this complex into specific components, we immediately find ourselves in difficulty. Is the pressure of the book on our hands one element, or is it ten elements for our ten fingers? If the temperature and the texture of the book's cover enter into the sensation, are these additional elements? It is a good example of Estes' model building that he does not concern himself with this question. If it is reasonable to suppose that there are such stimulus elements, Estes does not care just what the elements are, or how many there are, or how you decide where one element ends and another begins. He wants to know whether learning acts as if it is under the influence of such elements, not whether such elements "really" exist in the sense of being separately identifiable.

Another problem about this analysis of stimulus complexes into elements is that it implies that these elements operate separately, that there are no effects of patterns. Since we don't know what the elements are, it is hard to judge just how unrealistic this assumption is, but it certainly seems likely that there must be patterning effects of some sort. Estes has recently begun to concern himself with this issue, but most of his work has been done on the assumption that there are no patterning effects, that each element operates independently of each other one. Again the question is not whether this assumption is true but whether it is useful. To answer this question we must wait until we see the predictions Estes has been able to make from a model that included this assumption.

So far Estes has divided all the possible responses in a given situation into two classes, and he has divided all the possible aspects of the stimulus situation into an unspecified large number of elements. He now further assumes that each element is conditioned to one or the other of the two response classes. In other words, each stimulus element tends to evoke either A1 or A2. An element cannot be conditioned at the same time to *both* A1 and A2, nor can it ever be conditioned to *neither*. (If it seems unreasonable that all elements must be conditioned to one or the other of these response classes, keep in mind that all possible responses are included in one or the other class.) Accordingly, at any given moment, all elements can be classified as either conditioned to A1 or conditioned to A2.

The use of the word "conditioned" in this connection does not mean that there has necessarily been prior learning. It might be clearer just to say that every element is "attached" to one or the other response class, so that that stimulus element tends to produce that response. However, these connections are subject to change, with stimulus elements which were formerly attached to A1 becoming attached to A2, or vice versa. In fact, for Estes such changes are what is meant by learning. These changes are a proc-ess of conditioning, and hence Estes speaks of an element as being conditioned to a response when it tends to elicit that response.

Stimulus Sampling and Conditioning

To understand how the conditioning process operates in Estes' model, we must first look at the process of *stimulus sampling*. Estes assumes that only a small part of the stimulus elements in a given situation actually influence the response on any given trial. Estes refers to all of the stimulus elements in a given situation, taken collectively, as S. At any particular moment, only a small fraction of the elements in S are actually effective in determining the response. Which elements will they be? Estes assumes that the individual samples elements randomly from S. We need not assume that this sampling process is conscious and deliberate, as though the individual were window shopping before an array of stimuli. The sampling may be explained by momentary changes either in the environment or in the individual's attention. Again, however, it is important to note that Estes does not try to explain just how this sampling occurs. He assumes that it does occur, and whether it is a good or a bad assumption depends on whether it leads to valid predictions.

Each element has a certain probability of being sampled on a given trial. It is mathematically simpler to assume that all elements have the same probability of being sampled. Since the whole concept of stimulus elements is hypothetical anyway, there should be no objection to assuming that these probabilities are equal. Moreover, Estes has demonstrated that, at least for certain purposes, it makes very little difference whether one makes this assumption or not. He therefore assigns the Greek letter θ (theta) to represent the probability that any given element will be sampled on any given trial. Put another way, θ represents the proportion of all the elements in S that are sampled on any one trial.

On successive trials, different groups or elements are sampled. This sampling is random, so that each element has the same chance of being sampled on each trial. Whether or not an element was sampled last time has no effect on its chance of being sampled this time. Moreover, whether or not any one element is sampled this time has no effect on any other element's chances this time. Hence the degree of overlap among successive samples is determined solely by chance. This assumption, like so many others in Estes' model may seem unrealistic if we think of stimulus elements as particular identifiable sources of sensations. The important question, however, is whether Estes can use these oversimplified assumptions to make correct predictions about learning.

Let us consider two successive trials. For the sake of simplicity, let us say that in this situation θ is equal to 0.1. This means that one-tenth of the elements in S are sampled on each trial. Since the sampling is random, we can find the proportion of elements sampled on both trials by multiplying .1 times .1 to obtain .01. This means that one-hundredth of the elements in S are sampled on both trials. How many are not sampled on either trial? Since .9 of the elements (1 minus .1) are not sampled on the first trial, and .9 are not sampled on the second, we find the number not sampled on either trial by taking .9 times .9, which gives .81. By subtracting .81 from 1.0, we find that .19 of the elements *were* sampled on at least one of the two trials.

The stimulus elements sampled on a given trial are the ones that determine which response, A1 or A2, will occur on that trial. But if some elements are conditioned to A1 and others to A2, which of these two responses will occur? The answer to this question shows why this is called a statistical learning theory. Estes does not tell us definitely which response will occur; instead he gives the answer in the form of a probability statement. The probability of A1 is equal to the proportion of the elements in the sample that are conditioned to A1. Thus if 60 per cent of the elements that are sampled on a given trial are conditioned to A1 and the other 40 per cent to A2, there are 60 chances in 100 that A1 will occur on that trial and 40 chances that A2 will occur. Since the sample is drawn randomly from S, we could just as well say that the probability of A1 occurring on that trial is equal to the proportion of all the elements in S that are conditioned to A1.

Since the prediction of which response will occur is in the form of a probability, we can never say for sure which response will occur (unless the probability of A1 is either 1.00 or 0). This uncertainty of prediction may seem like a considerable weakness.

However, Estes is really only saying, a bit more bluntly, what the other theorists we have considered also said. Guthrie said that the combination of stimuli would "tend" to be followed by the movement. Skinner discussed the factors controlling rate of emission of an operant, but he never tried to predict exactly what that rate would be. Hull explicitly included the concept of oscillation, so that his exact statements about $_sE_R$ could not be converted into exact statements about momentary $_sE_R$ or about the characteristics of the response. Thus predictions from Estes' theory are no less definite than those from other theories. He has, however, put the whole theory in terms of probabilities: the probability that an element will be sampled and the probability that a given response will occur. (These probabilities can in principle be converted into speeds if desired.) Since probabilities are analyzed by statistical techniques, Estes' theory is called a statistical theory.

In his original formulation, Estes assumed that learning is by the principle of contiguity. This relation means, in his formulation, that whenever a response occurs, all the stimulus elements sampled on that trial become conditioned to that response. Nothing is said about reinforcement as such. This formulation is particularly well suited to classical conditioning. Consider a case of eyelid conditioning. We will call an eyeblink response A1 and the absence of a blink A2, so that on every trial either A1 or A2 but not both will occur. On the training trials the blink always occurs, since the unconditioned stimulus is always presented. As a result, all the stimulus elements sampled on a given trial become conditioned on that trial to A1 (the response of blinking). On successive trials, additional elements are sampled and become conditioned to A1, so that the proportion of the elements in S that are conditioned to A1 keeps increasing. Whenever an element is conditioned to A1 it is of course also unconditioned to (or "disconnected from") A2. Thus conditioning is a process of transferring elements from being conditioned to A2 to being conditioned to A1. As this process goes on, the probability of a *conditioned* eyeblink response (A1) increases. The unconditioned blink occurs on every trial, since it is elicited by the unconditioned stimulus, but the conditioned blink may or may not occur, its probability depending on the proportion of elements conditioned to A1.

Learning Curves

With all this background of assumptions, we are finally ready to look at the predictions which follow from them. First, what of the shape of the learning curve? Suppose we take the situation in which, at the beginning of learning, all the elements in S are conditioned to A2, so that the probability of a conditioned A1 response is zero. This case would be very near that in eyelid conditioning, where the chance that the subject will make a response to the conditioned stimulus before conditioning has begun is quite small. This condition means that all the elements sampled on the first trial will already be conditioned to A2 (not responding). However, on this trial they will become conditioned to A1. On the next trial another sample will be drawn. Most of the elements in this new sample will be conditioned to A2, but a few will be conditioned to A1 because they will have been sampled, and hence conditioned to A1, on the previous trial. Only those that are attached to A2 can become conditioned to A1, since the rest are already attached to A1. Thus the number of elements transferred from A2 to A1 will be less on the second trial than on the first. (Remember that the total number of elements sampled is the same on all trials.) On the third trial still more of the elements that are sampled will already have been conditioned to A1, so that even fewer will be transferred from A2 to A1. Learning will continue in this fashion, with fewer elements being transferred from A2 to A1 on each successive trial, until all the elements in S are conditioned to A1. At that point, no further learning can take place.

If we know the value of θ, we can make predictions about the proportion of elements in S that will be conditioned to A1 at the end of each trial. Let us return to the previous discussion of sampling in which we assumed for convenience that θ was equal to 0.1. At the end of the first trial, 0.1 of the elements in S had been sampled once. As a result, 0.1 of the elements were then attached to A1. After two trials, .19 of the elements had been sampled at least once, so that .19 of the elements were then conditioned to A1. The increase in the proportion of elements conditioned to A1 was .1 as a result of the first trial and .09 as a result of the second. In both cases, this increase was 0.1 of the elements still conditioned to A2. In other words, on each trial, 10 per cent of the elements still conditioned to A2 were transferred to A1. And this value, 0.1, is the value of θ. If we continued these calculations further, we would see that this ratio fits a general principle: on each trial the proportion of elements transferred from A2 to A1 is equal to θ times the proportion still conditioned to A2. However, since fewer and fewer are still conditioned to A2 on each trial, the actual number of elements transferred from A2 to A1 is less than on the previous trial.

This formulation has resemblances to both Guthrie's and Hull's discussions of the learning curve. Guthrie assumed that conditioning of a movement to a stimulus occurs on one trial, but that conditioning of an act requires many trials because it is made up of many stimulus-movement connections. Similarly, Estes assumes that an element is conditioned to A1 on one trial, but that the change in probability of A1 is gradual because there are so many elements to be conditioned. Thus in this respect Estes has taken an idea very much like Guthrie's and changed it from a loose verbal interpretation to a precise mathematical one. The mathematical description of the learning curve then turns out to be identical with Hull's. The advantage of Estes' formulation over Hull's is that instead of simply postulating that the curve should have this shape, he has derived this curve as a prediction from the more basic assumptions of sampling. He has, in a sense, out-Hulled Hull.

Other Aspects of Learning

Once a reader has grasped the fundamental assumptions ("postulates," in Hull's terms) of Estes' system, he can exercise his ingenuity by trying to predict how Estes will deal with various phenomena of learning. The phenomenon of generalization poses no problem. If a response has been learned to one set of stimuli, generalization is indicated by the occurrence of that same response when another, similar set of stimuli is presented. For Estes, a "similar set of stimuli" is one which has a number of the same stimulus elements as the original training set. If all of the elements in the first set are conditioned to A1, and if half of the elements in the second set are also in the first set, then at least half of the elements in the second set are conditioned to A1. The probability of an A1 response to the second stimulus set cannot then be less than .50.

Discrimination is more of a problem. If two stimulus sets have a number of elements in common, how can an individual learn consistently to give response A1 to one of these sets and response A2 to the other? For such perfect discrimination to be established, it would be necessary for all the elements in one set to be conditioned to A1 and all those in the other set to be conditioned to A2. This condition, however, is impossible, since some of the same elements are in both sets. Estes is not yet satisfied that he has found a completely adequate way of dealing with this problem. Probably the best suggestion has come from another statistical learning theorist, Frank Restle. Restle suggests that stimulus elements which are common to both sets become neutralized, that is, not conditioned to either A1 or A2. They are then irrelevant to the discrimination. The acceptance of this idea calls for some modification of the Estes model, but it seems difficult to avoid some such interpretation. Perhaps we need to consider not only responses A1 and A2 but also other kinds of responses that involve paying attention to certain stimulus elements and not others. This rather cognitive suggestion, which has implications beyond Estes' theory, will be considered in the next chapter.

Drive should be another easy concept to predict. For Estes, as for Guthrie and for Miller, drive is a stimulus (or, more precisely, a set of stimulus elements). Estes' principal contribution in this regard has been to argue that Hull's intervening variable D is unnecessary. Hull used D to refer to the general energizing function of all drives. In an ingenious mathematical example, Estes showed how what appears to be an over-all energizing effect of drive could be explained as simply a matter of the number of drive stimulus elements conditioned to different responses. This revision does not necessarily mean that drives do not have an energizing function, since Estes' example is hypothetical, but it throws the burden of the argument on Hull's supporters.

Extinction, for Estes, is simply another example of conditioning. If in acquisition, stimulus elements are conditioned to response class A1, then in extinction they are reconditioned to A2. The laws of learning are exactly the same in acquisition and extinction. This interpretation is essentially the same as Guthrie's. Guthrie says that extinction is learning to do something else, which raises the question, "what else?" Estes can dodge this question because, by definition, any response that is not A1 is A2. In extinction, A1 is being replaced by something else, but Estes considers only the rate at which that replacement goes on, not the details of what the "something else" looks like.

Forgetting and Spontaneous Recovery

Spontaneous recovery is a bit more of a challenge, but again Estes deals with it in a typically Guthrian fashion. To do so, he has to consider a larger category of stimulus elements than before. He assumes that S, the set of stimulus elements from which a learner samples in a given learning situation, is only a subset of all the elements that are sometimes available for sampling in that situation. In other words, if we consider all the stimulus elements that might be available for sampling in a certain learning situation, only some of them will actually be available for sampling on any given occasion. This seems like a quite plausible assumption. There are many characteristics of learners, teachers, and other aspects of a learning situation that vary from one occasion to another. If the learner is more tired or more distracted on one occasion than on another, for example, this difference could be expected to make some difference in what stimulus elements were available for sampling on the two occasions. We can therefore divide all the stimulus elements that might be available during this learning into two categories: S (those available on a given occasion) and S' (those not available on this particular occasion but potentially available on others). On any two occasions, some elements will be in S on both occasions, some in S the first time and in S' the second, some in S' the first time and in S the second, and some in S' on both. This assumption makes it possible to predict not only spontaneous recovery but also various other phenomena of learning.

Consider a learning situation in which originally all stimulus elements are conditioned to A1 (see Fig. 7, part A). In the course of conditioning, all of the elements in S are sampled at some time and become conditioned to A1. The next day the individual is tested for retention. By then, 20 per cent of the elements in S have moved into S' (i.e., are no longer available for sampling) and have been replaced by elements that were formerly in S' (Fig. 7, part B). Since all of these new elements in S are still conditioned to A2, 20 per cent of the elements now in S are conditioned to A2. As a result, the probability of an A1 response drops from 1.00 at the

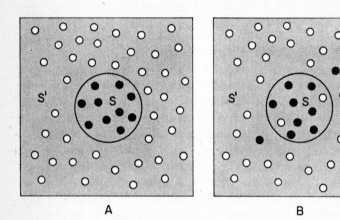

A   B

FIG. 7. *An analysis of forgetting in Estes' system*. Black circles represent elements conditioned to A1, open circles those conditioned to A2. In part A, all the elements in S have been conditioned to A1. In part B, a day later, 20% of these elements have drifted out of S into S' and have been replaced by elements still conditioned to A2. As a result, only 80% of the elements in S are now conditioned to A1. The probability of an A1 response has therefore dropped from 1.00 to .80 during the elapsed time.

end of the first day's training to .80 at the beginning of the session on the second day. This drop would ordinarily be described as 20 per cent forgetting. The more different the conditions are on the second day from what they were on the first, the more elements will leave S between the two days and the greater will be the amount of forgetting.

In this context, spontaneous recovery may be regarded simply as the forgetting of extinction. Suppose that over a series of days acquisition training is carried out until all the elements in both S and S' (i.e., all the potentially available elements) are conditioned to A1. Unless there was additional training involving some of the same elements, forgetting would thereafter be impossible. (This is an untestable assumption, since we could never be sure that no such training had taken place.) Suppose now that extinction is carried out for one day until all elements in S are conditioned to A2. If 20 per cent of the elements in S move into S' before the next test and are replaced, S will then be made up of 80 per cent elements conditioned to A2 and 20 per cent conditioned to A1. This means that 20 per cent of the response strength before extinction will have recovered spontaneously. A whole series of extinctions on successive days would be necessary in order to prevent any further spontaneous recovery.

This formulation of spontaneous recovery and forgetting emphasizes the importance of practice over a series of occasions. It takes not merely a lot of practice, but practice spaced in time to give maximum possible learning. Herein rests one of the difficulties with cramming and with very concentrated courses. Estes' theory, like Guthrie's, thus supports the view held by many educators that learning is most effective when there is time enough to spread the process out. Reviewing learned material every now and then, or taking a series of courses in which each begins with a review of the previous one, are procedures that fit well with this interpretation of learning.

Reinforcement

What does Estes have to say about reinforcement? Relative to many other theorists, not much. So far as he is concerned, a reinforcer is simply any event that determines to which response class the stimulus elements that are sampled will get conditioned. What other properties a reinforcer may have, such as perhaps being a reduction in drive, do not interest him. He is thus somewhat like Skinner in the way he interprets reinforcement, but he puts less emphasis on the importance of the topic than does Skinner.

Estes' treatment of reinforcement also resembles Skinner's in another respect: both are greatly interested in intermittent reinforcement. What happens, asks Estes, if some of the trials in a series end with reinforcement (thus conditioning all the elements

sampled on that trial to A1) and other trials end with nonrein-
forcement (conditioning all the sampled elements to A2)? A favorite learning situation for answering this question is the _light-
guessing experiment_. Here A1 and A2 are defined, not as making or not making a given response, but as making one of two possible guesses. The learner is seated in front of a board with two
light bulbs on it. On each trial he is instructed to guess which of the
two lights will be turned on. After he guesses, one and only one of
the lights does go on, and which one it is does not depend on
his guess. The two possible guesses are response classes A1 and
A2, and the two possible events (the left and the right light going
on) are called E1 and E2. Thus E1 reinforces A1 and E2 reinforces A2. However, Estes assumes that E1 conditions all the
sampled elements to A1 and E2 conditions all the sampled elements to A2, regardless of which response occurs on that trial.
In other words, the left light going on reinforces the response of
guessing "left," even if the guess the learner made was "right."
This assumption that a response which does not occur on a given
trial can nevertheless be reinforced on that trial is a departure
from the usual assumptions of connectionist reinforcement theories.

If E1 always occurs in this situation, the individual gradually
learns to make A1 consistently. (He also rapidly becomes bored
with the experiment.) What if E1 occurs 75 per cent of the time
and E2 25 per cent of the time, in a random order so that the
learner can never be sure which light will go on on any given
trial? What usually happens is that he comes to make A1 75 per
cent of the time and A2 25 per cent of the time. Any reader who is
ambitious enough to work through the mathematics can confirm
for himself that this is just what Estes' model predicts. (To do so,
the reader will have to ask himself what per cent of the sampled elements will be conditioned to A1 by E1 or to A2 by E2, when the
probability of A1 is greater than, equal to, and less than .75. It
will take a little thinking, but this opportunity to obtain an insight
experience while studying a connectionist theory really should not
be missed.)

This finding, so satisfying to Estes, has disconcerted many other
theorists because of its apparent irrationality. If the learner wants

to guess correctly as often as possible, his best strategy is to guess the more frequent event all the time. A cognitive theorist might expect him to follow such a rational strategy, since it would be the best possible insightful solution to the problem. Instead, however, subjects follow the irrational behavior that is predicted by Estes' conditioning model. Why? Many experiments have been done and many words written in attempts to explain this "irrational" behavior to other people's satisfaction. (A few special situations have been found in which learners do adopt the "rational" solution, but they are not typical.) Estes, however, can take pride in having correctly predicted an unexpected finding.

Another aspect of the theory has been confirmed in a different version of the light-guessing experiment. The object of this experiment was to provide a more direct test of the assumption that the probability of A1 is equal to the per cent of sampled elements that are conditioned to A1. Ordinarily we have no way of identifying the stimulus elements in any situation. This problem was partially solved by giving learners in the light-guessing situation a hint before each guess. The hint was a pattern of small lights on a board, separate from the lights being guessed. Some of these small lights were turned on only on trials when the left light was going to be correct, others only on trials when the right light would be correct. Thus some lights signaled E1 and others E2. These hints made it possible for the learner eventually to predict correctly every time which light would go on. This component made the experiment an example of discrimination learning. When the discrimination learning was complete, a test was given in which some of the signal lights from both sets were given before the learner made his guess. If each of the small signal lights acted as a stimulus element, what should Estes predict? The probability of guessing A1 should be equal to the per cent of signal lights on the test trial that had previously signaled E1. If, for example, two-thirds of the signal lights on the test trial were ones that had previously signaled E1, and one-third were lights that had previously signaled E2, A1 should occur two-thirds of the time. This and several other such predictions were confirmed in this experiment, thus giving additional support to Estes' assumption about stimulus elements and response probabilities.

Evaluation of Statistical Theory

How does Estes compare with other theorists we have considered? In his approach to theory construction he is most like Spence, building an abstract formal theory, but proceeding slowly, with a close eye both on new data and on the boundary conditions. However, he has put more emphasis on stimulus factors and less on the nature of reinforcement than has Spence, and the kinds of experiments he has done are rather different from Spence's. His interpretations of most topics are much like Guthrie's, but more detailed mathematically than Guthrie's. His interpretation of reinforcement, however, is most like Skinner's.

What have Estes and the other statistical learning theorists accomplished? They have shown how much of learning can be predicted from a formal, mathematical model. They have done new and interesting experiments. On the other hand, part of their success comes from having dealt with a fairly narrow range of learning situations, and many problems have arisen as they have expanded into new areas. Some of their mathematical precision, like Hull's, is more apparent than real, since we can never know the value of θ for any situation in advance, but must always get data in order to compute θ. Estes and his colleagues have almost nothing to say about the topics of most interest to cognitive psychologists. Statistical learning theory is an active, changing field today, and its eventual contribution remains to be seen. At least, it has provided psychology with a new set of conceptual tools and has perhaps pointed the way, by slow degrees, toward the kind of precise, general learning theory that Hull envisioned.

We have now completed our survey of the major theories of learning. We have seen how different psychologists have interpreted learning formally and informally, in cognitive and in connectionist terms, with reference to contiguity and to reinforcement. We have seen how different interests and different biases have led theorists in these various directions, and how the need to explain the results of experiments has to some extent drawn them together again. It remains for us to consider a number of developments in the study of learning that have not yet been incorporated into major theories, and to see what implications the theories we have studied have for our total understanding of the learning process.

Chapter 7

Recent Developments

IN OUR SURVEY of the major theoretical interpretations of learning, we have seen three issues on which theorists are divided: (1) whether connectionist or cognitive interpretations are more adequate for describing learning, (2) how the phenomenon of reinforcement should be explained, and (3) how broad and how formal theories of learning should be. On each of these topics there are valuable contributions which have been made, not by the major theorists so far discussed, but by researchers who have concentrated their investigations and their interpretations on narrower topics. The decision not to include these men among the major theorists is not intended to belittle their work, which is typically of the finest. Rather, the distinction is like that between the major and the minor prophets—in terms of the magnitude and scope of their systematic interpretations rather than their importance. The interpretations discussed in this chapter are more specialized than the more nearly all-encompassing systems that we have been looking at so far. This distinction is somewhat arbitrary, for systematic interpretations vary all the way from the broadest to the narrowest. Moreover, systems have a way of expanding. Estes would not have been listed in the major group ten years ago, and some of the men discussed in this chapter might be in the major group five or ten years hence. However, the intention is to group in this chapter those whose work consists more of contributions to particular theoretical topics than of theoretical system-building. This grouping will at least serve as a review of these issues and a preview of things to come.

MEDIATING RESPONSES

Perhaps the most striking trend that we observed in recent learning theory was the effort of connectionist theorists to broaden their systems so they could predict the flexible, insightful behaviors of most interest to cognitive theorists. This has been a concern, not only of the major theorists we have so far considered, but also of many other psychologists. A number of topics in human and animal learning and thinking seem to call for interpretations that are neither strictly connectionist nor strictly cognitive, but a combination of the two. We have seen that Hull and Spence made great use in their interpretations of fractional antedating goal responses and the stimuli they produced. Guthrie made somewhat similar use of movement-produced stimuli, while Miller's interpretation of secondary drive involved strong stimuli produced by the individual's own emotional responses. In all of these cases, the primary effect of a response was to produce the stimuli for further responses. A response which is of interest because of the stimuli it produces is called a *mediating response*.

Mediating responses are of two general sorts. One kind is called the *observing response* (Wyckoff, 1952). This is a response that changes the external stimulation one receives. A person staring at something and a dog pricking up its ears are making observing responses. Tolman's identification performance vectors represent tendencies to make such observing responses. In addition to those observing responses that are evident to someone else, there may be others inside the body, representing subtle changes in attention. What these observing responses have in common is that they change the stimuli we receive by helping to determine which external stimuli will be effective and which will not.

The other kind of mediating response is that which itself produces a stimulus. There is no one generally accepted term for these responses, but we may refer to them as *stimulus-producing responses*. The examples of mediating responses mentioned above from Spence, Miller, and Guthrie are all of this sort. The stimulus is actually produced by the response, rather than merely selectively received because of the response. Pinching oneself to keep awake would be an obvious example of this kind of mediating response.

Usually, however, these are not observable, external responses but unobservable intervening variables.

Observing Responses

We may now consider both kinds of mediating responses in more detail. Observing responses may be used as an explanation of a number of different learning phenomena. Since we usually do not know exactly what movements are involved in these observing responses, we could fairly speak of them simply as "responses of paying attention." One phenomenon that can be explained by such learning is the *acquired distinctiveness of cues.* This term refers to learning about which cues in a situation to pay attention to. When a first-grader discovers that it is the shape of letters rather than their size that is important in reading, the cue of form has acquired distinctiveness for him. This acquisition will then affect his subsequent learning of letters and words. Though it would be hard to demonstrate, it is reasonable to suppose that some observing response by the student is involved in his paying attention to form rather than to size. This response of paying attention to form is separate from any particular response that he makes to any particular form. This separateness has been demonstrated by D. H. Lawrence (no relation to the novelist) in several ingenious experiments with rats (Lawrence, 1949, 1950).

Another closely related example of a situation where observing responses are important is in the formation of *learning sets*. These were first demonstrated by Harry F. Harlow of the University of Wisconsin (Harlow, 1959). To demonstrate a learning set, an individual is given a long series of discrimination problems. On each problem he is presented with two objects. One of these has a reward behind it on every trial, the other not. The same one is correct on each trial. He has to find out by trial and error which one is correct, but once he has learned this he can be right on every subsequent trial of that problem. If he understands the principle, he can be correct on all but the first trial of every problem. All he has to do is to choose either stimulus at random on the first trial. If it is correct, he chooses the same one on all the other trials. If it is wrong, he chooses the other one on all the remaining trials. For the completely inexperienced learner, this solution is not as easy as it sounds. For one thing, the right-left position of the stimuli is changed from trial to trial, and some learners tend to respond to the position rather than to the object. There is also a widespread tendency to choose the other one on trial 2 regardless of whether the first one was rewarded on trial 1. Because of these and other *error factors,* inexperienced learners are likely to do poorly on the task. How are they to know that the same object, regardless of position, will be rewarded on every trial? Gradually, however, they do learn this principle, so that learning gets better and better from problem to problem. After having experience with enough different problems, all of which can be solved in the same way, learners commonly reach the point where their scores on new problems are nearly perfect. They are then said to have formed a learning set.

A learning set is an example of learning how to learn. It involves being set to approach the problem in a certain way. Since the approach to the problem requires paying attention to certain cues rather than others (form rather than position, for example), acquired distinctiveness of cues is one aspect of the formation of learning sets. In Tolman's terms, we are dealing with a field cognition mode. Most of the studies of learning sets have been with animals, particularly monkeys. There are large species differences and age differences in the rate at which learning sets are formed. Older animals and higher species of animals form learning sets faster, even though they may not be any faster at learning discriminations on the first few problems. The rate at which learning sets are formed has come to be regarded as one of the best measures of differences in intelligence among animals.

Much of education may be regarded as the formation of learning sets. We hope that in teaching students we are not merely providing them with specific stimulus-response connections, but are giving them the necessary background for continued learning after they leave school. We want them to be able, not merely to parrot answers to questions, but to solve problems by making use of what they have learned. Studies of learning sets show individuals going through such a process of learning how to solve problems. The solution to one problem cannot be transferred directly to another problem, but the general method of solution can. Just as the "intelligent" behavior of the experienced monkey solving a discrimination problem reflects his prior experience in forming a learning set, so the "intelligent" behavior of an adult human reflects his prior experience in learning how to solve problems.

Stimulus-Producing Responses

We have already considered a number of examples of stimulus-producing responses. It will be worthwhile to consider the variety of different functions that they are assumed to serve. First, there are drive functions. Conditioned emotional responses produce drive stimuli and thus serve as the basis of secondary drive. This function is emphasized by Miller and Dollard and by Mowrer. Second, there are incentive functions. Fractional antedating goal reactions produce stimuli that have secondary reinforcing properties. These serve as the basis of the incentive component in Spence's system. The anticipatory muscle readinesses that Guthrie discusses are similar. Third, there are cue functions. Whenever we carry on a skilled performance by using the stimuli from one response as the cues for the next response, we are taking advantage of stimulus-producing responses. A particularly striking example, however, is seen in Watson's view that thinking is merely subvocal speech. Thinking is then made up of fractional speech movements, responses of talking to oneself. These responses produce verbal stimuli that have cue functions. The cue function is thus very widespread.

This latter kind of cue function is particularly valuable for a rapprochement between connectionist and cognitive theory. If our own responses can provide us with cues and if these can include complex verbal cues, we are well on the way to a connectionist cognitive theory. If a man can make the responses of drawing a map on paper, can he not also make responses of imagining such a map? If he can give himself instructions in words, why not in images, in muscular sets, or in any other sort of stimulus-producing response? And if such nonverbal mediating responses are available to humans, why not to animals also? This line of reasoning can be carried to the point where nearly all of the cognitive theorists' statements about life space, sign-gestalt expectations, and cognitive maps are accepted, but all are reinterpreted as stimuli produced by the individual's own responses.

Clearly, not all of the suggestions about mediating responses that have been made by various connectionist psychologists have gone this far. Though Hull, Spence, Mowrer, and Guthrie all make use of mediating responses, none of them regards the response-produced stimuli involved as having the extensive gestalt properties that cognitive theorists favor. Nevertheless, there is room for such an extreme development of connectionist theory in the cognitive direction, and a number of such moves have been made.

The Study of Meaning

One of the best known recent developments of this sort is the work of Charles E. Osgood and his associates at the University of Illinois on the concept of meaning (Osgood, Suci, and Tannenbaum, 1957). They suggest that for every concept a person has, there is a mediating response which provides the meaning of that concept for him. (Actually they use the more general term "mediating process," but for consistency we will continue to speak of mediating responses.) These mediating responses are fractional parts of our response to the thing the word names. Thus our response to "sour" might be a slight tendency to pucker the lips and salivate, and our response to "mountain" might be a slight tendency to look upward. The mediating responses may also be part of the emotional response to the thing. We might, for example, smile slightly in response to the word "happy" or become tense in response to the word "danger."

Just what the particular mediating responses are is something we usually do not know. As Osgood and his associates are careful to point out, they may not be responses in the usual sense, like those in our examples, but may be unobservable processes in the central nervous system. We can, however, provide indirect evidence to support the view that the mediating response to a word is similar to the response to the thing that the word names. This view states that both the word and the thing are stimuli for a mediating response that produces further stimuli. These in turn may be the stimuli for some overt, measurable response. The mediating response and the stimuli it produces are similar whether they occur in response to the word or to the thing. This, indeed, is what we mean when we say that the word means the thing. Consequently the final overt response to the word should be similar to that to the thing. That it is so has been demonstrated by experiments in which a bell or a blue light is used as the conditioned stimulus for some response and then the word "bell" or "blue" is presented. A large amount of generalization is found from the stimulus to its name.

It seemed unlikely to Osgood and his associates that there are as many unique mediating responses for meanings as there are words in the English language. Considering the many ways in which the meanings of different words are related, they thought that a fairly small number of different mediating responses should be enough to explain most of the meaning of words. Since they could not study the mediating responses directly, they undertook instead to study the different mediating responses in terms of the *dimensions of meaning*. In order to make this study, they developed a technique known as the *semantic differential*.

In the semantic-differential method, one begins with several pairs of opposite words. These might be such pairs as good-bad, strong-weak, hard-soft, and wet-dry. Each of these pairs defines a dimension of meaning running from one extreme to the other, as from good to bad or from strong to weak. Any other word can then be rated according to where it falls on each of these dimensions. A given person might rate the word "friend" close to the good end of the first dimension, half way between strong and weak on the second, and a little closer to soft than to hard on the third. This pattern of points on the various dimensions then defines the meaning of the word "friend" for this person according to this method. With two words, or with two people rating the same word, the difference between the patterns indicates how different the meanings are.

Some of the dimensions that are used with this method turn out to be closely related, so that any word that is rated high on one is likely to be rated high on the other, and vice versa. Good-bad, for example, would be highly related to right-wrong. We can then conclude that these are really the same dimension. Over a long series of studies it is possible to determine how many really separate dimensions are needed to describe the meanings of words. It would then be plausible to suppose that each of these separate dimensions represented a separate mediating response. These several different mediating responses, occurring at the same time with different intensities in response to a stimulus word, would determine the meaning of that word. Osgood and his associates have found that a considerable part of the meaning of words can be accounted for with just one such dimension: the *evaluative dimension*. This includes such pairs as good-bad, beautiful-ugly, and kind-cruel, all of which are concerned with the desirability or value of the word being rated. Much of the remaining meaning is carried by two other major dimensions: strong-weak and active-passive. We can tell a great deal about the meaning of a word by seeing where it is rated on these three main dimensions.

There are, of course, limits to the meaning that can be given merely by placing a word the proper distance between good and bad, between strong and weak, and between active and passive. Some concrete descriptive words, such as "yellow" or "wet," have a good deal of meaning not accounted for by the three primary dimensions. Nevertheless, it is striking how much meaning is carried by the three, and especially by the evaluative dimension. How much real difference in meaning is there, for example, between "good," "fair," "honest," and "upstanding?" To the average person, probably very little, since they all are concerned primarily with evaluation. Whatever its limitations, the semantic differential has served both as a useful tool in practical studies and as a valuable approach to the quantitative understanding of meaning. Though a number of stimulus-response theorists have suggested that thinking involves the operation of mediating responses, Osgood's work on meaning is by far the most ambitious attempt to study the implications of this view in quantitative terms.

INTERPRETATIONS OF REINFORCEMENT AND DRIVE

The second topic on which there have been important recent developments is the nature of reinforcement. No theorist questions that the effects of our actions influence whether we will repeat these actions (which is the basic principle of reinforcement), but they disagree widely on how this influence should be interpreted. What, if anything, do all reinforcers have in common that makes them reinforcing? Guthrie, though he avoids the term "reinforcement," says in effect that all reinforcement involves is stimulus change. Skinner and Estes for the most part ignore the question, saying simply that whatever reinforces behavior is a reinforcer. Hull, Miller, Mowrer (as regards solution learning, even when it is reinterpreted as another kind of sign learning), Lewin, and Tolman all interpret reinforcement as some kind of drive reduction, even though some of them do not speak either of drive or of reinforcement. Miller's drive, cue, response, and reward can be roughly translated into Lewin's terminology as tension, path, approach vector, and valence, or into Tolman's as demand, sign, expectancy, and goal object. While these may not be the neatest of translations, they illustrate that the drive-reinforcement interpretation, in whatever words, is a widely recognized one.

New Descriptions of Drives

There are currently two trends in the interpretation of reinforcement, one that works within this drive-reduction framework and one that does not. Within the drive reduction framework, there has been a concentration on what drives are innate. In the past, connectionist psychologists who used the concept of drive have tended to treat as primary, or innate, only a few drives, such as hunger, thirst, sex, and pain, that are clearly physiological. Cognitive psychologists, on the other hand, have been more likely to discuss such motivational tendencies as pride, ambition, or affection, which have no apparent physiological basis. These latter motivational tendencies are regarded by connectionist theorists as the result of complex learning processes, including the acquisition of secondary drives. There is not necessarily any disagreement between these two points of view, since the cognitive theorists (other than Tolman) have not been much interested in the origins of the tensions or demands they discuss. The chief importance of these interpretations is that the connectionist theorists have had to make assumptions about the learning of motives that are extremely difficult to support by experiments. Although Miller was quite successful in demonstrating a secondary drive of fear, other secondary drives that are predicted by theory have proved impossible to demonstrate in the laboratory. As a result, there has been increasing interest in the possibility that there may be far more primary drives than have previously been recognized.

One such drive (or perhaps category of drives) that has received much attention is that which is satisfied by new experience. It is known variously as a drive of curiosity or exploration or manipulation or novelty seeking. Its existence is supported by many lines of evidence. Harlow (whom we have met before) showed that monkeys would work to unfasten a clasp device over and over again, even though neither food, escape, nor any other obvious reward was given for doing so. Butler showed that monkeys in a closed cage would press a lever to open a window so they could look out. If the monkeys were kept in the closed cage for several hours before the lever was made available, they would press more (indicating higher drive following deprivation). If the lever no longer opened the window, their rate of pressing would drop (indicating extinction). Such novelty-seeking behavior is found not only in monkeys, which have long been famous for their curiosity, but also in rats. Montgomery and Welker have made extensive studies of rats exploring new places and of the responses they will learn in order to be able to do such exploring. These and other related studies are discussed by Berlyne (1960) and by Welker (1961).

A second kind of drive that has recently been investigated is satisfied by activity. This is different from the kind of drive we have just discussed in that the activity does not have to produce any novel stimulation. Such activity occurs when a rat runs in an activity wheel, which is a sort of voluntary treadmill. A rat in such a wheel can, if he chooses, get exercise by running, but no exploration is involved, since the wheel just goes around without getting anywhere. Kagan and Berkun (1954) have shown that a chance to run in such a wheel will reinforce lever pressing, and Hill (1956) has shown that rats do more running in the wheel when they have been deprived of activity for a long time.

A third kind of drive has been referred to as contact hunger, first described, like to many interesting phenomena, by Harry Harlow. This is a drive which is satisfied by certain kinds of physical contact. Harlow originally studied it (Harlow, 1958) by rearing baby monkeys with *surrogate mothers*, wire models that gave milk like real mothers. He found that monkeys not only preferred a "mother" covered with terry cloth to one made of bare wire, but ran to the terry cloth "mofher" when frightened. They did so even if the wire "mother" supplied milk and the cloth "mother" did not. These and other findings in his experiments suggested to Harlow that contact hunger, exemplified by the baby monkeys' "hunger" for the cloth surrogate mother, is an important factor in personality development. It may well play an important part in personality development, not only in the attachment of infants to their mothers, but also in other aspects of love, in sex behavior, and in the development of social relationships.

The importance of these various drives is not simply in the recognition that people and animals seek new experience, activity, and pleasant sensations of touch. All of these tendencies have long been known. Rather, their importance is in the recognition, supported by experimental evidence, that they may well be just as much a part of our innate, biological nature as hunger, sex, or pain. This recognition does not by any means answer all our questions about why men seek companionship, achievement, or glory. Nevertheless, it helps to bridge the gap between the drives usually employed in laboratory studies of learning and the motives we all recognize in ourselves and others.

Responses as Reinforcers

The other trend in the interpretation of reinforcement, outside the drive-reduction framework, relates reinforcement to the learner's own responses at a goal. Reinforcement depends not on what happens to the individual (drive reduction, for example) but on what he does. This wording sounds like something Guthrie might say, though actually the idea is more like Spence's. The extent to which r_G is conditioned depends, in Spence's system, on the amount of goal activity that takes place. A lot of eating in a given place results in strong conditioning of r_G to that place. How reinforcing it is to get to a given place depends, therefore, on how much eating (or other goal activity) takes place there.

Two men besides Spence have advanced this idea. One, Fred Sheffield, drew his inspiration from Guthrie. Sheffield maintained that the act of consuming a goal object, rather than any form of drive reduction, is the essential factor in reinforcement. Will a response that leads to some goal object be reinforced by the goal object and learned? This depends, says Sheffield, on whether the goal object is consumed. Food, for example, is reinforcing to the extent that we eat it. Our own activity of eating provides the reinforcement for whatever response brings us to the food.

Sheffield did several experiments to support this position. For the most part, however, they were inconclusive. He showed, for example, that drinking a saccharine solution is reinforcing for rats, even though saccharine is completely non-nutritive (Sheffield and Roby, 1950). This finding certainly argues against the view that all reinforcers involve reduction in a body need, since saccharine does nothing to reduce the body's need for food. The study does not show, however, that the drinking activity was what produced the reinforcement. One could just as well say that the sweet taste of saccharine is the crucial reinforcing factor.

A more general formulation of this point of view has recently been presented by David Premack. He simply states that of any two responses, the one that occurs oftener when both are available can reinforce the one that occurs less often, but not vice versa. This relationship is illustrated by an experiment with children (Premack, 1959). The children were given an opportunity to engage in two activities, eating candy and playing a pinball machine. Some did one of these two oftener, some the other. Premack then arranged the apparatus so that for half the children the candy dispenser would work only if the child first operated the pinball machine. To the children who preferred playing, the new arrangement made little difference—they just went on happily playing the machine. For children who preferred eating to playing, however, this change did make a difference—their rate of playing went up, indicating that candy was reinforcing the playing. So far this is a familiar relationship—food reinforcing an instrumental activity. For the other half of the children, the arrangement was reversed, so that the pinball machine would work only if the child first took candy from the dispenser. To the children who preferred candy, this change made no difference. The children who preferred playing, however, ate more candy under this arrangement than before. In this case, playing reinforced eating.

From this study and several others, Premack concludes that there is no special class of consummatory responses that act as reinforcers. Playing could reinforce eating just as well as eating could reinforce playing. (At first glance, this conclusion seems like a disagreement with Sheffield, but Sheffield could agree with Premack by broadening his definition of "consummatory response" to include playing.) Any kind of response can reinforce any other kind of response, says Premack. All that is necessary is for the reinforcing response to be one that the learner makes more frequently than the response being reinforced.

Premack's interpretation has the same drawback as Sheffield's —that we do not know whether it is the activity itself or the consequences of the activity that acts as the real reinforcer. However, for many purposes this difference is unimportant. If we know how often an individual chooses to do any two things, we can predict (according to Premack) whether or not one of them will reinforce the other. To the extent that this relationship holds, it is a powerful predictive tool, regardless of how the relationship may finally be explained.

MINIATURE SYSTEMS IN VERBAL LEARNING

A third important development apart from the major theories is the increasing emphasis on *miniature systems*. These are systems with narrow boundary conditions—in other words, theories that seek to explain only a narrow range of laws. Actually, most of what we have talked about already in this chapter has involved miniature systems—theories of discrimination learning or of exploratory drives or of meaning. Moreover, some of the major theories we have discussed before originated as miniature systems. However, there is an additional area in which miniature systems have achieved particular prominence. This is also an area of particular interest in connection with the practical problems of human learning—the area of verbal rote memory.

Miniature theories of verbal learning, in contrast to most of the topics in this chapter, are nothing new. Many attempts have been made to explain the particular forms that rote memorization takes. Often these interpretations have drawn on the broader theories of learning, but they have still to some extent formed distinctive miniature systems. One of the outstanding contemporary students of verbal learning is Benton J. Underwood of Northwest-

ern University. We may consider him as an example of those mini-
ature-system builders who are concerned with the ways in which
rote verbal materials are memorized.

Underwood should certainly be classified as a connectionist
psychologist, for most of his analyses are in terms of verbal responses and the stimuli, usually also verbal, that elicit them. Many
of his experiments are simply concerned with finding the relationships between independent and dependent variables, with little interest in theoretical interpretations. In this respect he resembles
Skinner. When he does act as a theorist, however, his interpretations
are relatively formal: though he does not put them in the Hullian
form of postulates and theorems, he does make them specific enough
to be clearly testable with experiments. He uses the term reinforcement, but without much concern as to what the nature of reinforcement is; in this respect he is rather like Estes. A cautious, step-
by-step approach, with great emphasis on proper research methods, characterizes all of his work.

An Interpretation of Distributed Practice

One of Underwood's chief interests has been the question of
when and how _disturbed practice_ facilitates learning. One of the
best-known generalizations about learning is that it takes fewer
trials to learn something if there are rest periods between trials—
in other words, if practice is distributed. When the learning involves
a manual skill, distributed practice is usually far superior to
massed (no rests). Indeed, one may even learn more in a given total amount of time by spending much of the time resting than by
spending all of it in practicing the skill to be learned. However, lest
the reader optimistically jump to disastrous conclusions, it must
quickly be pointed out that distributed practice makes far less difference in verbal learning. Sometimes one can memorize a given
amount of material in slightly fewer trials if the trials are distributed, sometimes not, but time spent in practice is always more
useful than time spent in rest. Although distribution of practice is
not a particularly powerful variable for influencing the rate of
verbal memorization, the question of why it sometimes does and
sometimes does not make a difference intrigued Underwood.
Much of his work for over a decade has been aimed at determining

the effects of distributed practice on different kinds of rote learning and trying to construct an adequate theory to explain these effects.

The kinds of learning tasks Underwood has found most useful for experiments on distributed practice are those in which the items to be memorized are paired, one member of the pair always serving as the stimulus and the other as the correct response. (A familiar nonlaboratory example of this kind of learning is the memorization of a foreign-language vocabulary.) As many of these pairs as the experimenter wishes can be combined into a list to be memorized, with the pairs in different orders on different trials. These materials are presented to the learner on a memory drum, with the stimulus appearing alone long enough for him to guess the response, and then the response appearing for him to check himself. This procedure is known as the method of *paired associates*. The value of this method, in contrast to memorizing a series of items, is that the stimuli and the responses are clearly distinguished and can be analyzed separately. Underwood's experiments indicate that this contrast is very important. He has, in fact, analyzed the memorization process into two stages—the stage of learning the responses and the stage of attaching the responses to the appropriate stimuli. (In the foreign-language vocabulary, one must learn to write or pronounce each foreign word and must also learn to attach each to the correct English word as the stimulus.) This two-stage interpretation is essential to an understanding of when and how distributed practice produces its effects.

The crucial factor that determines what the effect of distributed practice will be is the difficulty of the response-learning stage (Underwood, 1961). This stage may be difficult for either of two reasons. One is that similarities among responses may make it difficult to give either of them correctly. For example, the two response words "rounded" and "crumbling" are sometimes given incorrectly as "rounding" and "crumbled." The other cause of difficulty is that the individual response items may be difficult to learn because they contain sequences of letters that are rare in English. Thus XBN is harder to learn as a response than LOR. Neither is a word, but LOR has a sequence of letters similar to what is often found in words, while the sequence XBN is not typical of English

H

words. This difference gives LOR an advantage both in familiarity and in pronounceability, and makes it easier to learn. If the responses in a given list are difficult to learn for either of these reasons, distributed practice will give faster learning. If, on the other hand, the responses themselves are easy to learn, so that the only problem is in attaching the responses to the appropriate stimuli, massed practice will be fully as effective as distributed.

How does distributed practice produce its facilitating effect on the learning of difficult responses? To answer this question, Underwood borrows several concepts from simpler forms of learning. He suggests that a major factor in the response-learning stage is learning not to give incorrect responses. In other words, incorrect response tendencies must be extinguished. During the rest intervals in distributed practice, these extinguished responses show spontaneous recovery. This recovery permits them to be re-extinguished. In massed practice they do not have time to recover. Since extinction requires that a response occur and not be reinforced, with massed practice there is less opportunity for extinction. However, these wrong-response tendencies continue to be strong and to interfere with the correct response tendencies, making it more likely that no response, right or wrong, will occur. Paradoxically, the phenomenon means that distributed practice results both in more errors and in more rapid learning.

This interpretation of paired-associate learning leads to several predictions about the effects of distributed practice. For one thing, as already noted, there should be more wrong responses with distributed practice but more failures to respond at all with massed practice. For another, the advantage of distributed practice should be primarily in the later stages of learning, when the wrong responses have had time to occur and receive extinction training several times. Finally, all of this expectation applies only to errors in which a response is given which would not be correct at any point in the list. Errors in which a response is given to the wrong stimulus, when it would be correct if given to a different stimulus, refer to the other stage of learning and are not relevant to this theory.

Most of the evidence for this theory is indirect; in fact, none of the above three predictions has been tested directly in a thoroughly adequate experiment. In addition, there is no explanation in the theory of why different principles should apply to the two stages of learning. What Underwood has done so far is to bring together a lot of evidence from previous studies and develop this theory to summarize it. It now remains for him to make the direct tests necessary to confirm it. Thus his approach is much like what Hull recommended. Though he has not used the language of postulates and theorems, he has developed a theory which goes beyond existing evidence, a theory from which he can deduce testable predictions. The testing of these propositions remains to be done.

CYBERNETICS

In addition to the three areas we have discussed, one other theoretical topic deserves mention here. This is the application of *feedback theory*, or *cybernetics*, to the study of learning. The term "cybernetics" was coined by Norbert Wiener (1948) to refer to the study of control mechanisms. The word is derived from the Greek for "steersman," since it is concerned with devices that keep some operation, like the sailing of a ship, on its proper course. In order to keep an operation on course, it is necessary to compensate for any deviation in either direction. If a ship drifts off course either to port or to starboard, the helmsman must move the rudder the proper amount and direction to bring the ship back on course. This illustration presents the general concept of *negative feedback*. Negative feedback involves adjustments in a system to keep it in a steady state by compensating for any deflections from that state.

The concepts of cybernetics emerged from the branch of engineering concerned with control mechanisms. Such mechanisms operate by negative feedback. A thermostat is an example. When the temperature falls, the thermostat turns on the furnace and thus makes the temperature rise. When the temperature rises to a certain point, the thermostat turns the furnace off and thus makes the temperature fall. In engineering terms, the thermostat and the furnace together make up a *system*. The temperature in the room is the input to the system, and the activity of the furnace is the *output* from the system. The effect of the output is fed back into the system as the input (hence the term feedback) and the effect of this feedback is to produce a change in the opposite direction from the input (so that the feedback is negative). There are many such mechanisms (they are often called servomechanisms), and cybernetics is an attempt to apply their principles to problems in psychology and related fields.

When a person performs any skilled act, he is constantly guided by sensations from his muscles, usually also from his eyes, and often from other sources. These sensations warn him whenever he is starting to make a mistake and thus enable him to return to the proper procedure. This response often happens so quickly and automatically that he is unaware of it, but it occurs nonetheless. This behavior is an example of negative feedback, with the output being fed back to control the operation and keep it on course. The important part that knowledge of results plays in skilled performances can thus be expressed in terms of feedback.

When we proceed to more complex purposive behaviors, the same principle applies. A student going through college may discover that he is getting failing grades. If the discovery leads him to work harder and thus bring up his grades, he affords an example of negative feedback. In the unlikely event that he studies so hard as to affect his health, he can cut down his studying. In both cases he discovers a deviation from his progress through college, one that threatens the success of his education, and he corrects the deviation so as to continue on his progress toward the degree.

The feedback model represents a middle position between connectionist and cognitive theory. Like connectionist theory, it is concerned with fairly mechanistic connections between stimuli and responses. Stimuli serve as the input, responses as the output, and the individual as the system. Negative feedback is the process by which stimuli control responses. Feedback theory resembles cognitive theory, however, in its concern with ways in which purposive behavior is maintained by a flexible control system that takes account of the structure of the environment. Moreover, feedback theory is useful not only in dealing with the behavior of individuals but also in analyzing the behavior of groups. The system it describes can as well be a club or a school class as an individual person.

The great weakness of feedback theory in the psychology of learning is that, like Lewin's system, it is not really a theory of learning at all. Feedback language is useful for describing any kind of purposive behavior, and thus will often apply to situations in which learning is taking place. The theory does not, however, make any distinction between learning and nonlearning situations. Consider, for example, an individual who is learning to use an axe. Each separate swing of the axe is controlled according to the feedback principle. If he observes that his blow will strike too high on the tree, he adjusts his swing to strike lower. This adjustment in itself is not learning. However, the axman also discovers that certain ways of standing, holding the axe, and swinging give better results than others. This discovery leads to changes within a session of chopping in the way he does these things. Both changes are examples of feedback. However, we can attribute most of the latter change to learning, and we can speak of the successful techniques as being reinforced. Finally, the person observes how well this activity of chopping is obtaining his goal, whether it is to earn money, to strengthen his shoulders, or to beautify his yard. If he notes a large discrepancy between his achievement and his goal, he may give up chopping altogether. This response would still be an example of feedback. It would also involve learning, but a different sort from the learning of skill with the axe.

So far, cybernetics as applied to learning is just another descriptive language. The starting point for a feedback analysis is a state of affairs that the system seeks to maintain. In many cases this situation would correspond to the concept of drive, since drive involves some disruption of the normal state either by the removal of something needed or by the presentation of something noxious. (The reader will recognize this as an oversimplified and somewhat controversial definition of drive.) The principal prediction which feedback theory makes is that the system will compensate for any deviations that occur, so as to maintain this state of affairs. The way in which it does so is a topic to be studied, not something about which the theory already makes predictions. Discrimination among cues, reinforcement of responses that reduce drive, the approaching of incentives with positive valence, and the following of paths in the life space can all be treated within this framework. Perhaps the most valuable aspect of this approach is that it emphasizes the continuous control of sequences of behavior, thus combining the fine detail of a molecular analysis with the flexible, purposive view of a molar analysis. To what extent the approach will prove useful in dealing specifically with questions of learning still largely remains to be seen.

Chapter 8

Learning Theory Present and Future

IN ANY SURVEY of an area of knowledge, such as that attempted in this book, there is a great danger that the reader will come away with a kaleidoscope of impressions—some, hopefully, interesting and enlightening—but with no over-all picture of the field. To a cognitive theorist, at least, such an outcome would seem most regrettable. In hopes of avoiding such an outcome, let us consider what the various interpretations we have examined can contribute to our understanding of learning.

THE HOPE FOR A BETTER THEORY OF LEARNING

First, as to the place of theory in general. All interpretations of learning are to some extent theoretical. No matter how hard one tries to "stick to the facts," he is bound to select certain facts at the expense of others and to generalize beyond his evidence, and he is very likely to talk about processes that he cannot directly observe. Our choice is not between facts and theories but between narrow theories and broad ones, and between casual theories and formal ones. The current trend in the psychological interpretation of learning seems to be both toward narrower and toward more formal theories. Such a generalization is risky, however, for there are many currents in psychological thought, and over-all trends are difficult to determine.

Most psychological interpreters of learning would probably recognize as ultimately desirable a broad, formal theory from which a wide range of learning laws could be predicted with a high degree of precision. There is, however, much skepticism about the practicality of such a system in the near future. For the present, there is room for many approaches to theory. Systems of classification, collections of very specific laws, broad rough-and-ready generalizations, and formal deductive theories all have a legitimate place in a young and growing field such as the psychology of learning.

There are two generalizations that we can make with a good deal of confidence. One is that narrow theories have a greater chance to be precise than do broader ones: the more situations one tries to encompass in a theoretical system, the more likely it is that one's predictions will apply more-or-less to many situations but not closely to any. The other generalization is that theories can be more precise when the situations they deal with are controlled experimental situations than when they are the variable situations of everyday life. Theories developed in the laboratory are, of course, applied to everyday life, but in this application they lose some of the precision that is their greatest asset.

The two above generalizations help to explain the variety of approaches to theory that we find in the study of learning. For a person who deals with a great variety of people in different situations, it may be both more useful and more satisfying to have such a broad generalization as, "Learning is most effective when the learner is motivated but not threatened." As a scientific law, this generalization is not very meaningful, since it leaves unspecified what we mean by "motivated" and by "threatened." It does, however, have a valuable use in telling us what to look for in a learning situation. Another person, dealing with one particular learning situation, might find it both more useful and more satisfying to know that "Infantrymen learn to use this weapon most effectively if they are trained three hours after breakfast, given knowledge of results after every shot, and told that their scores will go on their service record." This generalization permits more precise predictions than the previous one, and hence can be more easily and accurately used, but its range of application is too narrow to give it any general significance. Ideally, we would like to be able to combine the precision of the second generalization with the breadth of the first. This is a goal that keeps many theorists working. Until we can, however, theories that give us narrower predictions or vaguer ones will both have their place in psychology.

Apart from the general question of what form theories of learning should take, there are the various controversies about the terms in which learning should be interpreted. The most conspicuous is that between connectionist and cognitive interpretations, with those about the nature of reinforcement only less conspicuous, and a number of lesser ones much less noticed. Earlier in the history of modern psychology, these differences in interpretations were the basis of vigorous arguments among various theoretical schools of psychology. In recent years the differences have become less clear-cut and the controversies about them quieter. As new data were gathered, all the system builders who wanted to remain in business had to make adjustments in their systems to accommodate these data. In the process, they acquired more respect for the complexities of learning, more humility about their own systems, and more respect for the efforts of others.

This quieting does not mean that theoretical differences are disappearing—far from it. It does mean, however, that system builders are tending to be more tentative in their formulations. Rather than looking on theories as true or false statements about the nature of the world, they look on them as more or less adequate ways of summarizing present knowledge and of facilitating the gathering of new knowledge. Rather than saying, "I have the correct interpretation, and yours is wrong," they say, "Let's all see how far we can go with our theories in explaining the data, and I'm guessing that I can go farther than you."

Along with this change goes an increasing recognition of the boundary conditions of theories and an increasing respect for specialization. The difference between two theories is more likely to be seen as a reflection of different interests than as a disagreement about fundamental principles. Theorists now differ not so much in their biases about the nature of learning as in the areas they prefer to study and the methods they prefer to use. Theoretical controversy is by no means dead, but it tends to be both more muted and more closely related to specific topics than was once the case.

Criteria for an Ideal Theory of Learning

For all this increased modesty among theorists of learning, the goal of building a general theory of learning, broad yet precise, remains as an ultimate aspiration. What would such a theory be like? It would probably be formal, very likely stated much like Hull's: in terms of definitions, postulates, and theorems. This formality would serve both to make the theory more precise in its predictions and to reveal its inadequacies more clearly so that they could be corrected. It would be a theory constantly undergoing modification in its details with new data, yet so well conceived that its basic structure could accommodate a wide range of possible findings. Ideally, it would cover the whole range of learning phenomena in animals and men and the whole range of independent variables that affect learning; yet it would cover all this range with a small number of postulates. It is easy to see why most psychologists consider such a theory far in the future!

Such a theory would have to deal with the complexities of human symbolic learning and insightful problem solving. It would have to allow for the flexibility of behavior, for the way that the same knowledge or belief can be used in many different ways under different conditions. This means that it would have to go beyond any existing connectionist theory in dealing with cognitive processes. At the same time, it would have to recognize that such cognitive flexibility is far from universal even in the most intelligent of humans. It would have to deal with simple conditioning, with rote memorization, with skills that we can display without knowing how we do it, with blindly repetitive habits, and with lack of insight in situations where the opportunity for insight seems clear. And in addition to dealing with all of these forms of behavior when they occur, the theory must also tell under what conditions each of them will occur.

To accomplish such a monumental task, this ideal theory must undoubtedly take account of the developmental process. It must consider, in much more detail than any present theory, the great influence of earlier learning on later learning. What an individual will learn, how he will learn it, and what use he will make of the learning in any given situation, all depend greatly on his prior learning. Tolman recognized this fact in his concept of field cognition modes, and Harlow in his discussion of learning sets. Hull's concept of the habit-family hierarchy assumes the importance of prior learning. Learning to learn is a much discussed (though relatively little studied) topic in the field of rote memorization. Donald Hebb of McGill University, in a theory primarily concerned with perception and motivation (Hebb, 1949), has emphasized the importance of early experience on later learning, and this interest has recently led to much research. To predict whether a given individual's learning in a given situation will be flexible or stereotyped, insightful or rote, our "theory of the future" will certainly have to give much consideration to the effects of his prior experiences on his present learning processes.

Our ideal theory must also take into account the detailed stimulus situation. This aspect of learning has been most emphasized by Guthrie and by the gestalt psychologists. As might be expected from the great differences between these two systems, the forms that this emphasis takes in the two are in marked contrast to one another. Guthrie is concerned with getting a particular response that has occurred once to occur again, and he points out that it is most likely to occur again when the stimuli on the two occasions are most similar. The gestaltists, on the other hand, are interested in getting an appropriate new response to occur by a process of insight, and they point to the importance of having the situation so arranged that the desired response will form part of a good gestalt. These effects of the exact stimulus situation, both in the stereotyped use of old responses and in the insightful appearance of new ones, must be taken into account by any adequate theory.

The two factors we have just discussed—past experience and the present stimulus situation—interact through the process of paying attention. How the stimulus situation affects the individual depends on what aspects of it he pays attention to. Attention has been a relatively neglected concept in learning theory, but this neglect has recently begun to be repaired. Such concepts as "observing response" and "acquired distinctiveness of cues" testify to this new interest in attention. Lewin has carried this line of thought farther by noting that the effect of any experience depends on how we interpret it. This observation is undoubtedly true; the problem is to take account of this fact without losing track of the external stimulus and thus losing track of learning as well. None of the learning theories we have considered has an adequate answer to this problem, but our ideal theory would have to include one.

Finally, an ideal theory of learning would have to deal effectively with the topics of motivation and reinforcement. We know that learning (or at least learned behavior) depends on our needs and desires and on the positive and negative incentives around us. We also know that the consequences of an act are a major factor in whether we repeat that act. All theoretical interpretations of learning take account of these relationships in one way or another, but many unanswered questions remain. What needs or drives or demands are we born with, and how are they modified by learning to produce the multiplicity of adult motives? Do rewards act to reinforce responses, or to give positive valence to incentives, or both? Such questions as these remain unanswered, not because theories have failed to deal with them, but because different theories have dealt with them in so many conflicting ways that it is difficult to choose the most satisfactory. A truly adequate theory of learning would answer these questions in such a way as to sum up all our present knowledge about motivation.

Candidates for an Ideal Theory

What sort of theory could meet all the requirements we have set for it? At present the best guess seems to be that if one comes it will be a connectionist theory, but one in which symbolic mediating responses play a large part. It will interpret learning as basically a matter of stimulus-response connections, but with many of the connections being among mediating responses that serve to tie together complex patterns of behavior. It will recognize both the many innate sources of drive and reinforcement and the ways in which secondary drives and reinforcers are acquired. It will recognize both individual differences and age differences in learning abilities more than any current theory of learning. It will include a gradual increase in the complexity of mediating responses as a result of early learning. It might look somewhat like Spence's system, expanded and modified by Estes, Harlow, Osgood, and others, and with some features not found in any current learning theory. Both the vigor and the ingenuity of present-day connectionist theorists support the guess that they are most likely to provide the basis for the "theory of the future."

We certainly cannot rule out the possibility, however, that such an integrative theory might be more like present-day cognitive theories. The language of perceptions and beliefs is a more natural one for most people than the language of stimulus-response connections, and a theory based on such cognitive language might be less cumbersome than the kind of theory discussed above. Like Lewin's, such a theory would begin with our view of the world around us, and would treat learning as a modification in that view. It would, however, concern itself more than those theories do with the relation of the life space both to external stimuli and to overt responses. In this respect it would be more like Tolman's theory, as well as somewhat similar to Mowrer's latest interpretation. As regards external stimuli, it would have to include postulates about the ways that changes in stimuli produce changes in the phenomenal field. These postulates would deal both with the long-run changes in cognitions that we call learning and the short-run changes involving moods and momentary perceptions. They would also have to make allowance for differences in these effects according to heredity, age, and previous experience. As regards overt responses, the theory would have to recognize that cognitions exist at different levels of analysis. A cognition about how to get from one place to another includes not only a cognitive map of the route but also many tiny cognitions about the movements necessary to follow the route. These tiny cognitions are often ones that the individual is quite unable to describe, but they nevertheless have to be included somehow in his life space in order to give a complete explanation of his behavior. Finally, the ideal cognitive theory would require some way of dealing with those cases where what an individual tells us about his attitudes and motives fails to agree with his life space as we infer it from his deeds. There is little indication at present that any cognitive theory is likely to solve these problems and achieve the necessary combination of accuracy and breadth to qualify as an adequate theory of learning. If one should, however, it might well be more useful than the kind of connectionist theory discussed above.

A third possibility for an ideal theory of learning is a combination of the above two. Since cognitive theories deal best with complex symbolic behavior and connectionist theories do best with simpler behavior, a theory might make use of both interpretations. Such a two-part system might be even more like Tolman's than the purely cognitive one discussed above. For all its apparent advantages, it is unlikely that such a system would have a lasting vogue. Man's desire for consistency would keep urging that one kind of learning be explained in terms of the other. The result would probably be much like the ideal connectionist theory we have considered, in which cognitive processes are explained as the product of complex stimulus-response connections.

A final possibility is that the feedback model will be elaborated to the point where it can satisfactorily deal with the whole range of learning. This approach has the advantage of being well adapted to topics as diverse as muscular coordination and the attainment of life goals. It has, however, a very long way to go before it can fulfill the theoretical needs of the psychology of learning. The essence of learning, in cybernetic terms, is a *change* in the feedback mechanisms, a change in the way the system deals with a deviation from its course. What kinds of changes occur and what makes them occur are questions that cybernetics has done little to answer. How might it answer them? Perhaps when existing feedback mechanisms fail to keep the system on course, different new responses are tried out until one of them succeeds in bringing the system back on course. This response is then learned as a solution to that particular problem. This interpretation of learning sounds very much like a traditional connectionist interpretation. The question of how the system acquires its particular directions also remains to be answered. The prospect that an adequate theory of learning will develop out of cybernetics seems rather dim at present. However, the feedback model has the advantage of combining precise stimulus-response analysis with a recognition that behavior is not merely a collection of stimulus-response units but a continuously ongoing process. This advantage keeps it in the running as a possible basis for the learning theory of the future.

The reader may feel that the four above suggestions about possible future learning theories are not really very different. Such a feeling is not surprising. The problems that must be dealt with and the data that must be explained set limits to how different theories can profitably be. Whether a theory uses the language of habits and mediating responses or of perceptions and beliefs or of feedback mechanisms makes less difference than that it makes clear and accurate predictions about learning. It is by this criterion that we must judge different attempts to build a comprehensive theory of learning.

THE PRESENT-DAY VALUE OF LEARNING THEORY

Whatever form the theory of the future may take, most of us have to make the best of the theories we have today. Granted that all of them fall short of the ideals we have set for a truly adequate theory, what use can we make of them? For the most part, whatever exact predictions they make are applicable only to carefully controlled laboratory conditions. They can rarely predict directly to the complex, uncontrolled conditions of everyday life. Even with the most precise of scientific theories, engineers are needed who can use their ingenuity and experience to apply the theory to practical ends. Since theories of learning are not among the most precise, this "psychological engineering" is perhaps even more challenging than in other areas of science. Such "engineering" enters into many jobs, from animal training to psychological warfare, but above all it is the province of the educator.

The applied psychology of learning is important not only as a way of putting theories to practical use but also as a way of improving theories. Along with their other contributions, applied studies help to determine the boundary conditions of theories. If a theory based on laboratory data is used to make predictions to an applied situation, and the predictions are not confirmed, this event shows that the theory is not appropriate for that situation. It may still, however, be a perfectly good theory for predicting in other situations. In addition, applied studies reveal new laws that may then be used in the modification of old theories or the construction of new ones. Gagné (1962), for example, has recently presented some principles of learning that he has found valuable in military training. These principles are concerned with the hierarchical arrangement of component tasks and sequences of operations within a larger task. They are rather different from the principles that have been emphasized by most theories, and might serve as a basis for new theoretical work in the psychology of learning.

For most of us, the various learning theories have two chief values. One is in providing us with a vocabulary and a conceptual framework for interpreting the examples of learning that we observe. These are valuable for anyone who is alert to the world around him. The other, closely related, is in suggesting where to look for solutions to practical problems. The theories do not give us solutions, but they do direct our attention to those variables that are crucial in finding solutions.

Let us consider the ways in which various theoretical interpreters do these two things for us. Guthrie directs our attention to the importance of practicing the particular responses to be learned under the particular conditions in which they will be used, and also to the value of practicing them under varied conditions if they are to be firmly established. Skinner advises us always to find out what reinforces a given act, so that we can present that reinforcer if we want the act to occur or remove it if we want to extinguish the act. Miller and Dollard warn us to consider the secondary drives that may be learned in a situation and may then serve as the basis of new, often undesired, learning. Wertheimer and Köhler point out the importance of arranging learning situations so as to foster real, creative understanding rather than blind rote memorization. Lewin suggests that we try to reconstruct the learner's life space, with his tensions and goals and the paths and barriers that he perceives. Tolman, Hull, and Estes offer many of these same suggestions in more technical form. All of these suggestions require ingenuity if they are to be put to practical use. Each, however, serves to emphasize some aspect of the learning process that we would be wise to consider. Thus each serves both to enrich our understanding of the learning situations we observe and to help us find solutions to the practical learning problems with which we have to deal. While many theorists aspire to make a greater contribution than this, and to some extent succeed in doing so, this contribution alone is enough to make theories invaluable to the study of learning.

References

Berlyne, D. E. *Conflict, arousal, and curiosity*. New York: McGraw-Hill, 1960.

Buxton, C. E. Latent learning and the goal gradient hypothesis. *Contrib. psychol. Theor.*, 1940, 2, No. 6.

Dollard, J. C., and Miller, N. E. *Personality and psychotherapy*. New York: McGraw-Hill, 1950.

Estes, W. K. The statistical approach to learning theory. In Koch, S. (Ed.) *Psychology: a study of a science. Vol. 2. General systematic formulations, learning and special processes*. New York: McGraw-Hill, 1959, pp. 380-491.

Ferster, C. B., and Skinner, B. F. *Schedules of reinforcement*. New York: Appleton-Century-Crofts, 1957.

Gagné, R. M. Military training and principles of learning. *Amer. Psychol.*, 1962, 17, 83-91.

Greenspoon, J. The reinforcing effect of two spoken sounds on the frequency of two responses. *Amer. J. Psychol.*, 1955, 68, 409-416.

Guthrie, E. R. *The psychology of learning*. Rev. ed. New York: Harper, 1952.

Guthrie, E. R. Association by contiguity. In Koch, S. (Ed.) *Psychology: a study of a science. Vol. 2. General systematic formulations, learning, and special processes*. New York: McGraw-Hill, 1959, pp. 158-195.

Harlow, H. F. The nature of love. *Amer. Psychol.*, 1958, 13, 673-685.

Harlow, H. F. Learning set and error factor theory. In Koch, S. (Ed.) *Psychology: a study of a science. Vol. 2. General systematic formulations, learning, and special processes*. New York: McGraw-Hill, 1959, pp. 492-537.

Hebb, D. O. *The organization of behavior*. New York: Wiley, 1949.

Hill, W. F. Activity as an autonomous drive. *J. comp. physiol. Psychol.*, 1956, 49, 15-19.

213

Hull, C. L. *Principles of behavior*. New York: Appleton-Century-Crofts, 1943.

Hull, C. L. *A behavior system*. New Haven: Yale Univer. Press, 1952.

Kagan, J., and Berkun, M. The reward value of running activity. *J. comp. physiol. Psychol.*, 1954, 47, 108.

Koffka, K. *The growth of the mind*. Trans. by R. M. Ogden. New York: Harcourt, Brace, 1925.

Koffka, K. *Principles of gestalt psychology*. New York: Harcourt, Brace, 1935.

Köhler, W. *The mentality of apes*. Trans. from 2nd rev. ed. by Ella Winter. New York: Harcourt, Brace, 1925.

Lawrence, D. H. Acquired distinctiveness of cues: I. Transfer between discriminations on the basis of familiarity with the stimulus. *J. exp. Psychol.*, 1949, 39, 770-784.

Lawrence, D. H. Acquired distinctiveness of cues. II. Selective association in a constant stimulus situation. *J. exp. Psychol.*, 1950, 40, 175-188.

Lewin, K. *Dynamic theory of personality*. Trans. by D. K. Adams and K. E. Zener. New York: McGraw-Hill, 1935.

Lewin, K. *Principles of topological psychology*. Trans. by F. Heider and Grace M. Heider. New York: McGraw-Hill, 1936.

MacCorquodale, K., and Meehl, P. E. Preliminary suggestions as to a formalization of expectancy theory. *Psychol. Rev.*, 1953, 60, 55-63.

Miller, N. E., and Dollard, J. C. *Social learning and imitation*. New Haven: Yale Univer. Press, 1941.

Mowrer, O. H. On the dual nature of learning: a re-interpretation of "conditioning" and "problem-solving." *Harvard educ. Rev.*, 1947, 17, 102-148.

Mowrer, O. H. *Learning theory and behavior*. New York: Wiley, 1960.

Osgood, C. E., Suci, G. J., and Tannenbaum, P. H. *The measurement of meaning*. Urbana: Univer. of Illinois Press, 1957.

Premack, D. Toward empirical behavior laws: I. Positive reinforcement. *Psychol. Rev.*, 1959, 66, 219-233.

Seward, J. P. An experimental study of Guthrie's theory of reinforcement. *J. exp. Psychol.*, 1942, 30, 247-256.

Sheffield, F. D., and Roby, T. B. Reward value of a non-nutritive sweet taste. *J. comp. physiol. Psychol.*, 1950, 43, 471-481.

Skinner, B. F. *Walden II*. New York: Macmillan, 1948.

Skinner, B. F. *Science and human behavior*. New York: Macmillan, 1953.

Skinner, B. F. The experimental analysis of behavior. *Amer. Scient.*, 1957a, 45, 343-371.

Skinner, B. F. *Verbal behavior.* New York: Appleton-Century-Crofts, 1957b.

Skinner, B. F. Teaching machines. *Scient. Amer.,* 1961, 205, 90-102.

Spence, K. W. *Behavior theory and conditioning.* New Haven: Yale Univer. Press, 1956.

Thorndike, E. L. Animal intelligence: an experimental study of the associative processes in animals. *Psychol. Rev., Monogr. Suppl.,* 1898, 2, No. 8.

Thorndike, E. L. *The psychology of learning.* New York: Teachers College, 1913.

Tolman, E. C. *Purposive behavior in animals and men.* New York: D. Appleton-Century, 1932.

Tolman, E. C. *Drives toward war.* New York: D. Appleton-Century, 1942.

Tolman, E. C. There is more than one kind of learning. *Psychol. Rev.,* 1949, 56, 144-155.

Tolman, E. C. Principles of purposive behavior. In Koch, S. (Ed.) *Psychology: a study of a science. Vol. 2. General systematic formulations, learning, and special processes.* New York: McGraw-Hill, 1959, pp. 92-157.

Tolman, E. C., Ritchie, B. F., and Kalish, D. Studies in spatial learning. I. Orientation and the short-cut. *J. exp. Psychol.,* 1946, 36, 13-24.

Underwood, B. J. Ten years of massed practice on distributed practice. *Psychol. Rev.,* 1961, 68, 229-247.

Verplanck, W. S. The control of the content of conversation: reinforcement of statements of opinion. *J. abnorm. soc. Psychol.,* 1955, 51, 668-676.

Watson, J. B. Psychology as the behaviorist views it. *Psychol. Rev.,* 1913, 20, 158-177.

Watson, J. B. *Behaviorism.* 2nd ed. Chicago: Univer. of Chicago Press, 1930.

Welker, W. I. An analysis of exploratory and play behavior in animals. In Fiske, D. W., and Maddi, S. R. (Eds.) *Functions of varied experience.* Homewood, Ill.: Dorsey, 1961, pp. 175-226.

Wertheimer, M. *Productive thinking.* New York: Harper, 1945.

Wiener, N. *Cybernetics.* New York: Wiley, 1948.

Wulf, F. Über die Veränderung von Vorstellungen (Gedächtnis und Gestalt). *Psychol. Forsch.,* 1922, 1, 333-373. Trans. and condensed as "Tendencies in figural variation" in Ellis, W. D. *A source book of gestalt psychology.* London: Kegan Paul, Trench, Trubner, 1938, pp. 136-148.

Wyckoff, L. B. The role of observing responses in discrimination learning. *Psychol. Rev.,* 1952, 59, 431-442.

Suggestions for Further Readings

A. GENERAL READINGS

READERS WHO WANT to study the topics covered in this book more thoroughly will find the following references helpful.

Deese, J. *The psychology of learning*. 2nd ed. New York: McGraw-Hill, 1958. — Though not oriented toward theoretical systems, this book provides a broad coverage of the psychology of learning, including a number of theoretical issues and the data bearing on them.

Hilgard, E. R. *Theories of learning*. 2nd ed. New York: Appleton-Century-Crofts, 1956. — The standard secondary reference on contemporary theories of learning, providing both authoritative descriptions and critical evaluations of the outstanding theories. The chapters on Hull and on mathematical models are rather difficult; otherwise the book is highly readable throughout.

Koch, S. (Ed.) *Psychology: a study of a science. Vol. 2. General systematic formulations, learning, and special processes*. New York: McGraw-Hill, 1959. — A collection of 12 readings on various modern learning theories, most of them written by the theorists themselves. The study of which this volume forms a part emphasizes certain topics in the philosophy of science, with the result that the distinctive styles of some of the authors are partly lost. However, this is the most complete and up-to-date source book available. The chapters vary in difficulty, but most of them are harder reading than Hilgard.

Woodworth, R. S. *Contemporary schools of psychology*. Rev. ed. New York: Ronald, 1948. — A short, easy, secondary reference for the recent historical background of contemporary psychological theory.

B. PARTICULAR THEORISTS

Among the primary sources mentioned in the text, the following are especially recommended for their readability and their concern with the applications of learning theory.

Dollard, J. C., and Miller, N. E. *Personality and psychotherapy*. New York: McGraw-Hill, 1950. — An outline of Miller's learning theory, followed by its application to the development of personality and the learning and unlearning of neuroses.

Guthrie, E. R. *The psychology of learning*. Rev. ed. New York: Harper, 1952. — The author's interpretation of a number of learning situations and his comments on several other theorists.

Skinner, B. F. *Science and human behavior*. New York: Macmillan, 1953. — A popular summary of the chief variables in learning as studied by the author, followed by the interpretation of organized social behavior in terms of reinforced learning.

Wertheimer, M. *Productive thinking*. New York: Harper, 1945. — A consideration of education, problem-solving, and creativity from the gestalt point of view.

Index of Names

219

Index of Topics and Partial Glossary

FOR EACH TECHNICAL term, the reference that explains the meaning of the term is given in italics. In addition, a few terms are defined here for quick reference or for increased clarity. However, the reader should keep in mind that these are rough-and-ready definitions and that usually the best way to understand the meaning of a term is to read the discussion of it in context.

Methuen's University Paperbacks

writing days, and are especially interesting as evidence
of his ideas on literature at that time.

UP 24 **An Introduction to Ethics**
WILLIAM LILLIE
'Mr Lillie must be congratulated . . . I shall unhesi-
tatingly recommend his book to first-year students.'
Adult Education

UP 25 **Elements of Metaphysics**
A. E. TAYLOR
Professor Taylor's work has held its own for fifty
years as the best comprehensive account of the main
principles of metaphysics.

UP 26 **Mathematics of Engineering Systems**
DEREK F. LAWDEN
'It is undoubtedly a valuable addition to the literature
of engineering mathematics and should prove helpful
not only to students, but also to practising engineers
and physicists.' *Journal of Applied Physics*

UP 27 **Life and Thought in the Greek and Roman
World**
M. CARY and T. J. HAARHOFF
The aim of this book is to provide a brief but com-
prehensive outline sketch of Greek and Roman
civilization.

UP 28 **The Growth of the English Novel**
RICHARD CHURCH
This study, by an author who is himself a novelist
as well as a poet and critic, presents a continuous story
of the progress of the English novel.

of one million lire for the best popular scientific book published in the previous five years.

UP 35 **Byzantine Civilization**
STEVEN RUNCIMAN
Sir Steven Runciman gives a general picture of the Orientalized Graeco-Roman civilization which represented the last phase of the Roman Empire and had its capital at Constantinople.

UP 36 **The Wound and the Bow**
EDMUND WILSON
A wide and penetrating study of artistic creation, this book contains detailed studies of Dickens and Kipling, and shorter pieces on Casanova, Edith Wharton, Ernest Hemingway and James Joyce.

UP 37 **The Course of German History**
A. J. P. TAYLOR
'He is not only a brilliant but a profound historian.'
R. H. S. Crossman, *New Statesman*

UP 38 **King Solomon's Ring**
KONRAD LORENZ
'A book opening a whole series of doors upon enthralling and enchanting aspects of the animal world ... decorated with sketches as charming, as compassionate, as sensitive and humorous as his prose.'
Daily Telegraph

UP 39 **A History of England**
E. L. WOODWARD
'A brilliant little book: it combines a concise record of events with an absorbing picture of England's

evolution in the political, social, economic and cultural
spheres.'   *Sunday Times*

UP 40 **Cromwell's Army**
CHARLES FIRTH
Sir Charles Firth's classic work is now made available
again after many years.

UP 41 **The Theory of Beauty**
E. F. CARRITT
Mr. Carritt's examination of the various aesthetic
theories has been the standard book in English on
the subject for two generations.

UP 42 **The Instruments of Music**
ROBERT DONINGTON
A full account of the mechanics and physics of hearing
and of the history of musical instruments.

UP 43 **Shakespeare's Tragic Heroes**
LILY B. CAMPBELL
A unique account of the connection between Shakespeare's conception of passion and tragedy and his
familiarity with the learning and philosophy of his
day.

UP 44 **Introduction to Money**
HONOR CROOME
'Mrs Croome has written an attractive book dealing
principally with the nature and development of
money, but ranging also over a wide field of national
and international economic activity.'
                                        Economic Journal

UP 61 **A Short History of the Middle East**

G. KIRK

'This . . . has become perhaps the most useful short guide to the tangled affairs of the Middle East during the last forty years or so.'

Royal Asian Society Journal

UP 62 **Political Theory**

G. C. FIELD

After sketching the historical development of political ideas Professor Field analyses and discusses some basic concepts of modern political theory, in particular the notions of the State, of Sovereignty and the Law.

UP 63 **Medieval People**

EILEEN POWER

Many writers have recounted the lives of the heroes of the Middle Ages. This book is about ordinary folk who are so often left out of history. In it are described the lives of some typical people ranging from Bodo, a Frankish peasant, to a housewife of fourteenth-century Paris.

UP 64 **Outlines of Tudor and Stuart Plays: 1497-1642**

KARL J. HOLZKNECHT

A student of Elizabethan and Jacobean drama will find this book a help to his studies. It provides synopses of eighty plays of the main dramatists, excluding Shakespeare. It will serve as a handy guide to readers who have difficulty in following the tangled plots and who wish to refresh their memories about plays they have read or seen on the stage.

UP 65 **Aristotle**

SIR DAVID ROSS

Sir David Ross gives here a straightforward account of Aristotle's philosophy as it stands before us in his works. Attention has been paid both to Aristotle's general principles and to the working out of these into a connected and detailed system.

UP 66 **Economic Theory and Under-Developed Regions**

GUNNAR MYRDAL

'Around the central argument there cluster loosely a
number of disquisitions on value judgements in
economics, on colonialism, the criteria of national
planning, and on international trade. All are stimulating, all are valuable . . . a good book.'

The Economist

UP 67 **The English Bible**

F. F. BRUCE

Professor Bruce, in this comprehensive study of the
various translations of the Bible into the English
language, traces the story from its earliest days up to
1961, the year of publication of the new English Bible.
This history of the translation brings together facts and
information which have previously appeared only in
specialized accounts of the separate translations.

UP 68 **Art and Artifice in Shakespeare**

ERIC STOLL

This examination of the structural design of four plays
– *Othello, Macbeth, Hamlet,* and *King Lear* – shows
how Shakespeare obtained his effects by the repeated
use of certain artistic devices.

UP 69 **A Handbook of Greek Literature**

H. J ROSE

This famous account of Greek literature is a continuous narrative, complete in itself and assuming
no previous acquaintance with Greek writings. It
includes every author, from Homer to Lucian, who
was Greek in both language and spirit.

it has already been hailed in France, the best modern one-volume history of France.'

UP 74 **The Industrial Revolution in the Eighteenth Century**

PAUL MANTOUX

Professor T. S. Ashton, who supervised this new edition of the work, says in his preface 'in both its architecture and detail this volume is by far the best introduction to the subject in any language . . . one of a few works on economic history that can justly be spoken of as classics'.

UP 75 **Maps and Diagrams**

F. J. MONKHOUSE AND H. R. WILKINSON

A reference book which is intended to help in the compilation and construction of a wide range of geographical maps and diagrams.

UP 76 **Thackeray the Novelist**

GEOFFREY TILLOTSON

An investigation of Thackeray's novels carried out with the object of discovering how he wrote them and what they tell us of his thoughts and attitudes.

UP 77 **The Medieval Centuries**

DENYS HAY

The changes which took place in Europe during the thousand years lying between the fifth and fifteenth centuries are the subject of this book.

UP 78 **The Psychology of Society**

MORRIS GINSBERG

In this book the author confines himself to a discussion of the fundamental problems of Social Psychology and offers a critical account as to the nature of the social mind.